Sent and
Gathered

engaging
worship

series editors
Clayton J. Schmit
Todd E. Johnson

Engaging Worship, a Brehm Center series, is designed to promote reflection on the practice of Christian worship by scholars, artists, and practitioners, often in conversation with each other. Each volume addresses a particular liturgical issue from one or multiple academic disciplines, while exploring ways in which worship practice and leadership can be renewed. Volumes in this series include monographs and edited collections from authors of diverse theological and ecclesial communities. The goal of this series is to bring scholars, students, artists, and church leaders into conversation around vital issues of theology and worship.

The Brehm Center for Worship, Theology, and the Arts is an innovative space for the creative integration of worship, theology, and arts in culture. It is located at Fuller Theological Seminary in Pasadena, California.

Sent and *Gathered*

A Worship Manual
for the Missional Church

Clayton J. Schmit

Baker Academic

a division of Baker Publishing Group
Grand Rapids, Michigan

Published by Baker Academic
a division of Baker Publishing Group
P.O. Box 6287, Grand Rapids, MI 49516-6287
www.bakeracademic.com

Printed in the United States of America

Library of Congress Cataloging-in-Publication Data
Schmit, Clayton J.
    Sent and gathered : a worship manual for the missional church / Clayton J. Schmit.
        p.   cm. — (Engaging worship)
    Includes bibliographical references and index.
    ISBN 978-0-8010-3165-6 (pbk.)
    1. Worship. 2. Mission of the church. 3. Missions—Theory. I. Title.
BV15.S334 2009
264.001—dc22   2009017724

For Carol, Kyrie, and Jacob

Contents

Acknowledgments

This book represents a conversation about worship and the missional church. The major voice in this dialogue, with all its opinions and preachments, is mine. Where I have borrowed insights from others or sought to represent their parts of the conversation, I pray I have done so fairly and with accuracy. If there are misrepresentations, the errata are mine.

I am deeply grateful for my many conversation partners. Not all of them can be acknowledged. Some have enriched my view of worship without their knowing it and some have done so without my own knowledge. Such is the school of the church, wherein we are tutored by preachers, worship leaders, prayer leaders, musicians, and countless servants whose names we may not know.

There are, nevertheless, numerous people who have been active partners in dialogue and who have helped to shape the thoughts captured on these pages. I wish to thank these colleagues, pastors, scholars, and lay ministers who have helped formulate and reform both my thinking and my prose: Diane Dardón, Dennis Tollefson, Bob Kaul, Bruce Hanstedt, Tim Kellgren, Rick Lischer, Ryan Marsh, Karen Ward, Bishops Will Willimon and Gideon Maghina, Lisa Lamb, Jeff Frymire, Agnes Lee, Noel Snyder, Bill Brehm, Dee Brehm, Lloyd Ogilvie, Mark Lau Branson, Marguerite Shuster, Chap Clark, David Scholer, Bill Pannell, Jeff Bjork, Melinda Quivik, Diane Jacobsen, Michael Aune, Mons Teig, Gordon Lathrop, Mark Bangert, Jerry Evenrud, Jana Childers, Richard Ward, Todd Farley, Doug McConnell, Ron Kernaghan, Doug Nason, Moses Pulei, Mary Hulst, Mel Robeck, Mike Pasquarello, Rein Bos, Richard Mouw, and John Witvliet. I am especially grateful to the Brehm Center for Worship, Theology, and the Arts and its core faculty and leaders who are my constant companions in dialogue at Fuller Seminary: Fred Davison, Todd Johnson, Ed Willmington, Eddie Gibbs, Bill Dyrness, Rob Johnston, Roberta King, Craig

Detweiler, Alexis Abernethy, and Carolyn Gordon. Lynn Reynolds and the rest of the Brehm Center staff have added a strong measure of support as this manuscript was prepared, for which I am highly appreciative. I thank Bob Hosack, editor at Baker Academic, both for his patient encouragement for this project and for his partnership in establishing the Engaging Worship series, of which this book is a part. I am also grateful to Charles Bartow and the echo of his mentoring voice, which stands behind all my academic projects. Finally, and most ardently, I am grateful to my son Jacob who wrestles with angels and teaches me daily how to see God in laughter, music, and technology; my daughter Kyrie, whose name is a prayer, who provided editorial assistance, and who adds dance and music and light to my days; and my beloved Carol who is a song and whose love and support are the foundation on which my life and work are set.

Introduction

What we call the beginning is often the end
And to make an end is to make a beginning.
The end is where we start from.

. . . .

We shall not cease from exploration
And the end of all our exploring
Will be to arrive where we started
And know the place for the first time.

T. S. Eliot, "Little Gidding"

The era of fighting over worship styles and musical preferences in worship is, in some camps, drawing to a close. There is a refreshing breeze of worship renewal blowing through the Christian church not only in North America but also in many places across the planet. It is characterized by churches—local, national, and global—seeking to learn from their historical and denominational roots as well as from the liturgical expressions of Christians in other places. At times, this occurs as one congregation borrows from the resources and practices of a church across town. At other times, it happens when a congregation borrows worship ideas or music from another culture or country. Sometimes both happen at once.[1] But the interest is not merely in borrowing from others. It also involves rethinking patterns of the

1. The kind of borrowing I am speaking of and advocating here is not the kind that is often found in churches in the non-Western world that import sermons, preaching styles, and music from the West, especially from agencies eager for a world market for their products. I am speaking, rather, of the mutual sharing of indigenous ideas and idioms that inform the worship in one place with a sense of global awareness in another. While colonialism and missionary activity over the years have been quick to impose Western hymns and preaching styles on developing

past and finding in them value for present use. This book addresses the current situation by describing the nature of this liturgical convergence and providing principles for shaping liturgies that are missionally focused, creative, dynamic, theologically congruent, and appropriate to each local setting. It addresses the question of Christian worship in a general way and does not presume to speak particularly to a single worship tradition or denomination. The hope is that we can explore the common ground that unites us as Christian worshipers who gather regularly for prayer, praise, and communion with our Creator.

"Constancy" and "Diversity"

The concept for this book emerged through many conversations with scholars, pastors, and leaders of worship. It also derived from participation in innumerable worship services that represent the diversity of today's worship idioms. What these conversations and frequent occasions of being a participant/observer proved to me is that there is as much commonality among worship practices in Christian churches as there is diversity. Moreover, the things we hold in common appear to be fundamental to Christian worship and are practiced by thoughtful, disciplined believers in all places where God's people gather.

The location for many of these worship conversations and much of the field research has been the fascinating liturgical laboratory known as Fuller Theological Seminary, which is among the world's largest multidenominational institutions. In this rich environment I teach preaching, worship, and church music. Given that there are students and faculty representing more than one hundred Christian denominations and more than sixty countries, worship at Fuller is amazingly diverse. One week, there may be an all-seminary chapel service that is led by charismatic Africans. The next week, a Eucharistic service may be hosted by a British Anglican priest. That evening, a Taizé prayer service may be held, followed the next night by an emerging worship experience.

Fuller's diversity notwithstanding, conversations about worship in the classroom, with faculty colleagues, and with scholars and pastors elsewhere have demonstrated to me that concerns relating to our diversity of practice are often needlessly exaggerated.[2] To be sure, each of us has a set of worship idioms we feel comfortable with, and it is not surprising that we are sometimes

---

churches, there is a refreshing trend among Western churches to enrich their worship by borrowing global music and art.

2. I do not mean to underestimate the extent to which the church is still battling over worship. Liturgical theologian Todd Johnson observes, for example, that "particularly in the past two decades with the proliferation of so many 'new' forms of worship, the question of what is truly worship and what is 'a lot like worship' is hotly contested in liturgical circles" ("Liturgical Links"). Similarly, Christian songwriter Gloria Gaither laments that in her international travels she is seeing evidence in churches everywhere of people battling over musical styles in worship, a dispute that, she surmises, "breaks the heart of God" ("Worship Wars"). Nonetheless, there

suspicious of patterns that are foreign to our own practice. Yet it is self-serving for any one group to insist that its worship is the most authentic or proper. It may be true that some services of worship are more lively than others or that some services seem more chaotic than others. But that has less to do with worship *style* than it does with the way liturgies are prepared and presented. The most high-church worship may be vivid and engaging, while the most low-church or contemporary worship service might be dull and uninspired. One of the things Christians of all traditions have in common is that we can design and execute worship services in any idiom poorly—or well. Coming from a strong liturgical background (I was raised and remain a Lutheran—a tradition that has often been fairly criticized for snubbing those who practice so-called free forms of worship), I have been humbled while doing the field research of singing and praying with Christians from vastly different backgrounds and traditions. I have learned that the Spirit of God is alive in many places and in many ways in worship. As I have moved to a place of positive reception for the faithful worship of people in so-called nonliturgical settings, others, like Robert Webber, have moved in the opposite direction. "I began to see," he observes, "that 'free worship' is not necessarily free."[3] To test my understanding of the liturgical commonalities I hoped to discuss as I began this book, I made a point of having a conversation about worship with a faculty colleague who is a leading ecumenist from the Pentecostal tradition. We spoke about the worship principles we held in common and in the end concluded that if a Lutheran and a scholar from the Assemblies of God can agree on certain matters of worship, there is certainly something to build on.

This book is an attempt to broaden that conversation and reveal things learned in the living laboratory of the church at worship in the world.[4] Essentially, the book will argue for a common understanding regarding a theology of worship that can lead us to acknowledge our shared foundations for worship practice, and it will celebrate the idea of Christian diversity.

As a young Christian, I often wondered why there were so many different denominations in the church. I reflected that there must be many because not all people could come to the faith in the same way that I did and not all would want to express their faith in my own limited way. Accordingly, I surmised, it should not be a surprise that there might be perhaps a dozen denominations in the world. It would be, in fact, a matter to celebrate that God could work in people's lives in so many ways. Little did I know then of diversity. But now that I am more seasoned in my understanding of the church's breadth, I find

---

are strong voices urging recognition of the worship forms, patterns, and theological principles that we have in common. It is on these observations that the present discussion is built.

3. Webber, *Worship Is a Verb*, 4.

4. While none of us can have experienced worship in every corner of the church, I have had the opportunity to do so on four continents and among people from countless denominations and faith traditions.

those early assumptions still hold. The church is vastly diverse—and must be. We must also be a church at worship. There are some liturgical foundations and formulations we hold in common. They will be brought to expression in various ways, depending on who we are, where we come from, and where we worship. Finding the proper local liturgical equilibrium is to strike a balance between what Pedrito Maynard-Reid calls "constancy" and "diversity."[5]

This book will also argue for the renewal of worship in all places by a firmer knowledge of the worship practices of Christians in many places. It will suggest that worship can be enriched by the careful appreciation and thoughtful reception of worship expressions of people from many countries and cultures. I do not advocate indiscriminate borrowing of worship expressions, but I do argue for what might be called an "informed eclecticism."[6] It may not be necessary for worship to incorporate expressions from other cultures in order for it to be appropriate and lively. But, historically, the church has borrowed things from many places and baptized them for liturgical use. That it continues to do so, especially in an age of worldwide communication, is fitting and proper.

One of the places worship draws its expression from is contemporary culture. This, too, is important, for we are not the church of another age. We are the church of the twenty-first century and need to provide worship opportunities that engage people of this culture. "It will no longer do," said liturgical historian Todd Johnson, "to prepare people for a church that does not exist."[7] Ethnomusicologist C. Michael Hawn has said that the worship of the church is a centuries-old hymn to which every generation adds a new stanza.[8] The new stanza may take a musical form, may incorporate other art forms, may be a surprise—or even an offense—to some believers. But if the new stanza is thoughtfully wrought and theologically appropriate, it will have its place among our diverse expressions of worship.

This book is not without its opinions. There are some issues that can be decided as we think about the shape of worship in the twenty-first century. Accordingly, I attempt to draw some conclusions about how worship can be shaped for a missional, diverse church. For this reason, the project strives to be both a practical theology of worship and a manual for worship. Those

5. See Maynard-Reid, *Diverse Worship*, esp. chap. 3, "Constancy and Diversity."

6. I am indebted to liturgical scholar Michael Aune for the suggestion of this term.

7. This statement came from a private conversation regarding the practice of teaching worship in seminaries. It is representative of the kinds of conversations that gave shape to this project.

8. Hawn borrows this concept from United Methodist Bishop Joel Martínez who said (in 1996): "Each generation must add its stanza to the great hymn of the church." Hawn takes this to mean that "each generation needs to speak to and of God according to the realities and time in which it lives. However, like a good hymn, we should sing the earlier stanzas too—our inheritance from the saints. Yet, we should not stop on the penultimate stanza, afraid to venture into the concerns and needs of our own time, but finish the hymn and see what God has to say to us today." From private correspondence with C. Michael Hawn (September 2008).

familiar with traditional worship manuals know that they typically seek to prescribe rubrics and offer detailed explanations regarding appropriate language, gesture, and form in worship. This manual is less specific and seeks to be useful to a diverse church. The rubrics or guidelines I will consider are those that reflect shared practices rather than the established practices of an individual worshiping community. The explanations regarding specific forms and practices will be open to interpretation, depending on various matters of context.

At the heart of this project lies a hypothesis that I hope the research and discussion will prove. My sense is that, regardless of tradition or denomination, worship in our churches can be renewed when we attend to the theological issues that place us on solid footing and the contextual issues that make us unique. In other words, if a practical theology of worship bears a certain structural footprint, it is not hard to imagine that numerous architectural expressions might appropriately rise from it. The foundation will yield worship structures that vary according to where, when, and how they are built.

I envision a church where a person from a strictly liturgical tradition might happen into the worship of a charismatic church and both understand what it is about and feel compelled to participate. Conversely, I can imagine—and in fact, have occasionally seen—incidents where those from free church traditions feel at ease and at home in very formal modes of liturgy that were highly engaging. To give one example, an African American Baptist colleague once told of presiding over the Eucharist in a multidenominational setting. He chose to use the familiar (to some) words of a Eucharistic prayer as a means of praying over the elements. When he reached the words, "Pour out your Holy Spirit upon this bread and this wine," he noted that worshipers from traditionally liturgical churches attended to them in familiar ways. But so, too, did those from Pentecostal traditions. For them, the words prompted an eruption of vocalized responses common to their own worship. The *epiclesis* (prayer for the coming of the Holy Spirit) is a form of prayer liturgically appropriate to both traditions and equally familiar to them (even if not understood in such terms by the Pentecostal participants). This book seeks to initiate conversation that searches out and celebrates—and learns to build on—similar commonalities.

The Shape of the Conversation

This book is presented in two parts. Part 1, which includes the first six chapters, makes several grounding observations about worship for the twenty-first century and represents the theological heart of the book.

In order to establish a meaningful conversation about worship, several key terms will be identified and clarified. Some terms common to the worship discussion will also be considered briefly and dismissed from the dialogue as too vague or multivalent in meaning to be useful. Among those things placed on the table for discussion will be the fourfold pattern of worship that is commonly used by churches of many denominations, though more freely in some than in others. The establishment of these terms and forms will be undertaken in the first chapter.

Chapter 2 explains why the book has a contrary title, *Sent and Gathered*. (We are obviously gathered together for worship *before* we are sent back into the world in Christian service.) It reviews the case that the Christian church is now in a post-Christian mission era and recognizes that there is a two-part rhythm to worship. Borrowing from Miroslav Volf, worship is described as both adoration and action. Christians typically gather for an hour or two of adoration on Sunday mornings. But, as the service ends, there is the moment of sending wherein God's people are compelled outward toward Christian action and mission in the world. The sending is the fulcrum where worship turns from its interior focus to its outward thrust.[9] This chapter builds a case for missional worship that does not end with the benediction but that uses the sending as a compelling liturgical moment empowering believers for missionary activity in the world.

The third and fourth chapters examine the shape of the liturgical reunification that is at work in many parts of the church. Whereas the history of the Protestant church is the story of how the Reformers sought increasing freedom from the theological and liturgical constraints of the late-medieval Catholic Church, today there are aspects of convergence in liturgical thought and practice. Chapter 3 explores the biblical and historic wisdom behind the simple, four-part pattern of worship that is increasingly being recognized as the blueprint for Christian liturgy. Chapter 4 considers the role of art in worship and describes how leadership in the artistic renewal of worship is happening in surprising places. Those churches and traditions that were once most opposed to the supposedly idolatrous use of the arts in the Reformation period are now proving to be guides in creating worship that is rich with artistic expression. Additionally, the church today, with its capacity for instantaneous communication, is becoming increasingly aware that there is much to be learned from the artistic expressions of Christians in other congregations, denominations, and geographic locations.

The fifth chapter reviews the concepts that worship always involves communication and that a goal of worship leadership is to communicate precisely what is intended. There is often a gap between what a church expresses as its beliefs and what is being expressed locally by the language or actions of those

---

9. By *interior focus* I mean the attention placed by believers on adoration of God and God's focus on the people gathered to be centered in worship. It is interior in that it takes place within and is the larger part of the hour of adoration.

leading worship. This chapter argues for the careful and proper use of gesture and rhetoric that congruently bespeak a church's theology.

The focus of the sixth chapter is the context of worship. It concludes part 1 by summarizing basic worship principles and describing a matrix, or a set of categories, that can guide worship planning and theological critique. It argues that Christian worship, regardless of denomination and tradition, can be built on theological foundations and that the particularities of local contexts are key factors in determining the proper forms and expressions for a given setting.

Part 2 of the book turns to the practical matters of worship planning and leadership. Following the four-part fundamental pattern of the liturgy, each of the four chapters offers specific guidance in the form of a worship manual.[10] Building on the foundational issues discussed in part 1, particular theological principles for worship will be reviewed and specific guidelines for the implementation of worship practices will be presented. The suggestions proffered derive from common worship principles yet demonstrate how they might be variously employed depending on context. In keeping with the book's upside-down (or inside-out) approach, part 2 begins at the end as it reviews the importance of the *sending* portion of the liturgy. As T. S. Eliot observed, "to make an end is to make a beginning." Chapter 7 suggests ways for missionally oriented worship to be planned and executed with intention and force. In chapter 8 we return to where worship begins, with an exploration of the principles for assembling as a worshiping community. Chapter 9 considers issues relating to the proclamation of the Word, both read and preached, and chapter 10 takes up the celebration and remembrance of sacramental actions.

Toward a Practical Theology of Worship

Before we get to the heart of the material, it will be useful to address a foundational issue. The field of liturgical studies is a vast and growing area of

10. Manuals for guiding worship leaders in the graceful execution of liturgies have been in use for centuries. The Sacramentary, developed in the Middle Ages, contained collections of prayers and liturgical formulas, but few directions for implementation of liturgies. Full liturgical instructions were contained in separate volumes known as *ordines*. Missals, in use from the tenth century to the present, are books that combine Roman Catholic services of worship with clerical instructions for liturgical execution. They, too, contain limited instructions and rely on separately published customaries for additional directions. The Protestant church has produced countless worship books, some incorporating manual instructions (such as *A Directory for the Public Worship of God*, the so-called Westminster Directory of the Church of Scotland, published in 1645), others published with companion manuals giving detailed background and guidance for liturgical practice (e.g., *The Lutheran Book of Worship*, 1978, and its companion *Manual on the Liturgy*, 1979). Even free church denominations have produced manuals for worship. For example, the *Minister's Manual* (three volumes) by William E. Pickthorn was published by the Assemblies of God. See Bradshaw, *The New Westminster Dictionary of Liturgy and Worship*, 66–86.

research. It springs from the liturgical movement that began, as some argue, in the early twentieth century and that gave rise to the disciplined study of Christian liturgy.[11] In *What Is Liturgical Theology?* David Fagerberg has identified scholarship in four categories: theology of worship, theology from worship, liturgical theology, and secondary reflections on liturgical theology.[12] In discussing what he calls "liturgics," Fagerberg implies but does not name a fifth category, practical theology of worship.

"Up to quite recent times," wrote liturgical scholar Alexander Schmemann in 1960, "liturgics has belonged to the category of 'supplementary' or 'practical' disciplines."[13] Schmemann admits to a neglect of this area by liturgical scholars because as "an applied science," it is "of interest for the most part to the clergy, but not to theologians."[14] In other words, he admits of longstanding tension between what is considered genuine theology and what is considered practical theology. Fagerberg reflects this opinion in his own writing: "When a strict dichotomy is imposed between theology and liturgy, the latter is usually treated as mere expression of faith in pious, esthetic and emotive forms, itself void of theological content. It is as if theology exists for academicians and liturgy exists for pure-hearted (but simple-minded) believers."[15]

This book holds no bias against things written for pastors and other liturgical practitioners. At the same time, it seeks to be theologically critical with regard to the practical science of liturgics. It is, in fact, a practical theology. It is written for clergy and others who seek to understand the practice of worship and how it relates to their own denominational or traditional theology. It is also written for those who seek to understand how the practice of worship relates to the unique cultural situation the church currently hopes to thrive in. In addition, this practical theology of worship is written with the hope that it can be used in seminary classrooms as a tool for getting at the physical practices of leading worship and proclaiming the gospel. The book seeks, moreover, to be part of an ongoing discussion by liturgiologists and practical theologians who want Christian worship to have a distinct character in the twenty-first century yet a clear connection to the practices of the millennia that precede it. The book is written by one who is a clergyman, a scholar, and

---

11. Some scholars indicate that, though it has nineteenth-century roots, the movement actually began in the early twentieth century. Renowned Orthodox liturgical theologian Alexander Schmemann, for example, says it "began almost simultaneously in different parts of the Christian world in the years following the First World War." See *Introduction to Liturgical Theology*, 13. Others, as Patrick Keifert demonstrates, argue that the movement "came in two waves, the first originating in the nineteenth century with liturgical reforms on the European continent and separate movements at Oxford and Cambridge." See *Welcoming the Stranger*, 39.

12. For an understanding of the nuanced differences between these categories, see Fagerberg, *What Is Liturgical Theology?* 11–12.

13. Schmemann, *Introduction to Liturgical Theology*, 9.

14. Ibid., 9–10.

15. Fagerberg, *What Is Liturgical Theology?* 13.

a continuing student of worship who does research in the field each time he observes and joins God's people at prayer and praise.

Penultimately, it should be said that this book intends to work *toward* a practical theology of worship. It is not the final word, nor even my final word, on the topic. It is, rather, part of the continuing conversation about the practice of worship. Readers join in the conversation when they examine the pages that follow and when they experiment with the manual suggestions that conclude this work. If the suggestions prove to be useful, the conversation will have succeeded in one way. Insofar as these pages spark disagreement or are poorly conceived or articulated, the conversation will succeed when practitioners and practical theologians take up the debate, adding their own opinions and offering rebuttal with regard to the nature of worship in an age of mission. Either way, the discussion is about something that is of ultimate importance to the future of the church: how God's people are led into an encounter with the One who made them, who restores them, and who inspires them for active service in the world.

Finally, it needs to be acknowledged that this book represents a stroll through the gardens of a number of academic disciplines. For example, it has to do with ritual studies, semiotics, anthropology, phenomenology, musicology, aesthetics, cultural studies, liturgics, missiology (and other branches of theology), and certainly more. The purpose of the book is to survey, rather than contribute to, the work of these disciplines as it relates to worship. My hope is that by searching through many fruitful acres, we can harvest the things about Christian worship that represent our commonalities and assemble a cornucopia from them for the sake of Christian unity. The ultimate goal is to contribute to ecumenical worship renewal, which can only be done by "love and invitation," as the Faith and Order Commission of the World Council of Churches rightly insists. I invite readers into the conversation and hope that my side of the discussion is made charitably.

One

Worship and the
Mission of God

1

Foundations

> The missio Dei is God's revelation of God's self as irrevocably bound to this world. It is about God's own passionate desire, which will not be frustrated, to move more and more into the world and more and more into each human heart.[1]
>
> Michael Aune

As we begin this conversation, we need to establish the foundations our thought is based on. For this, I will identify the four common building blocks that give worship its shape. Second, I will place before us the vocabulary for worship that will be used throughout the book. Finally, I will consider the missional character of the church in the twenty-first century, the church whose worship we seek to inform.

The Fourfold Common Pattern for Worship

The church in North America is enjoying a period of increasing liturgical convergence. Not long ago, there was frequent and heated discussion about the so-called worship wars, where the liturgical practices of traditional churches were challenged by those employing various forms of contemporary wor-

---

1. Aune, "Ritual Practice," in Schattauer, *Inside Out*, 174.

ship.[2] Now, as the smoke from the battlefield clears, we find that people are attempting to learn from one another: traditionally liturgical churches are adopting contemporary modes of liturgical expression from megachurches; megachurches and emerging church networks are embracing the use of arts in worship; all churches are exploring ways to use media, moving images, and technology in worship and ministry; and the worlds of the evangelical and free churches are embracing once-eschewed patterns of formal liturgy. In part, this comes as the fruit of a longstanding movement toward liturgical renewal.[3] This convergence also results from the desire among churches of many kinds to accept some of the gifts of postmodern culture: renewed interest in symbol and mystery, emphasis on personal experience, capacity for instantaneous worldwide communication, eclecticism, a search for authenticity, and so forth. The result of this confluence of liturgical streams is that many churches are settling on a shared but broadly construed pattern of worship that will be familiar to those who worship within traditional liturgical settings.

The pattern that is being widely embraced emerges from the fact that when the people of God assemble, they do so as a local configuration of the body of Christ. This makes *gathering* a key feature of any form of worship. When assembled, the people of God gather around the traditional Christian symbols and their related liturgical actions, *Word* and *sacrament*.[4] Having been gathered and fed by fellowship, Scripture, and sacramental practices (or remembrances), God's people of every denomination and tradition are *sent* forth at the close of worship, dispersing back into the communities where they live and work. This increasingly accepted liturgical format is identified in four movements: *gathering, Word, sacraments, sending*.[5] Graham Hughes gives this description of the recent trend toward liturgical unity:

> Across the remarkable proliferation of new orders of service in western Christianity through the concluding decades of the twentieth century—as a response to, and manifestation of, the so-called Liturgical Movement in western churches—there is an equally remarkable uniformity, both in their basic, and in their more detailed, structures. They are commonly arranged in four components: an opening or introductory rite, followed by what is called the Service

2. Patrick Keifert defines the worship wars as "the intense conflict within churches trying to develop Christian worship appropriate for this transitional time between Christendom and the New Missional Era" (*We Are Here Now*, 169). The battles continue in some places. Armistice has been reached in others.

3. A brief history of the Liturgical Renewal movement in the church in the West can be found in Keifert, *Welcoming the Stranger*, 41–53. A culminating effect of the movement in the Roman Catholic Church was the liturgical reform that resulted from the Second Vatican Council. Its relationship to "contemporary worship" is explored helpfully by Plantinga and Rozeboom in *Discerning the Spirits*, 23–27.

4. Lathrop, *What Are the Essentials of Christian Worship?* 7.

5. See Webber, *Planning Blended Worship*.

of the Word, a rite for the celebration [of] the Eucharist, and a "dismissal" or "sending" rite. The term *ordo* is sometimes invoked for this near universal "shape of the liturgy."[6]

It may seem bold to claim that this pattern or ordo is common to most Christian traditions of worship. The claim may be especially suspicious to those in free churches. Yet when one analyzes the shape of worship in most traditions (setting aside typical Quaker worship, which gathers, prays, and leaves in silence), the pattern holds. Even churches whose worship derives from frontier revival meetings are characterized by rites of assembly, proclamation of and response to the Word, at least occasional sacramental action or remembrance, and songs and rites of dispersal.[7] The sacramental portions may not always fall in the traditional place, but nearly all churches celebrate baptisms and communions in some form.[8]

While this common pattern for worship is useful insofar as it brings a layer of unity to the Christian church that is welcome after as much as a half century of division over musical and worship idioms, it does not automatically solve all worship problems and does not guarantee that worship will necessarily unfold in a way that is conducive to the mission of God. Some people have voiced challenges to the idea of a common order of worship. Interestingly, they come chiefly from those who most appreciate its value and are sensitive about overstating its usefulness. Lutheran liturgical theologian Gordon Lathrop, who says that "we may call this simple and widely affirmed pattern 'the ecumenical *ordo*,'" is aware of a number of concerns arising from postmodern thought: "For one thing, there is the question, 'Whose *ordo*?' That is, what communities in fact follow this pattern? But also, who gains power by the privileging of this pattern?" Second, Lathrop admits to the possibility that this generally useful pattern for worship may be "painted with too broad a brush," that it may be "only applicable in some places," and that it might be nothing more than "a mental construct forced upon the actual facts," an "unwarranted 'meta-narrative' intending to indicate a widespread similarity of practice where none exists." His most searching question is this: "How does *ordo* avoid becoming ideology?" These questions remain sensitive to what goes on in local worshiping communities, "to the local particularities and the locally thick and thin moments" of Christian worship.[9]

6. Hughes, *Worship as Meaning*, 166.

7. Frank Senn describes the shape of such liturgies in his magisterial *Christian Liturgy*, referring to the so-called seeker service associated with certain megachurches as "a form of the old frontier or revival pattern of worship with a gathering including songs, testimonies, concerns, and prayers, followed by the reading of Scripture and preaching, and a response to the word" (688).

8. There are exceptions; for example, the Salvation Army and the Society of Friends (commonly known as the Quakers) do not typically practice baptism and Holy Communion.

9. Lathrop, "Bath, Word, Prayer, Table," in Lange and Vogel, *Ordo*, 218, 219.

In response to these worthy challenges to the claim that there is such a thing as a common pattern that is ecumenically pertinent, Lathrop concludes:

> Indeed, the postmodern challenges may help us to treasure the ecumenical *ordo* the more, especially when it is noted that an open meeting around a multivalent pool, around an interesting set of words and around an inviting supper is not, in the first place, designed to compel [usage]. Healthy liturgy, focused on strong central signs and not individual personal decisions, makes a way of ever deeper significance available to its participants, but it also lets those participants be free.[10]

Michael Aune also observes that there are a couple of problems associated with the way this fourfold pattern relates to a church's pattern of ministry. For one, we may be sent out for mission at the end of a service, but "most likely once the liturgy has ended, we go downstairs to the coffee hour instead."[11] The second and larger problem, Aune notes, is that when we are sent forth from worship to ministry in the world, the sending can carry a tone of agenda that might be at odds with God's purpose. This has "the potential result that the missio Dei, what God is doing in the world, has been subsumed under our own agendas." Still, Aune, a liturgical theologian doing work on worship and mission, argues that we need to shape our worship rituals with "considerable care and attention—not for the sake of exhibiting some flawless [ritual or ritualizing] technique, but for the sake of evoking an ongoing recognition of God's presence and activity in the world."[12]

The liturgical convergence that is characterized by this fourfold construction brings a welcome respite after years of warring over liturgical idioms and music. Churches of many denominations and traditions find it useful to craft their liturgies with these four movements clearly marked.[13] Whether traditionally ordered or free, richly figured or spare, the pattern provides for worship that has a reasoned sense of plot and flow. The gathering, whether it contains a single entrance hymn or a twenty-minute set of songs, draws the people together in the place and moment of corporate worship. Assembled, they hear the Word of God read and proclaimed, increasingly through the use of arts. The sermon and/or artistic proclamation of the Word bring the assembly to a liturgical culmination. When the sacraments or ordinances are celebrated, a second climax is attained.[14] The sending is the liturgical denouement.

Each of these liturgical actions has its own power and purpose. What I seek to demonstrate in this book is that whereas the final movement, the

---

10. Ibid.
11. Aune, "Ritual Practice," in Schattauer, *Inside Out*, 170–71.
12. Ibid., 72–73.
13. See, for example, the communion liturgies published in *The United Methodist Book of Worship*; *The Book of Common Worship* of the Presbyterian Church (USA) and the Evangelical Lutheran Church's African American hymnal, *This Far by Faith*.
14. Lathrop, *Holy Things*, 50.

sending, is often considered to be the least important part of worship, it has the potential to connect the hour of Sunday worship to the rest of the work we do as Christians in our daily lives of witness and service.[15] This will be the subject of chapter 2.

Our conversation about the common patterns of worship will relate principally to the ecumenical ordo described above. But there are other aspects of ecumenical practice that will come under consideration as we proceed. Among them are the liturgical qualities of time and space.

Liturgical Time and Space

Even though some churches disregard much of the church calendar, all communities of faith acknowledge the need for Sabbath, a common day (whether it is Saturday or Sunday) for worship. Most acknowledge at least two liturgical seasons, Christmas and Easter. There are many more days and seasons that can be observed, and some faith traditions adhere strictly to a full structuring of liturgical time. Monastic communities still pray the daily hours in addition to celebrating weekly and seasonal observances. For some faith communities, daily, yearly, and three-year lectionaries guide the use of biblical texts in worship. The use of the liturgical calendar and both the values and problems relating to the use of lectionaries will be addressed in part 2 of this book.

There is also some level of ecumenical agreement as to the shaping of liturgical space. Generally, we establish our assembly seating before or around a pulpit, a table, and perhaps a baptismal font or pool. The ways that space communicates, facilitates, and sometimes dominates worship will also be discussed in part 2.

Rehabilitating Our Vocabulary

One of the most taxing issues in liturgical studies in recent years has been developing a meaningful vocabulary with which to discuss the range of worship practices today. Some old terms, such as *ritual*, *rubric*, and *liturgy*, have been so closely associated with medieval Roman Catholic worship or its contemporary cousins that they have been eschewed by those in free church traditions. Meanwhile, terms like *contemporary* and *blended worship* have been so widely used that there is little agreement as to what they mean. What

15. As elsewhere in this book, certain terms will be used as shorthand to refer to complex issues. In this case, *Sunday worship* is used as a metaphor for the regular, weekly gathering of God's people, whether that occurs on Saturday (as on the biblical Sabbath) or midweek, as in seeker-sensitive churches whose Sunday seeker services are followed by worship for the faithful on Wednesday evenings. Seventh-day Adventists provide an example of the former; Willow Creek Community Church is an example of the latter.

Sidebar 1.1: The One, the Few, and the Many

Who is present for worship? Those who assemble are the body of Christ, made up of people with differing roles and varying degrees of spiritual engagement. They are the *many* who come to participate in the songs and prayer, listen to the Word as read and preached, give assent to the community's place in baptism, be nourished by the Eucharist, and be sent out into service to Christ. Among them may be both the initiated and those inquiring into the faith; some, spiritually mature and well versed in the local patterns unfolding about them; others, newly initiated and still learning the forms, songs, and patterns of prayer. They will be people diverse in age, culture, and circumstance.

Also present are the *few* with specialized roles. They may be people in the choir. . . . They may also include the trained laypeople who perform the ministerial functions of canting, accompanying music, reading Scripture, leading in prayer, and serving as acolytes, banner bearers, and crucifers. In more central roles, there are usually the preaching minister and the presiding minister. . . .

These are the constituency of worship, people who are present to one another as the community of faith. But the list is incomplete, for they cannot gather as the people of faith unless the center and focus of that faith is also present. Worship cannot be godly, or God-pleasing, unless it is the gathering of God's people in the presence of God. Christian worship is the assembly and active participation of the *many*, the *few*, and the *One*.

Clayton J. Schmit, Too Deep for Words: A Theology of Liturgical Expression *(Louisville: Westminster John Knox, 2002), 27–28.*

passes as contemporary in some places incorporates music and forms that are anachronistic by a quarter century. What appears as blended worship in one place may pass as a traditional liturgy in another. As we begin, it is necessary to identify the terms that will be used in this discussion and those that, for the sake of clarity, will be avoided.

Worship and Worship Leader

We start with the word *worship* itself, which is reduced in certain settings to mean nothing more than a set of worship songs sung by the congregation and led by a *worship leader*.[16] It is not uncommon to hear a musical worship

16. See, for example, Navarro, *The Complete Worship Leader*. In this book the author refers to many kinds of worship leadership, including preaching, selecting liturgical art, setting the communion table, providing for sensory input in worship, etc. Yet as the following quotation makes clear, the art of music is privileged in his account, and the term *worship leadership* suggests musical leadership exclusively: "There are many ways to engage the five senses in the worship experience, but we must explore with good judgment and not do anything inappropriate. . . . As

leader say that following the worship, the service will continue with the reading of Scripture and the sermon, as if these were not fundamental elements of Christian worship since biblical times. In this discussion, *worship* will refer to two broad categories: (1) the full complex of activities (song, prayer, praise, lament, proclamation, silence, offerings, meditation, fellowship, announcements, etc.) that make up our public adoration of God and (2) those actions that relate to the work of Christian discipleship in the world. The Sunday morning worship leaders, then, are not just the musical leaders; so too are pastors, preachers, readers, ushers, choirs, instrumentalists, acolytes, altar servers, media technicians, and so forth. They are the *few* whose job it is to prepare carefully for the moment when *many* gather to come into the presence of the *One* God (see sidebar 1.1).

Presiding and Assisting Ministers

The few who prepare in advance for the gathering of the worshiping community may consist of quite a number of individuals. Some choirs, for example, have a hundred voices. Not all worship leaders, however, have central leadership roles. In fact, usually, there is one central leader. That person is known by a number of names. *Presider* is common in reference to an ordained leader, but it is not intended to mean presidential in the powerful sense: "not with the massive authority of a 'president,'" says Gordon Lathrop. Presiders in worship do not draw attention but give it. They point "beyond themselves to the One who lives at the heart of the assembly's symbols."[17] Another common word for an ordained central leader is *celebrant*, the person who leads celebrations of the Eucharist and of festive worship services such as baptisms and weddings. Both terms will be employed in the pages that follow. A less common and more officious term (literally) is *officiant*, the one who provides official—even legal—oversight to proceedings such as weddings; this term will not be used.

There are several useful terms for nonordained leaders in worship (e.g., *deacon*, *presbyter*, and *cantor*). Preferred here will be the use of *assisting minister*. This captures the egalitarian sense that all servants in worship are ministers. Assisting ministers execute their roles not in assistance of the celebrant but in assistance of the assembly. The worshipers are the ones for whom the few rehearse. Regardless of the centrality of their roles, both presiding and assisting ministers have a duty to learn their roles well and to practice their words—whether they are scripted or improvised—in order to lead worship gracefully. When they do so, they "invest" their words and actions "with the gift of oneself."[18]

---

worship leaders, we need to distinguish great works of art from average art. We need to begin to expose our churches to great art whether *pre-composed* or *self-composed*. God deserves our best!" (93; my italics, to highlight the conflation of *art* and *music*).

17. Lathrop, *The Pastor*, 10, 11.
18. Ibid., 25.

Liturgy

The term *liturgy* has been used in the church since biblical days. It derives from the Greek *leitourgia*. In its first setting, the word referred to the work of the people, specifically, the civic work that citizens performed in their communities: public service or public works.[19] The expression was adopted in the Greek version of the Hebrew Scriptures (the Septuagint) and by New Testament writers to refer to priestly actions performed during public worship. Through the years, *liturgy* has come to mean the specific rites involved in services of worship. It is especially associated with the sacraments, for example, communion liturgies and baptism liturgies. But, beyond reference to specific rites, the term is also used today as a way to emphasize the egalitarian quality of worship. If liturgy is the work of the people, then it is not something performed solely by ordained priests for the sake of gathered worshipers. It is something done by the entire priesthood of believers (1 Pet. 2:9). The public work of the people is to sing and pray together, listen to and participate in the proclamation of the Word, join in fellowship and communion, and be sent into the broader ministry of the church as a community of faith.

For some, the word *liturgy* suggests worship that is executed in rote and mechanical ways. Clearly, this is not its intended meaning.[20] I sense that the time is right to rehabilitate the use of *liturgy* as a descriptor for the forms and actions of worshiping people when they gather. This is done based on a growing impression that the word has declining negative associations. One sign of the convergence that will be described in chapter 3 is that there appears to be greater openness today for things *liturgical*. A classroom anecdote may elucidate. As I begin to teach Christian worship, I typically ask students how many of them grew up in worship traditions where the term *liturgy* was interpreted negatively. As few as three years ago, half of the class would raise their hands. Recently, this number has been reduced to a few persons.

In this book, the use of the term *liturgy* is maintained with reference to the usual matters: (1) theological issues relating to worship (as in the study of liturgy), (2) specific forms or orders of worship (such as Taizé liturgies or communion liturgies), (3) the body of worship services belonging to a church or denomination (such as the Orthodox liturgy), or (4) the egalitarian work of the people who gather to worship God. The latter meaning relates to the characteristic Protestant theological emphasis on the priesthood of all believers. By these definitions, we can see that all people who gather for Christian worship, regardless of tradition or denomination, have forms of prayer and

19. As Todd Johnson once put it informally, "If a person dug a community well, that was a liturgical act."

20. Eddie Gibbs has helpfully quipped that liturgy intends to provide "a structure, not a corset."

Sidebar 1.2: Liturgy Is the Enacted Expectations of the Gathering

Every act of worship has some structure. Common sense suggests that someone has decided what time the meeting will start, who will lead, what music there will be, and who will speak. Even a community which has decided to make a worship time completely open has actually *decided* to do this, and gradually habits form as to who will do what. Congregations which worship regularly together get into a rhythm and develop a style, not only because a desire for some kind of order is part of our humanity, but also because the Spirit gifts people to offer complementary ministries which the same people tend to express (some are prophets, others teachers, etc.). In this sense the liturgy is about the enacted expectations of the gathering: "what have we gathered for and who will put it into practice?"

Jeremy Fletcher and Christopher Cocksworth, The Spirit and Liturgy (Cambridge, UK: Grove Books, 1998), 14.

---

practice that can be described as liturgies. In other words, from this perspective there are no *nonliturgical* traditions of worship.[21]

Churches that have historically considered themselves to be nonliturgical, liberated from what they have seen as the constraints of liturgy, are sometimes called *free churches* or practice *free worship*. While I argue that even these churches have a liturgy, given that any organizational pattern for worship can rightly be termed a liturgy, I find that the term *free* in relation to these churches and their liturgies is a useful distinction. Therefore, I will use *traditional liturgy* for those that follow a more conservative line and *free liturgy* for those that are more freely structured.[22]

In addition to *liturgy*, several related terms will be used as we proceed. Referring to the specific actions that make up the activities of worship, they are employed somewhat interchangeably: *pattern* or *order of worship*, *ordo* (the classic Latin term for the shape of the Roman Catholic Mass), *form of worship*, and *worship service*.

Ritual

As with the word *liturgy*, some Christians have historically sought to avoid using the term *ritual*[23] in relation to what takes place in worship. It suggests

---

21. A Pentecostal pastor once confessed to me, "In my church, we do not have a liturgy. Of course, we do the same things every week, and if I dare to change them around, I will probably need to look for a new job."

22. I do not mean to imply, by the use of *free church*, the European distinction between state (or established) churches and those free from state control and support.

23. The field of ritual studies has strong ties to the study of the liturgy. Growing out of the modern assumption that anything can be understood through study, it began in the nineteenth

for them lack of creativity, rote participation, and cold and formal enactment of prescribed events. Often, the meaning of the word has been linked with certain negative modifiers, as in *dead ritual* or *mere ritual*.

As with *liturgy*, the time is right to recapture the use of a powerful idea and its referent word. People are coming to realize that ritual is not lifeless but an inextricable part of life. Mark Bangert explains:

> Rituals establish patterns for the way things really are, patterns that continue well beyond the holy time and space. They unveil the deep, hence real, dynamics of personal relationship; they carefully mark the doorways to . . . life, so that participants might perceive meaning and purpose in ordinary life. Through repeated conventions, rituals show us how to act, reveal what is valuable, and provide patterns of behavior toward the creation and all those who have not yet tasted the goodness of God.[24]

We have rituals in every aspect of life, and they exist in every culture.[25] It is no surprise that rituals are at work in worship. They give us corporate actions that draw us into movements in worship that stand for life and faith. "Ritual reduces in order that it might expand."[26] The use of *ritual* and the related *rite* will also be rehabilitated for this conversation.

Ordinaries and Propers

The terms *ordinaries* and *propers* have specific meaning in the context of liturgical studies. They refer, generally in relation to the church calendar, to those elements of worship that are constant and those that are variable. In churches where a traditional liturgy is commonly used, the elements that are employed on a regular or *ordinary* basis are known as the *ordinaries*. For example, when such churches gather for worship, they ordinarily recite the Lord's Prayer as part of the service. They might also sing or say a *Kyrie eleison* (the historic Latin prayer featuring the words "Lord have mercy, Christ have mercy") and recite a creed. These elements of worship are among the ordinaries used by those churches. The *propers* refer to portions of a service that are

---

century to look at the rituals of global peoples through numerous lenses, including ethnology, phenomenology, anthropology, and psychology. Its relationship to liturgy has focused especially on the sacramental rites of Christians. For a review of the connection between liturgiology and ritual studies, see Lange and Vogel, *Ordo: Bath, Word, Prayer, Table*, esp. chap. 1, "Towards a Rediscovery of the Christian Sacrament," by Schillebeeckx. The study of ritual has also been an important part of missiology. See, for example, Hiebert, Shaw, and Tiénou, *Understanding Folk Religion*.

24. Bangert, "Holy Communion," in Schattauer, *Inside Out*, 69.

25. Examples are all around us: bedtime prayers with children, saying the Pledge of Allegiance in school, standing during baseball's seventh inning stretch, punching a time clock at work, and lighting fireworks on Independence Day, to name a few.

26. Bangert, "Holy Communion," in Schattauer, *Inside Out*, 69.

selected as appropriate for the day. For example, Scripture lessons for Christmas Day will be different from those that would be proper for the season of Lent. Other propers include songs or hymns selected for a given occasion, prayers pertaining to a worship theme or season, the sermon's particular focus, and so forth. The historic use of the ordinaries and propers is explored in chapter 6. There, too, the notion of what is proper in worship today is expanded to include broad liturgical issues, such as what kinds of language or music are proper for people who worship in a given denomination or tradition? Is it proper for the worship of Episcopalians to be identical to that practiced by followers of the Willow Creek model? Is it proper for North American Christians to borrow songs or prayers from Christians in Asia or South America? What kinds of art are proper for worship in various traditions, or at certain times of year? How does a church determine whether the use of technological media is proper for its worship? We shall see that the multifaceted issue of context is a key determinant of what should be considered ordinary and proper in a given worship setting.

Style and Idiom

The preferred term in this conversation for what is typically called worship *style* will be *idiom*. It relates to the specific character of expression involved in a given kind of worship. *Style* suggests a number of unhelpful connotations. Style can be transitory, as when something is *in style*. It can be subjective, as in someone's *personal style*. It can also be dependent on cultural trends, as in *stylish* or *out of style*. *Idiom* is a less worn, thus more convenient term for the issues under consideration. As Jeremy Begbie says of music, "Idioms, limiting and defining possibilities, . . . are inextricably bound up with social meanings and codes, and sometimes with large-scale interpretive frameworks."[27] Worship idioms are also limited and defined by certain modes of expression that can be identified, categorized, and evaluated.

Sacraments and Ordinances

The Reformation began a debate over the nature of Christian sacraments that continues to this day. The medieval Roman Catholic Church identified seven pastoral actions as sacraments: baptism, communion, ordination, penance, confirmation, marriage, and last rites for dying persons. Luther and the other Reformers reduced the sacraments to two, baptism and communion, although Luther was open to the inclusion of penance among the sacraments. The Protestant church settled on baptism and communion as the only sacraments,[28]

---

27. Begbie, *Theology, Music, and Time*, 214–15.

28. Anglicans, it should be noted, distinguish between these two *dominical sacraments* and the other five that are also embraced by the Catholic Church.

with an understanding that they were biblical actions mandated by Christ himself and that involved mundane elements (water, bread, and wine). For Lutherans and others (e.g., Anglicans and Episcopalians), the sacraments are rituals that execute strong divine action. Baptism is God's incorporation of persons into the body of Christ. Communion brings the physical presence of Christ and his forgiveness. The sacraments are understood as *means of grace*. For churches that have followed Ulrich Zwingli's sacramental theology, the sacraments are not indicators of any presence or activity of God. They are simply remembrances of God's saving actions. Still seen as having been ordained by Christ himself, they are practiced as symbolic gestures that bring to mind what God has done for God's people.

In order to create distance between these two theological understandings (divine presence and remembrance of God's acts), certain traditions began to use the term *ordinance* in place of *sacrament*. According to these churches, ordinances are practiced not because God uses them to bring Christ's presence but because Christ *ordained* that we do them. This term was established in relation to baptism and communion by the Baptist church in England and was used interchangeably with *sacrament* during the seventeenth century.[29] It is used today by other free church traditions that follow the Zwinglian theology. Nonetheless, there is ongoing debate within Baptist circles about establishing "a sacramental theology that is in dialogue with other parts of the Christian Church."[30]

Because baptism and communion are central actions of Christian worship, regardless of how they are theologically construed, it will be useful to speak of them in a common way. The term *sacrament* will be used throughout this book to refer to baptism and communion. The use of this term does not intend to disregard the theological issues at stake that are signified by *ordinance*. It does, however, suggest a further means by which we can find commonality despite the diversity of our worship traditions. As an indication of this accommodating approach, Robert Webber says of the Eucharist, "Although it is impossible to give a rational explanation for what happens, it is possible to agree with Justin Martyr (150 AD) that the bread and wine consecrated is no 'common food or common drink.' Through the bread and wine, Christ becomes present in his church and to his people."[31]

Relevance and Pertinence

Finally, our conversation will proceed without engaging the question of the apparent *relevance* of worship. This well-used category of evaluation suggests

29. Ellis, "Baptists in Britain," in Tucker and Wainwright, *The Oxford History of Christian Worship*, 569–70.

30. Ibid., 570. I am grateful to Ryan Bailey for alerting me to the state of this conversation within Baptist churches.

31. Webber, *Worship Is a Verb*, 52.

that worship can be judged on the basis of its relationship to human needs and expectations. Is the music something that I can relate to? Does the preaching give me something to take home? Do I feel welcome or feel that I belong? Are the people friendly? Do I feel like I have had a spiritual experience? While worship must *pertain* to the human person and properly *relates* to the corporate as well as the individual context, it is not first about making people feel involved or moved or good about themselves. Worship is first about God and what God is doing as we join with the body of Christ and enter into the divine presence. The true relevance of worship is the understanding that *God chooses to relate to us.* If worship is relevant in that sense, the implication is that every service of worship can be a renewed setting in which the Creator comes into communion with human creatures. The relevance of worship is not something that pastors, preachers, or worship leaders can build into the experience. They can only pray for it. If worship enables the relationship between God and God's people, that is a gift of grace, for God is the one who chooses to show up when we worship.[32] The focus of worship, whether in the church or in active discipleship, is upward and outward. Worship may inspire us, feed us, restore us. But it is not designed to be *relevant.* Rather, it should be designed so as to *pertain* to us. It has us in mind as active participants in the encounter with God. It is inclusive and seeks to engage us in the work of the liturgy. It calls out in us the deep resonance between our world and the world of Scripture. It draws us into solidarity with Christians of all times and all places. It engages us on a sentient level. It places us on the path toward what God is doing in the church and in the world. And pertinent worship involves people in culturally and contextually fitting ways. Pastors and worship planning teams prepare services of worship that are filled with the potential for a rich encounter with God; when we succeed in being inspired, fed, and restored, it is by the Holy Spirit working through our worship activities. Pertinence is something we *can* plan on. But relevance is not something that worship leaders can add as an ingredient for worship to make it authentic or real. Relevance is, once again, that divine reach whereby the One who made us bends down to interact with the many who gather in prayer, praise, and lament.

In what ways can worship be designed to be pertinent to individuals and to the body of Christ? That is the subject of the worship manual in part 2. It demonstrates that through the use of the arts, an appreciation for and some level of employment of conventional forms, and the intentional utilization of spiritual gifts, worship can appertain to God's people.

Shopworn Terms

Some terms bear continued use because they make clear and strong reference to matters relating to worship. Others have become so overused as to have lost

---

32. For a discussion of God's presence (or absence) in worship, see Schmit, *Too Deep for Words*, 32–34.

their referential power. *Contemporary* is chief among the latter.[33] For some people, *contemporary worship* is synonymous with *seeker sensitive*. For others, it is merely conventional worship in which the hymns are replaced by *contemporary* Christian songs. Often, these songs are decades old. Contemporary worship is understood as *praise and worship* in some settings and *tabernacle worship* in others.[34] Still others are concerned that *contemporary* ought to apply to any worship that is undertaken in the present day. "If worship," says Mark Bangert, "is not contemporary—deliberately concerned in preaching, prayer, and offering with issues of this life and the world as it is now—then it is dead."[35] Another classroom anecdote demonstrates the typical confusion associated with the term. The course was called "Issues in Contemporary Worship." After a field trip to a Methodist church that claimed its worship idiom to be *contemporary*, an African American Baptist student remarked, "Oh, so that's what contemporary worship means. My church has been doing it like that for over one hundred fifty years!" While the term *contemporary worship* is still employed gainfully in many settings, it will not be in use here.

Similarly, the term *blended worship* is sufficiently overused so as to mean many things. It, too, shall be avoided, along with *authentic worship*,[36] *real worship*,[37] and *true worship*.[38] (For a depiction of the confusion surrounding these terms, see sidebar 1.3.)

Another term that is used too frequently, though usually with decent intentions, is *liturgically correct*. It comes up when thoughtful worship planners and leaders are concerned for making sure their liturgies and actions in worship are proper, according to some imagined standard. For example, we might hear someone ask, "What is the liturgically correct way to reverence the altar?"

The problem with this approach to worship planning is that it assumes that worship is best understood as a prescribed set of activities that are known to an elite college of liturgical scholars. Those who study such things (so the thinking goes) must know precisely how the church has historically done these things and can teach the rest of us the exact procedures. Often the holders of this view have equal disdain for worship that is not properly conducted according to a historic template.

---

33. In recent years I was asked by Wesley Seminary in Washington, DC, to teach a summer course called "Contemporary Worship." I said I would instead teach a course called "Issues in Contemporary Worship." The first issue on the discussion table was the overuse and confusing use of the word *contemporary*.

34. Webber, *The Renewal of Sunday Worship*, 212. Tabernacle worship is described as a pattern wherein leaders select music that takes participants on an emotional journey "through the [tabernacle] gates into the outer court, into the inner court, and finally into the Holy of Holies."

35. Bangert, "Holy Communion," 73.

36. See Bateman, *Authentic Worship*.

37. See Wiersbe, *Real Worship*.

38. See Hustad, *True Worship*.

Sidebar 1.3: Idioms of Worship in Use in North America

What is the difference between *traditional*, *contemporary*, and *blended* worship? Lester Ruth has captured the complexity of the issue:

How would you classify the worship of your church or parish? Is it "contemporary" or "traditional"? Are those forms too limited? In that case, would the terms "linear" or "organic," as found in some recent youth ministry training materials, be more helpful? Still at a loss for the right classification? Maybe the terms from a recent online worship forum would be more accurate: "multisensory worship," "indigenous worship," "innovative worship," "transformational worship," "blended worship," "praise services," "spirited traditional," "creative," or "classic worship"? Or are ethnic or racial designators more descriptive of your service's character: "African American," "Hispanic," "Euro-American," or some other similar designation?

Has the term exactly right for your church's worship not been mentioned yet? If so, then how about "multimedia worship," "authentic worship," "liturgical worship," "praise and worship," or "seeker services"? Perhaps terms rooted in various intended "audiences" would be better: "believer-oriented worship," "believer-oriented worship made visitor-friendly," or "visitor-oriented worship." Some scholars now advocate classifications by generations. And so, is your worship service "boomer," "buster," "Gen-X," or "millennials'" worship?

Lester Ruth, "A Rose by Any Other Name: Attempts at Classifying North American Protestant Worship," in The Conviction of Things Not Seen: Worship and Ministry in the Twenty-First Century, ed. Todd E. Johnson (Grand Rapids: Brazos, 2002), 33.

A more useful approach is to understand that worship can be undertaken in any number of ways, for God's people are immensely creative and only God can determine when worship is false. There is no liturgically correct way to do anything. There are, however, means of execution in worship that are informed by best practices, or by historic practice—what I will describe in chapter 3 as the historic wisdom of the church at worship—as well as by contextual considerations. The only correct approach to worship is to seek what is right for a given place and time. The shape of such a liturgy will be determined by considering many factors, including the denomination or tradition of the worshiping community, their demographic makeup, the capacity of local leaders, the spiritual gifts available within the community, the season, the portions of Scripture to be employed in proclamation, the availability and training of artists and musicians, and so forth. No outside expert can make a determination on a question of worship without firm knowledge of these kinds of concerns. The best persons to make determinations are local leaders when they are familiar with historic practices, worship theology, the use of the voice and body in ritual expression, and all manner of local issues. Even though every pattern of worship can rightly be called a liturgy, there can be no liturgically correct way to perform the rites within a given liturgy. There certainly are communication issues that make some practices more useful than others, but there is no pharisaical standard by which to judge the texts, words, and actions of worship.

Mission and Missio Dei

This chapter concludes with the description of a final key term: *mission*. In the past, mission and missionary activity had principally to do with sending evangelists to places in the world where the gospel had not been heard. The theological field of missiology grew out of these activities. But mission today is not merely something that local churches support in foreign territories. Mission today recognizes that Western society, once firmly understood as Christendom, is now more like the early church in its pluralism and its state of needing to hear the gospel of Jesus Christ. The change in the use of the word indicates a turn in present-day thinking about the nature of church that is not merely another fad or passing theological trend. It returns us to the biblical idea that mission is central to God's purpose in history. It is *missio Dei*.

The mission of God, and thus, the mission of the church, has been made clear from the outset. What Christ set in place as the Great Commission has guided the church's activities ever since. "The importance of Christ's command to his followers to go into all the world to proclaim the gospel and make disciples," says Eddie Gibbs, "is evidenced by the fact that this command occurs in all four Gospels."[39] As the disciples followed this command first locally, then by spreading out into the known world, they took the good news of Christ to a Jewish and Greco-Roman world that had many other religious options. Everywhere the followers of Jesus turned, they were faced with missionary opportunities. When they spoke to the Jews, they were contending with people who often considered the message of Christ an aberration and a weakening of the concept of one God. When they dealt with Romans and Greeks, they were offering a monotheistic choice that was incompatible with the easygoing worship of multiple gods, as was common in those cultures.[40] The local churches that were established by the disciples of Jesus and by Paul

---

39. Gibbs, *Church Next*, 55. The Great Commission is found most explicitly in Matthew 28:18–20. It is included in some form in Mark 16:15–18; Luke 24:45–49; and John 17:18 and 20:21. It must be noted that the best Markan manuscripts end at 16:8 and do not contain the commission. Acts 1:8 also implies the commission when Jesus says, "You will be my witnesses in Jerusalem, in all Judea and Samaria, and to the ends of the earth."

40. Larry Hurtado has shown the nature of this pervasively religious environment: "it is clear that the religious environment of earliest Christianity was diverse, vigorous and flourishing. . . . Christianity had to compete in a very active religious 'market', and if it won adherents it did so by offering 'products' and 'services' that could be perceived as comparing favourably with what else was on offer" (*At the Origins of Christian Worship*, 37).

became "mission outposts within the mission of God" that gave witness to Christ in cultures of vast diversity.[41] They found themselves, as Patrick Keifert puts it, "caught up into God's movement and life. They did not imagine mission as something or somewhere other than their primal activity as a called, gathered, centered, and sent people of God. This is the core characteristic of a missional church: being, not just doing, mission."[42]

The church continued being and doing mission by establishing churches in the Latin West, the Greek East, and in North Africa. The missionary status of the church continued until the fourth century when what is known as Christendom made Christianity a dominant part of the culture. Once faith in Christ became common, even the social norm, the need for evangelization and mission changed. "Evangelism was done by [people] having babies."[43]

The state of Christendom and its apparent demise have been well explored in a body of missional literature that has flooded the theological landscape during the past several decades.[44] While there is no need to rearticulate the reasons for and seasons of Christendom's destabilization, it is necessary for our purposes to state the general conclusions that these writers reach. They can be summed up in these words from Darrell Guder: it has become "a truism to speak of North America as a mission field" and an "obvious fact that what we once regarded as Christendom is now a post-Constantinian, post-Christendom, and even post-Christian mission field."[45]

Whereas post-Christendom in North America and Europe suggests that we are living in what some call post-Christian times (as Guder does), it must be recognized that this is not the case in the majority world. In Asia, Africa, and South America the church is growing at a nearly incalculable rate. The mission of God is alive on these continents, demonstrating that there is nothing post-Christian about the beginning of the twenty-first century. There is more missionary activity and more growth of the church than in any other time in history.[46] What *post-Christendom* means is that those places once viewed as culturally Christian are now part of world missions. This is certainly true in

41. Keifert, *We Are Here Now*, 28.

42. Ibid.

43. Ibid., 31.

44. Craig Van Gelder traces this movement back to 1952, when Wilhelm Anderson proposed a new look at mission theology at the International Missionary Council at Willingen, Germany. The title of his proposal was *Missio Dei*. In the following decades, the theme was undertaken ecumenically, including work by writers from the Roman Catholic and Orthodox Churches and the World Council of Churches. See Van Gelder, *The Essence of the Church*, 33.

45. Guder, *Missional Church*, 2, 7.

46. "In the year 2000, Christians of all kinds constituted one-third of the world's 2 billion people. . . . During the last decade of the 1900s, the Christian movement grew worldwide by 16.4 million people a year. . . . Majority world Christians made up 16.7 percent of all Christians in 1900 but 59.4 percent in 2000" (Pocock, van Rheenen, and McConnell, *The Changing Face of World Missions*, 135–36).

Europe and North America where Christians from Asia and Africa are now coming to revitalize the faith of those living in the West's religiously pluralistic and antagonistic mission field.[47] Some observers consider the end of Christendom a matter of failure and something to fear. Others see it as a season of epochal change in the church.[48] Keifert chooses to describe the situation today in positive and hopeful terms. While grieving the loss of Christendom, he prefers to speak of our age as a "New Missional Era," which represents "God's invitation to join in this new adventure in the life of God and world, gospel, church, and culture."[49]

The conclusion that must be drawn from consideration of the missional status of the church today is that all churches, whether they know it or not, exist in a missional era. They need, therefore, to have a missional thrust to their ministry if they are to survive—or to thrive. Just as in the apostolic age, the mission field is directly outside the door of the church, regardless of whether the congregation is located in Moshi, Tanzania, or Memphis, Tennessee. The purpose of this book is not to convince churches that they need to become missional in their approach to ministry (others do that forcefully). It is to assist them in thinking about worship in an age of mission. No other age currently exists.

Conclusion

This chapter has placed before us the key terms and ideas upon which this book is built. Central to our discussion are two key observations: that there is an increasing awareness among the denominations and traditions that public Christian worship consists of the faithful gathering themselves around the Word and the sacraments, and that from those gatherings we are sent out into the fields of mission that lie beyond each church door. Along the way, several key theological ideas have been identified:

1. Worship is relevant only because God chooses to relate to humanity and to invest God's self in our gatherings.
2. Liturgy consists of the egalitarian activities engaged in by people who gather for worship and who go forth in service to the world; worship is always a set of rituals that, however free, have some liturgical shape.

47. "Virtually every continent in the world participates in the modern migratory 'dance.' It should be our prayer that the fervor of majority world believers will be infectious and will reignite the lost passions of the Western World. There are solid indications that this is already happening" (ibid., 151).

48. It should be noted that not all consider Christendom to be at an end. Philip Jenkins considers the current situation to be the "next Christendom." See Jenkins, The Next Christendom.

49. Keifert, We Are Here Now, 36.

3. The role of worship leaders is to serve, drawing the assembly into an encounter with the One who made, redeems, and sustains them.

4. The *missio Dei* is the mission of the church today: to be called and gathered as the body of Christ, centered through Word and rites, and sent forth as the active people of God.

2

Sending Is Mission

> Mission is the result of God's initiative, rooted in God's purposes
> to restore and heal creation. "Mission" means "sending," and
> is the central biblical theme describing the purpose of God's
> action in human history.[1]
>
> Darrell L. Guder

I n the last chapter I considered the basic terms and concepts this conversation will employ. Additionally, two key observations were made. The first is that public worship is increasingly being understood as the gathering of God's people around the central symbols of Word and sacrament and their being sent to do the mission of God. The second is that the church in North America today no longer exists in the privileged era of Christendom. Post-Christendom means that the church in the West, just as in every other part of the world, is a church in mission. In this chapter, I will examine the relationship between the shape of worship and the shape of the missional church's ministry and will demonstrate how rethinking the use of the sending portion of the liturgy can revitalize worship's connection to the *missio Dei*. I begin with a fundamental observation.

Worship Is Mission

"Worship and mission are the same," declares Mark Bangert.[2] This is perhaps not apparent at first glance. Christians seem to be about two public things.

1. Guder, *Missional Church*, 4.
2. Bangert, "Holy Communion," in Schattauer, *Inside Out*, 69.

We gather for worship on Sundays and other occasions where we praise God, hear the Word read and proclaimed, participate in the sacraments (or at least remember them as baptized people), and are dismissed for other activities at worship's end. Mission seems to be what Christians do in the world when we are not at worship. We witness to and serve humanity in our workplaces, schools, and neighborhoods. Both missional and liturgical theologians, however, are eager to declare that these are not two independent activities but one complex thing called worship.

Each activity that takes place inside the Lord's Day assembly is interwoven with the life outside the church doors. Gathering assumes that we have not been together before we begin. We are outside, in the world, coming together into churches and other places of worship as a concentrated local configuration of the body of Christ. Gathering draws us spatially from the world in which we engage in Christian action. But it does not disconnect us from the world. It connects the world to worship through us. When we attend to the reading and proclamation of the Word in worship, this also connects us to mission. It tells us what God is about in the world and transforms us into people who are sent to cooperate with God's projects in the world. Likewise, the sacraments claim us as God's people, give us renewed peace and forgiveness, and provide signs of how life is to be lived. The way we live inside church is to be identical to the way we live outside. The sending is the point of integration whereby worship and mission flow together. "Liturgy and mission . . . are one and the same. . . . What is inside is out and what is outside is in."[3] These are the convictions held by those who understand that we live in a new missional era and that all ministry is missional.

The Pattern of Mission

What is the pattern of missional ministry? It is characterized by the use of four verbs that derive from biblical witness. Patrick Keifert describes them this way: "In this New Missional Era, this time of the missional church, those congregations that are faithful, effective, and efficient will be part of a transforming mission. They will be transformed by the mission—*called, gathered,* and *centered in Word and sacrament*, and *sent* into the mission of God in daily life."[4]

3. Ibid., 68 and 70.
4. Keifert, *We Are Here Now*, 37, my italics. Other writers on the missional church use similar terms, especially *called, centered*, and *sent*. These terms run throughout the missional church literature. Eddie Gibbs provides attribution for the origin of their use: "Following Leslie Newbigin and others, a church that is missional understands that God's mission calls and sends the church of Jesus Christ to be a missionary church in its own society and in the cultures in which it finds itself" (*Church Next*, 51).

Notice that the italicized words above resonate strongly with two other sets of terms. I have made reference to the first set in the previous chapter where the fourfold pattern of worship is identified. We will return to this directly. But there is another set of terms that need to be recognized as germane to this discussion. They come from the church's first evangelical: Martin Luther. When describing in his Small Catechism the work of the Holy Spirit in the church, he says that the Spirit "calls, gathers, enlightens, and sanctifies the whole Christian church on earth."[5] While not perfectly identical, Luther's and Keifert's terms share strong resonances. Luther uses these words to describe the activities of the Holy Spirit; Keifert uses his to describe the activities of congregations in the missional church. It is, perhaps, no coincidence that Keifert is himself a Lutheran systematic theologian, steeped in Luther's understanding of the Trinity. For Luther, the Spirit is God's verb, the present active part of the Trinity that calls people into faith, gathers them for worship and Christian service, enlightens them through proclamation of the Word, and sanctifies them through participation in the means of grace (which include the sacraments). These two writers agree that God calls and gathers people into the church. What Keifert identifies as being centered is implied in Luther's use of enlightened and sanctified. The resonance between these lists of activities suggests that Keifert (along with other missional theologians) identifies the work of the missional church as the work of God in the Holy Spirit. This implication is made explicit when Keifert later says:

> So the Holy Spirit dwells in and creates many structures and forms but also breaks them open to the release of God's preferred and promised future. . . . Adjusting focus from the church's mission to God's mission massively changes everything. It is God's mission, not the church's. It is God's mission that reflects the very nature and being, movement, and action of God. The very life of God as Father, Son, and Holy Spirit is a process of mission. A Father who sends a Son, a Son who sends a Spirit. In this very likeness of God, we are called, gathered, centered, and sent within the life of the triune God and God's mission, an infinite journey of being called and sent.[6]

One observation about the pattern of mission is that it is the pattern of God's activity in the world and a manifestation of the Spirit's predicate power in the church. A second observation is that these inspired activities of missional congregations that are called, gathered, centered, and sent correspond precisely with the fourfold pattern of Christian worship. Those who are called to be Christians are gathered for worship, centered in Word and sacraments, and sent out to be agents of Christ's mission. The parallel here is no coincidence. It indicates that the activities of worship are the activities of the missional church.

5. Martin Luther, "Small Catechism," in Tappert, *The Book of Concord*, 345.
6. Keifert, *We Are Here Now*, 65–66.

In other words, worship is a fundamental part of God's mission. It is the place where God acts to draw people together as the body of Christ; centers, enriches, and sustains them with spiritual nourishment in the form of Word and sacrament; and sends them out into the external activities of mission that take place beyond the church doors. To put it simply, worship is the adoration of God on Sunday morning *and* the activity of Christians in the world. Engaging in these things is engaging in God's mission. Worship as adoration and action, a theme developed by Miroslav Volf, is one to which I will soon return.

The Pattern of Worship

I have identified the common shape of Christian worship as gathering, Word, sacraments, and sending. While they appear, when listed, to be of equal significance, there is a clear disproportion in the ways the rites are typically executed in worship. This is especially the case with regard to the sending portion of our liturgies. I am not speaking in terms of duration here, for it would be absurd for a liturgical sending to last as long as a typical sermon. I am speaking, rather, in the sense that the presider should have a clear intention and a deliberateness of execution in this relatively brief rite. Placing too little emphasis on the ways that the sending rites are constructed and performed sends a strong signal to worshipers that runs counter to the sense that worship is a key part of God's mission in the church and in the world. It suggests, rather, that worship ends when the church doors open and the gathered disperse.

The natural flow of energy in this four-part liturgical scheme is linear, beginning with the actions of assembly. It might be compared, to use a musical metaphor, to the first beat of a musical measure in which there are four beats or pulses.[7] Gathering is the downbeat, the first and leading pulse among four equally engaging pulsations. It sets the stage for what is to follow; typically, it announces a theme and launches a liturgical trajectory that is played out through hearing the Word and, at least occasionally, celebrating the sacraments. Word and sacramental celebration (and remembrance) are the second and third beats of our musical measure. By the time the sending occurs—the final, often deflated fourth beat—the service of worship is all but over. At this ultimate point, people have offered their praise, heard the Word, released their petitions, and been enriched by an encounter with God and God's people. Liturgy completed, they are dismissed.

---

7. The four-beat measure (also known as a *bar*) is the most common rhythmic structure in Western music. There are other common patterns (the three-beat waltz pattern, the two-beat march, etc.). The use of the four-beat pattern is referenced here and in the following sections because there is something inherent in the structure of music that can shed light on our understanding of how the fourfold pattern of worship can be connected to that which follows as the mission of the church in the world.

Sending or Dismissal?

While this four-part action is a useful blueprint for worship, we need to give special attention to the final segment of worship if it is to be missionally engaging. Wrongly construed, the moment of sending can give the sense that worship is a containable set of activities bracketed by a musical prelude and postlude, and complete within itself. This is the message conveyed when worship's final action is understood not as sending but as dismissal, the term often used for the concluding rites.[8] For example, in Robert Webber's book in which he celebrates the fourfold common pattern of worship, he introduces the sending rites as the dismissal.[9]

The problem with dismissal language is that it suggests finality, rather than movement from one state to another. To be dismissed is to be set free from participation in an activity. Dismissal at the close of worship has the power of adjournment, where the activities of worship are suspended until the worshipers reconvene at a later time. The implication is that nothing relating to worship will occur until the resumption of liturgical activities the following Sunday morning. This type of liturgical release heightens the sense that worship is something removed from the rest of life, reserved for those inside the faith community, and separated from the mission of God outside the church walls. Thomas Schattauer identifies this conventional view as an *inside and out* approach to worship and mission. It occurs where "liturgy is understood as the quintessential activity for those inside the church community. Mission is what takes place on the outside when the gospel is proclaimed to those who have not heard or received it or . . . when the neighbor is served in acts of love and justice."[10]

When the final liturgical movement is understood as dismissal, its action is often nearly imperceptible, forgotten, or a mere afterthought. Illustrations abound: a hasty benediction is uttered, without care given as to poetic language or gesture; a rote blessing is recited without consideration for that which came before or that which is to follow; a closing song is sung while the worship leaders beat a hurried exit. The following practice, though witnessed in Southern California, has become regrettably routine: a megachurch service of worship concluded with the pastor, wearing nonliturgical mufti, standing before his people. He raised his hand in an awkward farewell gesture and said clumsily, "Ah, okay, see you all next week." The practical implications of this action are clear: we have now concluded what we gathered for; with no further agenda, we disperse with a casual *auf wiedersehen*. (For a description of what a worship leader might prefer to communicate in the final moments of worship, see

---

8. The English word *mass* comes from the Latin phrase that concluded the Roman Catholic rite: *Ite, missa est*, "Go, it is the dismissal."

9. Webber, *Worship Is a Verb*, 54.

10. Schattauer, "Liturgical Assembly as Locus of Mission," in Schattauer, *Inside Out*, 2.

sidebar 2.1.) The theological message, in such cases, is equally clear, though problematic. The action implies that worship is a distinct set of activities that begin with people drawing together and end with people dispersing. There is no indication in the dismissal that God's presence goes with people beyond the church door. There is no apparent expectation that God's people will be the church beyond the congregational campus or that the mission work they might engage in is connected to the Sunday service of worship. Nevertheless, faithful believers know that it *is* an act of worship to live continually in God's presence while engaging in secular pursuits as well as in Christian service.

One of the key motifs of missional church theology is that all of life is worship.[11] It comes from Paul's description of life in faith in Romans 12, where he appeals to believers to present their entire lives as "spiritual worship." Paul makes an impressive list of spiritual gifts to be employed in our spiritual worship: prophecy, service, teaching, exhortation, generosity in giving, lending aid, and doing acts of mercy. He then lists the behaviors of one living a life of worship, regardless of spiritual gifts. They include blessing our persecutors, rejoicing and weeping with others, harmonious living, humility, and forgiveness. Missional theologian Craig Van Gelder summarizes *all of life as worship* and as consisting of these activities: gathering for specific occasions of worship, discipling, fellowshiping, serving, witness, visioning, and stewarding.[12]

In pondering the question of whether a believer's worship in church is distinct from his or her engagement in the world, Miroslav Volf says:

> The answer to this question depends on where God is to be found. It is a consistent teaching of the Bible that God's presence is not limited to a particular locale. God is present in the whole created reality. No segment of it is secular in the sense that the transcendent God is absent from it. All dimensions of life in the world have what one might call a sacramental dimension: they can be places of meeting God in gratitude and adoration.[13]

If there is a dimension of worship that occurs in the world, then a liturgical dismissal sends entirely the wrong signal. It suggests that God's presence and purpose only occur to believers when they gather. A richer view of worship emerges when the final movement in the liturgy is understood as *sending*, whereby the people of God are sent forth into the world to engage in the ongoing work that has begun in the assembly. The implication is that worship consists of two kinds of activities, those within the church walls and those without. Worship is, as Volf asserts, both "adoration and action." He observes: "The sacrifice of praise and the sacrifice of good works are two fundamental aspects of the Christian way of being-in-the-world. They are at the same time

11. Van Gelder, *The Essence of the Church*, 151.
12. Ibid., 151–54.
13. Volf, "Worship as Adoration and Action," in Carson, *Worship*, 208.

Sidebar 2.1: What Does a Meaningful Sending Communicate?

Instead of a hasty or casual statement of release from worship, what would the thoughtful presider want to communicate in the moment of sending? Perhaps his or her words and gestures can imply the following:

"Now that we have gathered for a time of adoration, fellowship, and spiritual enlightenment, you are being sent forth to be the church in the world. What we do here in adoring God is connected to the action you will engage in as the worship of your life in all you do. You are not alone in this; as God is present in our gathering, so God will be with us in our homes, neighborhoods, schools, and workplaces. God go with you, and empower you for the mission that lies before you. God keep you safe and strong, committed and focused, filled with faith and love. Go in peace; serve the Lord."

All of this can be implied in a sending moment. It need not be said in so many words, and probably ought rarely to be so explicit, or it, too, can be rote and verbose. But this perspective can inform every word and gesture used to conclude a service of worship. It can be the attitude of the presider who knows what is to follow once the doors are opened to the world; it can be the stance of the one who, having led in a time of adoration, is turning now to lead in the time of service.

---

the two constitutive elements of Christian worship: authentic Christian worship takes place in a rhythm of adoration and action."[14]

This rhythm suggests that the two movements are organically related. Adoration and action are not to be separated into inward and outward functions, but maintained as a single operation enacted in two spheres: within the assembly of believers and throughout their dispersal in the world. The organic nature of this connection has been captured by Schattauer, who contends that the conventional *inside and out* approach to worship and mission must, in this new age of mission, be supplanted by an *inside-out* approach: "This [inside-out] approach locates the liturgical assembly itself within the arena of the missio Dei. The focus is on God's mission toward the world, to which the church witnesses and into which it is drawn, rather than on specific activities of the church undertaken in response to the divine saving initiative [the inside and out approach]. The missio Dei is God's own movement outward in relation to the world."[15] This connection between mission and worship is underscored by Darrell Guder, who says: "Our postmodern society has come to regard worship as the private, internal, and often arcane activity of religionists who retreat from the world to practice their mystical rites. By definition, however, the *ekklesia* is a public assembly, and its worship is its first form of mission. . . .

14. Ibid., 203–7.
15. Schattauer, "Liturgical Assembly," in Schattauer, *Inside Out*, 3.

The reality of God that is proclaimed in worship is to be announced to and for the entire world."[16]

Similarly, Carolyn Headley and Mark Earey urge a break from the conventional approach to worship in mission, which "assumes that worship only operates when 'they' come to 'us.'" Continuing, they imply an understanding and support of the inside-out approach: "But worship also has a role in forming Christians for mission 'out there.' By energizing and envisioning worshipers, by proclaiming the gospel, by shaping an alternative worldview and by modeling aspects of the kingdom, regular worship plays a significant part in the mission of a local church even before a visitor enters the building."[17] Adoration and action, worship as the first form of mission, worship inside out: what these images hold in common is an understanding that there is no such thing as an adjournment of worship. That which concludes the Sunday service is not dismissal, but dispersal, in the sense of going forth, being driven or distributed: it is a sending. To be sent from corporate worship is to be released for and reengaged in the mission of the church in the world. Eddie Gibbs puts it succinctly: "mission *means* sending."[18]

A Musical Interlude

One way to strengthen the perception of a connection between sending and mission is to examine the issue from the perspective of a parallel but independent discipline.[19] In this case, I will consider the ways of music as a metaphor for what is happening in liturgy.

To say that sending is mission is to suggest that the customary downbeat stress within a four-part pattern of worship is at odds with the missional church's purpose.[20] Conventionally, we think of the gathering as the first element in our worship, our first step toward adoration. Adoration continues through hearing the Word read and proclaimed and culminates in the mysteries of the sacraments. With the sending, the adoration concludes in its most explicit sense and gives way to action. From the conventional perspective, the sending represents finality: "Go, it is the dismissal," and worship has come to its completion. But, if adoration and action are understood as equal liturgical engagements, the sending is not a mere ending but a *compelling*. It both

16. Guder, *Missional Church*, 243.

17. Headley and Earey, *Mission and Liturgical Worship*, 10.

18. Gibbs, following Guder, in *Church Next*, 51; my italics.

19. This line of inquiry follows the trajectory of the Music and Theology Colloquium, instituted by Jeremy Begbie in Cambridge, England. It seeks to use music as a tool for doing theology.

20. The strong first beat of a musical measure is called the *downbeat* because within the conductor's gestural pattern, the baton travels emphatically downward to mark the beginning of each measure.

concludes corporate adoration and inaugurates action. Sending engages the church for mission. While it is the downbeat of gathering that sets the tone and the course for the church's adoration, it is the fourth pulse, the sending, that propels the church toward its missionary work. The mission is the *leitourgia*, the "work of the people" in their communities.

If sending engages worshipers in mission, then to complete the imagery of the four-beat musical bar, the stress of the strong first beat no longer dominates. While the downbeat of worship inaugurates adoration, the fourth beat initiates action.

The success of this musical image draws on the compelling quality of the final beat in a musical bar. The final beat might seem to signify the end of something (the end of a measure, or the end of a performance). In fact, it actually always signals that something significant is to follow. There is, in fact, more generated at the ending of a measure than there is completed. Within a given four-beat bar, there flows a limited amount of musical material—precisely of the duration of four beats. The shape of the measure, with its strong leading impulse on the first beat and a secondary stress occurring on the third beat, imbues a musical performance with shape and coherence. But the fourth beat in a bar, though the last and least stressed, is also critical. While it serves to conclude, the last beat is also weighted with anticipation. It is the pier from which is launched the next musical moment and all that succeeds it. This applies even when the final beat of a measure occurs at the end of a musical piece. Even there, the final beat leans toward something: not music, in this case, but silence. Every musical performance ends in a hush, an aural vacuum. The final cutoff from the conductor is not followed by immediate applause from the audience, nor even the intake of breath by the singers or players. (Indeed, even the listeners may be left momentarily breathless.) There is an unwritten tacet in the music, the one that follows everything, the silence that signifies the end of the piece, the pause that echoes the emotive power of the final musical moment. The more powerful the musical experience, typically, the longer the post-musical pause. The final beat of the last measure in the music leans directly toward this pregnant hush.

In relation to the measures of music that follow within a musical piece, each final beat of a measure can be construed as an upbeat. The upbeat is the unwritten beat *before* the music, the moment of preparation. The conductor raises the baton; the singer draws breath; the violinist extends the bow over the strings, making it ready to be drawn into play at the downbeat. The final beat in a measure has the same power: it leans toward the next bar and raises its musical possibilities; it strains forward with an expectation of musical completion.

It is this leaning-forward quality of the fourth beat of a musical bar that makes it an intriguing metaphor for liturgical sending. Like the sending, the final beat of the musical bar brings to an end one period. At the same time, it is intrinsically connected to what precedes it, and it leads forcefully into all that follows. It creates a moment filled with anticipation, with leaning toward what will be fulfilled. The sending is an upbeat, not divorced from what precedes or follows, but organically part of the whole of adoration and action; the sending is a culminating moment of adoration and the inauguration of the worship action that proceeds from it.

For this reason, it may be useful for worship planners and leaders to think of the sequence of liturgical actions in this way: sending is not a hasty afterthought; it is the primary element of preparation for a demanding aspect of worship (action) that lasts typically from one Sunday morning to the next. During the week the faithful are engaged in outward worship, the work of God's people, which might be called "the living liturgy of discipleship." The week of work in Christian mission is followed by the gathering of God's people who, now spent, draw earnestly together to be centered through fellowship, the refreshment of the "bread of life," and the nourishment of the sacraments. In short, worship consists of God's people being sent and gathered, that is, sent out for action in the world and gathered again for the hour of adoration.

Sending God's People Forth in Mission

In practice, what would it mean to see sendings as the beginning of worship in the world? It would not mean that the sending would compete in duration with the other liturgical movements. (Here, the musical metaphor breaks down, as all must when stretched beyond their useful limits. The beats in a musical bar have different kinds of stress, but each are necessarily of equal relative duration.) Like the denouement in any drama, the sending should always be brief and summary. But to see the sending as a powerful liturgical moment means that it is prepared intentionally and conducted with vitality. It is not an afterthought nor a casual "see ya later," but a force-filled word of compulsion. It contains a sense of the impending action that is ahead, and it is grounded in the sense that God is present in the world of action even as in the place of adoration. We are sent forth, not on our own, to make the best of the coming days, but with God. We are blessed, benedicted; we are infused with the conviction that God is with us in the journey from interior activities (of centering) to exterior activities (of serving), that God's Spirit is leading us from adoration into action, and that Christ's love in its embrace has redeemed the body of Christ and in its outward reaching will continue his mission of healing, peace, justice, and salvation in the world. A strong sending will bless God's people on their way but will also propel us insistently into the world of living discipleship.[21]

21. Graham Hughes, in *Worship as Meaning*, makes the point with force:
> The critical note [in sending] is the divine blessing as people make ready to return to their familiar world. As the commentary [*Book of Common Worship*] has it: "Assured

A common liturgical misinterpretation of the sending occurs when the celebrant offers a concluding prayer instead of a benediction. There is nothing wrong with a final prayer, but when it replaces the benediction or blessing, it deflates the compelling moment of sending and makes of it an ending and dismissal. The language of prayer is directed toward God, not God's people. Though the prayer may ask for God's presence during the coming week, or for God's guidance in the mission of the church, it does not *send* God's people into mission. A prayer in place of a benediction represents an *inside and out* model of worship. The alternative *inside-out* model requires a firm word to the people. The benediction is not a concluding prayer. It is a declarative statement of blessing spoken directly to those who are to go forth in action. The Aaronic blessing (Num. 6:23–26), as an example, is unequivocal in its pronouncement of God's ongoing presence and blessing. "The Lord bless you and keep you," it declares in the present tense. It has explicit performative force in that it performs a powerful action in its very enunciation.[22] Blessed by God's action in fulfilling this pronouncement, the people go out to worship in the world.

Worship Is about God and What God Is Doing in the World

One of the valid criticisms of worship today is that it often has more to do with people and their perceived needs than with God. In some churches this takes the shape of worship that satisfies market forces in musical taste, architecture, sermon forms, seating, and even the type of coffee served during fellowship times. In other places, it seems that worship is designed to serve the ego needs of pastors, preachers, musicians, media technicians, or other leaders. Another prevalent flaw in certain worshiping communities is that the language of prayer and song is focused on the worshiper rather than on God's relationship to God's people. One of my colleagues once remarked during seminary chapel that he was tired of worship songs that seemed to be all about "me and what's-his-name." Worshipers, laments Keifert, "almost always describe worship . . . as something 'we do' or 'I do.' I worship God. I participate in fellowship. We sing hymns and pray." In reference to the results of his field research, he adds, "God, in the vast majority of these descriptions

---

of God's peace and blessing, we are confident that God goes with us to our tasks." By all means, "mission" (i.e., people's glad acceptance of their responsibilities as disciples) is not out of sight in this section (the very name "sending," in its allusion to "apostolicity," ensures this). But without empowerment—and the grace of God— given in "blessing," this can only be variously resigned or strident commitment to philanthropic humanism. Blessing is thus the *sine qua non* of mission. (168–69)

22. The word *performative* is used here in the illocutionary sense of J. L. Austin, as developed in *How to Do Things with Words*. For an explanation of the explicit performative power of pastoral pronouncements, see Schmit, *Too Deep for Words*, 45–53.

by churches' own members and in their own words, is best the object of human action. Rarely did we hear of God doing something in worship, much less in the community or neighborhood around them."[23]

Missional church theologians remind us that worship is about God and God's mission in the world. Keifert puts it this way: "God is the chief actor in Christian worship, and God is calling, gathering, centering, and sending people into the movement and practices of Christian worship. Christian worship follows from the movement and sending of God, the very life of the Trinity."[24]

What does a missional worshiping community look like? Linford Stutzman and George Hunsberger have identified the characteristics of churches whose worship is missionally focused. "Worship is by its very nature God-directed," they say.[25] Accordingly, it has these four marks:

1. Worship is a public witness about what God is doing in the world. The activities of worship are defined by three New Testament words selected by the authors for their strong public implications:

    ekklesia: an assembly gathered for decision making, a town meeting

    kerygma: a public proclamation heralded in the name of one who has ultimate authority

    leitourgia: a public works project, works on behalf of the people and their public good

    Worship, say Stutzman and Hunsberger, has a "public horizon. . . . This is what is so inherently missional about worship."[26]
2. Worship declares God's reign. "Whatever else may be happening, the words and actions of worship declare that God rules, in Jesus Christ, through the power of the Holy Spirit."[27]
3. Worship sustains the identity of the Christian community. Mission-minded people of God don't come to worship seeking to get something out of it. They come, instead, to give something to God: "their adoration, their confession, their faith, their loyalty, and their obedience." By focusing on God and giving these sacrifices of praise and submission, they are being formed as a people of God, and as Christian disciples.[28]
4. Worship in missional churches infuses the entire public life of the congregation. Worship, for these communities of faith, "motivates and

23. Keifert, *We Are Here Now*, 62.
24. Ibid., 120.
25. Stutzman and Hunsberger, "The Public Witness of Worship," in Barrett, *Treasure in Clay Jars*, 102.
26. Ibid., 106–7.
27. Ibid., 106–8.
28. Ibid., 109–10.

permeates public action, for it is an encounter with the God who both calls his people out of the world and sends them into it."[29]

The conclusions drawn by Stutzman and Hunsberger about missional worship are representative of what missional theologians have to say about the relationship of worship to mission. To summarize, worship is a public act of adoration in which God's people are formed as a community of faith and a public act of allegiance to God's reign as they do God's work in the world. It is the liturgy of being gathered for Word and sacrament, and the liturgy of being sent as disciples. These things are inextricably bound. Volf says it clearly: "By aligning with God's character and purpose in adoration one aligns oneself also with God's projects in the world. By praising God who renews the face of the earth and redeems the peoples one affirms at the same time one's desire to be a cooperator with God in the Word. Adoration is the well-spring of action."[30]

Conclusion

The theme of this chapter is that worship is intricately connected with our mission as God's people. Accordingly, I have argued that it is prudent to rethink how we plan and execute our worship services. They need to be imbued throughout with the understanding that we gather to give ourselves to God, not to gain satisfaction or pleasure; that we are centered and shaped by involvement with God's gifts of Word and sacrament; and that we are sent as we have been called, to be the hands, hearts, and voices of God's mission immediately beyond the church doors. The sending is anything but final. It is weighted with anticipation, leaning toward the reality that God's reign is at hand and that we are the agents of its fulfillment in our neighborhoods and communities.

I have attempted in this chapter to bring together two patterns of activity: the shape of worship and the shape of mission. The following theological convictions have become apparent:

1. The *missio Dei* and the worship of God are interrelated, Spirit-led activities of the church.
2. Worship is both the weekly adoration of God in public gatherings and the daily service of God in Christian action.
3. The liturgical sending is a pivotal action connecting the inward adoration of God to the outward service of God.

---

29. Ibid., 113.
30. Volf, "Worship as Adoration and Action," in Carson, *Worship*, 210.

3

There Is a River

There is a river whose streams make glad the city of God, the holy habitation of the Most High. God is in the midst of the city; it shall not be moved; God will help it when the morning dawns.

Psalm 46:4–5

Rivers both run together and divide. Tributaries feed rivers to make them large and full. Deltas spread the flow out into the sea. I am borrowing the psalmist's metaphor of river here to make reference to the confluence of liturgical practice I have been describing as a welcome development in worship renewal. The Reformation began a process of worship renewal that unleashed a flood of innovation that has now taken us far from what most would recognize as a common Christian practice of worship. If Luther's reforms regarding the sacrifice of the Mass were the crack in the dam, then the growing liturgical freedom expressed by Andreas Carlstadt, Ulrich Zwingli, Martin Bucer, John Calvin, John Smyth, and others spread the breach and let the waters of liturgical innovation flood the Protestant landscape.[1] The flow reached its alluvial breadth as the Quaker church reduced the actions of public worship to an

---

1. Carlstadt was a follower of Luther but was less conservative in his reforms of the Roman Mass. Zwingli, Bucer, and Calvin were the Swiss Reformers who each produced services of worship and accompanying theologies that further eroded the shape and theology of the monolithic Mass. John Smyth was the British founder of the Baptist Church in England, a group that followed the Radical Reformation of the Anabaptists in Europe.

Sidebar 3.1: Four Descriptions of Liturgical Accord

A new reformation of Word and sacrament is occurring in North American Prot-
estantism. Yet so unnoticed has this movement been that it lacks a name. . . .
One could designate the present movement as a "reformation of Word and sacrament." It is certainly an effort at reforming current practice in almost every
aspect of worship. Or one might speak of it as the "renewal of worship" in the
sense of efforts to infuse new vigor into it. Yet another dimension is represented
by the phrase "recovery of worship." Much of the new is also very old. Many practices long dormant in Christian worship now seem relevant and useful. Greater
knowledge of the first four Christian centuries has provided much impetus for
recent reforms.

James F. White, "A Protestant Worship Manifesto," in Twenty Centuries of Christian Worship, *ed. Robert E. Webber, The Complete Library
of Christian Worship 2 (Peabody, MA: Hendrickson, 1994), 333.*

In the 1980s and 1990s a movement that converges the liturgical and the contemporary forms and experiences of worship has emerged. The antecedents of this
movement are clearly found in the twentieth century liturgical renewal movement
and in both the charismatic and praise and worship movements. . . . The convergence movement also draws from the evangelical and reformed movements as
well, clearly making it eclectic.

Robert Webber, Worship Old and New, *rev. ed. (Grand Rapids: Zondervan, 1994), 249.*

continued

---

assembly that sits and waits silently on the Lord. "Be still, and know that I
am God" (Ps. 46:10) would be a fitting rubric for their worship. And the flow
achieved its greatest departure from the formal Roman Mass when the Azusa
Street revival in 1906 embraced a Pentecostal-style (as on the Day of Pentecost)
return of the free exercise of the Holy Spirit to worship.[2]

The spreading waters of liturgical innovation now seem to be drawing back
to a central stream. (See sidebar 3.1 for descriptions of the contours of movement toward liturgical consensus.) This is apparent not so much in that there
is broad embrace of the traditional liturgical pattern that would be familiar
to Roman Catholics, Episcopalians, Lutherans, and others (the specific shape
of this pattern will be presented later in this chapter); rather, it is apparent
in the ways that churches are finding common ground for conversation, for
describing and shaping their worship, and for seeking useful resources from a
range of ecumenical and global sources. As we have been saying, the broadly
conceived four-part ordo gives us a common means by which to speak of how

---

2. See Robeck, *Azusa Street Mission and Revival*, esp. chap. 4, "Worship at the Azusa
Street Mission."

Those who are being drawn into this convergence of streams can be character-ized by several common elements. While these are not exhaustive or in any order of importance, they form the basis for the focus and direction of the convergence movement. (1) A restored commitment to the sacraments, especially the Lord's Table.... (2) An increased motivation to know more about the early church.... (3) A love for the whole church and a desire to see the church as one.... (4) The blending in the practice of all three streams is evident, yet each church approaches convergence from a unique point of view.... (5) An interest in integrating structure with spontaneity in worship.... (6) A greater involvement of sign and symbol in worship.... (7) A continuing commitment to personal salvation, biblical teaching, and the work and ministry of the Holy Spirit."

Randy Sly and Wayne Boosahda, "The Convergence Movement," in Twenty Centuries of Christian Worship, *ed. Robert E. Webber, The Complete Library of Christian Worship 2 (Peabody, MA: Hendrickson, 1994), 333.*

Some churches are reclaiming ancient patterns for worship, including the Christian year, lectionaries, and traditional structures of the Eucharistic prayer. Indeed, this liturgical movement has led Methodists and Presbyterians to sing their Eucharistic prayers, evangelicals to light Advent candles, Roman Catholics and Episcopalians to nurture congregational participation in psalmody, and some Mennonites, Brethren, and Nazarenes to form lectionary study groups.

John D. Witvliet, "Beyond Style: Rethinking the Role of Music in Worship," in The Conviction of Things Not Seen: Worship and Ministry in the Twenty-first Century, *ed. Todd Johnson (Grand Rapids: Brazos, 2002), 68.*

Christians shape missionally oriented worship, regardless of denomination or tradition. As for the shared worship resources, there is wide-ranging appreciation today for music from the Taizé and Iona communities, the use of dance and other arts in worship, the careful use of poetic language in prayer and preaching, and so forth. Surely the unity in faith these things signal is something that makes glad the city of God.

In this chapter I will take a brief look at the spreading and drawing together of worship's watercourses, showing that the central channel of liturgical practice is something given to the church as a gift of historical wisdom. Nothing could be wiser than exercising the gifts that God has given. Frank Senn reminds us that the actions of Christian liturgy are "acts of rite and prayer instituted by Jesus the Christ and inspired by the Holy Spirit in the history of the church."[3] The patterns of the historic liturgy are a gift that must be received today, though used with flexibility, as the Spirit continues to lead us.

3. Senn, *The People's Work,* 6.

Following the discussion of the historic wisdom of worship, I will consider the use of these forms as sources for creativity for those who seek to make worship a lively, missional activity.

The Historic Wisdom of the Church at Worship

The book of Proverbs makes it clear that wisdom comes from obeying God ("the fear of the Lord is the beginning of wisdom," Prov. 9:10) and listening to one's elders ("Hear, my child, your father's instruction, and do not reject your mother's teaching," Prov. 1:8). The practices of Jews and Christians through the ages have revealed a wisdom about worship that today we are prudent to apprehend. From this wisdom comes the understanding that public worship consists of four types of actions: gathering together as God's people, hearing God's Word, being physically connected to God's presence through mystery and rite, and being sent forth to be God's people among the nations. For each of these actions, let us consider the wisdom behind them, wisdom that comes from both obeying God, as we know God's intent from Scripture, and listening to our elders.

Gathering

The gathering of God's people for public worship is a biblical practice:

But Moses said to God, "Who am I that I should go to Pharaoh, and bring the Israelites out of Egypt?"
 He said, "I will be with you; and this shall be the sign for you that it is I who sent you: when you have brought the people out of Egypt, you shall worship God on this mountain." (Exod. 3:11–12)

Ascribe to the Lord the glory due his name; bring an offering, and come before him. Worship the Lord in holy splendor. (1 Chron. 16:29)

Assemble, all of you, and hear! (Isa. 48:14)

Let this be recorded . . . so that the name of the Lord may be declared in Zion, and his praise in Jerusalem, when peoples gather together, and kingdoms, to worship the Lord. (Ps. 102:18–22)

Blow the trumpet in Zion; sanctify a fast: call a solemn assembly; gather the people. (Joel 2:15–17)

[Jesus] began to teach in their synagogues and was praised by everyone.
 When he came to Nazareth, where he had been brought up, he went to the synagogue on the sabbath day, as was his custom. (Luke 4:15–16)

Remember that the word *synagogue* derives from the Greek verb meaning to gather (*synágō*). The practice of assembling in these local meeting places began during a time of displacement, when the Israelites, exiled in Babylon, found themselves cut off from the central place of worship in Jerusalem.

Most conspicuously, we also have this word from Jesus about gathering:

> For where two or three are gathered in my name, I am there among them. (Matt. 18:20)

Gathering is also the first action of worship historically described by our faith elders. Justin Martyr, for example, reports that "on the day called Sunday there is a meeting in one place of those who live in cities or the country," as believers assembled to hear the Word and celebrate the Eucharist.[4] Another example comes from Egeria, the fourth-century traveling nun, who describes the worship of Jerusalem as the repeated daily gathering ("all the people congregate once more") of monks, nuns, and laypeople for the offices of daily prayer.[5] She also says, "But on the seventh day, the Lord's Day, there gather in the courtyard before cock-crow all the people, as many as can get in, as if it was Easter."[6]

The counsel of the ages on the need for and nature of gathering is manifold. Some interesting points made by various of our elders are worth noting. St. Basil assures of the need for believers to worship together, even if circumstances require that people meet in small gatherings: "But if some, perhaps, are not in attendance because the nature or place of their work keeps them at too great a distance, they are strictly obliged to carry out wherever they are, with promptitude, all that is prescribed for common observance, for 'Where there are two or three gathered together in my name,' says the Lord, 'there am I in the midst of them.'"[7]

John Chrysostom, in his *Baptismal Instructions*, teaches that gathering for worship is more important than all other things in life: "And when the hour for gathering in church summons him [the baptized], let him hold this gathering and all spiritual things in higher regard than anything else."[8] The Church of Scotland required the gathering of families for home worship, and warned: "The head of the family is to take care that none of the family withdraw himself from any part of family-worship."[9] Puritan worship, as might be expected, was marked by the most sober kind of gathering: "Let all enter the Assembly, not irreverently, but in a grave and seemly manner."[10]

4. Justin Martyr, *First Apology*, in Richardson, *Early Christian Fathers*, 287.
5. Egeria, quoted in White, *Documents*, 86.
6. Ibid., 87.
7. St. Basil, *The Long Rules*, in White, *Documents*, 89–90.
8. John Chrysostom, *Baptismal Instructions*, in White, *Documents*, 85.
9. Church of Scotland, *The Directory for Family-Worship*, in White, *Documents*, 97.
10. *A Directory for the Publique Worship of God* [Westminster *Directory*], in White, *Documents*, 108.

One of our more recent elders, from whom we have learned much about worship, is James F. White, who offers this caution on the importance of gathering: "In recent years liturgists have become more sensitive to the need for gathering space, in which the people come together to discern the body of Christ. This may be the most important single action of worship, and failure to take it seriously could have dire consequences as Paul warns (1 Cor. 11:29)."[11]

Word

Also, like the gathering of God's people, the place of the Word as central to worship is biblical:

> Then the king [Josiah] directed that all the elders of Judah and Jerusalem should be gathered to him. The king went up to the house of the Lord, and with him went all the people of Judah, all the inhabitants of Jerusalem, the priests, the prophets, and all the people, both small and great; he read in their hearing all the words of the book of the covenant that had been found in the house of the Lord. (2 Kings 23:1–2)

> And on the sabbath day [Paul and Silas] went into the synagogue and sat down. After the reading of the law and the prophets, the officials of the synagogue sent them a message, saying, "Brothers, if you have any word of exhortation for the people, give it." So Paul stood up and with a gesture began to speak. (Acts 13:14–16)

> Give attention to the public reading of scripture, to exhorting, to teaching. (1 Tim. 4:13)

The centrality of the Word in worship is attested to by our historic elders as well. Justin Martyr reports that after people gather in cities or the countryside, "the memoirs of the apostles or the writings of the prophets are read as long as time permits. When the reader has finished, the president in a discourse urges and invites [us] to the imitation of these noble things."[12] St. Augustine considered exposition of Scripture so central to Christian life and worship that he authored a book on preaching. *On Christian Teaching* is considered the first Christian homiletics textbook and is still instructive today. In it, he advocates that preachers make good use of the rules of classic rhetoric: "The eloquent divine, then, when he is urging a practical truth, must not only teach so as to give instruction, and please so as to keep up the attention, but he must also sway the mind so as to subdue the will."[13]

11. White, "The Spatial Setting," in Tucker and Wainwright, *The Oxford History of Christian Worship*, 799.
12. Justin Martyr, *First Apology*, in Richardson, *Early Christian Fathers*, 287.
13. Augustine, *On Christian Teaching*, excerpted in Edwards, *A History of Preaching*, 2:82–83.

Listening to the wisdom of our mothers in faith has been made difficult because of Paul's early teaching that "women should be silent in churches" (1 Cor. 14:34). Yet, as O. C. Edwards Jr. observes, the twelfth century provided an exception to the church's following of this rule. He notes several female preachers, including Rose of Viterbo and Umiltá of Faenza. Most notable, however, was Hildegard of Bingen. She was widely known for her preaching and provided scriptural exposition for clergy, monks, and laity alike. She left behind a collection of sermons called *Expositions of the Gospels*, sermons for twenty-four services of worship within the liturgical calendar.[14]

During the Reformation period, when many liturgical freedoms were spawned, the Word remained central to worship in Protestant churches. Luther certainly kept both the reading of the Epistles and Gospels and preaching as the key second movement within the liturgy: "the time has not come to attempt revision here, as nothing unevangelical is read," he said in the introduction of his 1523 Formula of the Mass. He added, "If in the future the vernacular be used in the mass (which Christ may grant), one must see to it that Epistles and Gospels chosen from the best and most weighty parts of these writings be read." And "in the meantime, the sermon in the vernacular will have to supply what is lacking."[15]

If Luther preserved the place of the reading of lessons and vernacular preaching in Protestant worship, John Calvin reinvigorated worship with a renewed emphasis on use of the Psalms: "There are psalms which we desire to be sung in the Church, as we have it exemplified in the ancient Church and in the evidence of Paul himself, who says it is good to sing in the congregation with mouth and heart. . . . The psalms can incite us to lift up our hearts to God and to move us to an ardor in invoking and exalting with praises the glory of his name."[16]

Throughout the medieval Roman and the early Reformation churches, use of the Old Testament in worship was spotty (except for the book of Psalms). The 1645 Westminster Directory revitalized the use of the Old Testament readings in the worship of Anglicans, Scottish Presbyterians, and the Puritan Independents: "How large a portion [of Scripture] shall be read at once, is left to the wisdome of the Minister: but it is convenient, that ordinarily one chapter of each Testament be read at every meeting: and sometimes more, where the chapters be short, or the coherence of the matter requireth it."[17]

14. Edwards, *A History of Preaching*, 1:197–200.

15. Martin Luther, "Introduction to *Formula Missae*," in *Luther's Works: Liturgy and Hymns*, trans. Leupold, Lehmann, and Zeller Strodach, 53:24.

16. John Calvin, *Articles Concerning the Organization of the Church and of Worship at Geneva Proposed by the Ministers at the Council January 16, 1537*, quoted in White, *Documents*, 105.

17. *A Directory for the Publique Worship of God*, as quoted in White, *Documents*, 109.

Johann Sebastian Bach adorned the Word with music, as is clear from his journal entry describing the service of worship for the first Sunday in Advent in 1714. The center of this service included "Reading of the Epistle, Singing of the Litany, Preluding on the Chorale, Reading of the Gospel, Preluding on the principal composition [cantata], Singing of the Creed, The Sermon, After the Sermon, as usual, singing of several verses of a hymn."[18]

Among the Protestants who advocated freedom in worship form was Charles G. Finney (1792–1875). Under his leadership a new idea developed, that the Sunday congregational service become oriented principally to the production of converts. Accordingly, preaching was retained as central to the worship experience and was made "more exciting, to meet the character and wants of the age."[19]

Sacraments: Baptism

Holy Baptism is a key biblical practice, mandated by Christ and exercised by nearly every tradition within the Christian faith.

Go therefore and make disciples of all nations, baptizing them in the name of the Father and of the Son and of the Holy Spirit. (Matt. 28:19)

But when they believed Philip, who was proclaiming the good news about the kingdom of God and the name of Jesus Christ, they were baptized, both men and women. (Acts 8:12)

As they were going along the road, they came to some water; and the eunuch said, "Look, here is water! What is to prevent me from being baptized?"
    He commanded the chariot to stop, and both of them, Philip and the eunuch, went down into the water, and Philip baptized him. (Acts 8:36, 38)

For in the one Spirit we were all baptized into one body—Jews or Greeks, slaves or free—and we were all made to drink of one Spirit. (1 Cor. 12:13)

The *Didache*, a collection of teachings from the early second century about the faith, gives instruction on how to baptize, employing the use of the trinitarian formula mandated by Christ: "This is how to baptize: Give public instruction on all these points, and then 'baptize' in running water, 'in the name of the Father and of the Son and of the Holy Spirit.'"[20]

Many other church fathers and mothers gave instruction on the place of baptism in Christian worship.[21] Representative is what Egeria reported as hap-

---

18. Bach, "Order of Divine Service in Leipzig," in David and Mendel, *The Bach Reader*, 70.
19. Charles G. Finney, "Measures to Promote Revivals," quoted in White, *Documents*, 115.
20. "The Didache," in Richardson, *Early Christian Fathers*, 174.
21. These include Justin Martyr, Irenaeus of Lyons, Clement of Alexandria, Tertullian, Cyril of Jerusalem, Ambrose of Milan, John Chrysostom, Egeria, and Augustine of Hippo. There statements are contained in White, *Documents*, 147–66.

pening in Jerusalem, indicating that preaching on baptism occurred in worship services during the week following baptisms that took place on Easter: "[After Easter, the bishop] interprets all that takes place in Baptism. . . . Indeed the way he expounds the mysteries and interprets them cannot fail to move his hearers."[22] An especially interesting statement was made by the Roman Catholic Church in the fifteenth century in The Decree for the Armenians, which declared that "holy baptism holds the first place of all the sacraments, which is the doorway to the life of the spirit, and through it we are made members of Christ and his body, the Church."[23]

Luther brought few changes to the practice of baptism in his worship renewal program. Of note, however, is this suggestion to return to the use of full immersion: "Although in many places it is no longer customary to thrust and dip infants into the font, but only with the hand to pour the baptismal water upon them out of the font, nevertheless the former is what should be done."[24] Luther also provided the well-known "Flood Prayer" for the 1526 version of his baptismal liturgy. This prayer, in various translations and paraphrases, has been incorporated into numerous baptismal rites by churches of many denominations and is widely used today. (See sidebar 3.2 for its text.)

The Radical Reformation taught that infant baptism was wrong and that only persons who first understood and confessed the faith were to receive the sacrament. Still, as Menno Simons makes clear, baptism is connected to preaching and the worship of the church: "Here we have the Lord's commandment concerning baptism, as to when according to the ordinance of God it shall be administered and received; namely, that the gospel must first be preached, and then those baptized who believe it. . . . Thus the Lord commanded and ordained; therefore, no other baptism may be taught or practiced forever. The Word of God abideth forever."[25]

Sacraments: Holy Communion

The holy meal is also a biblical practice, commanded by Christ and exercised by the whole Christian church.

> This is my body which is given for you. Do this in remembrance of me. . . . This cup that is poured out for you is the new covenant in my blood. (Luke 22:19–20)

22. Egeria, quoted in White, *Documents*, 163.
23. "The Decree for the Armenians," in White, *Documents*, 164.
24. Martin Luther, "The Holy and Blessed Sacrament of Baptism," in *Luther's Works*, trans. Jacobs and Bachmann, 35:29.
25. Menno Simons, "Foundation of Christian Doctrine," in Verduin, *The Complete Writings of Menno Simons*, 126.

For I received from the Lord what I also handed on to you. . . . For as often as you eat this bread and drink the cup, you proclaim the Lord's death until he comes. (1 Cor. 11:23, 26)

They devoted themselves to the apostles' teaching and fellowship, to the break-ing of bread and the prayers. (Acts 2:42)

The early church fathers and mothers had much to say about the place of the Eucharist within the service of worship. Again, a single example is rep-resentative. To the church in Ephesus, Ignatius of Antioch wrote, "At these meetings you should heed the bishop and presbytery attentively, and break one loaf, which is the medicine of immortality, and the antidote which wards off death but yields continuous life in union with Jesus Christ."[26]

The teaching of the elders of faith on the question of the presence of Christ in Holy Communion began to diverge in the ninth century, where writings by monks Paschasius Radbertus and Rastramnus disputed whether the bread and wine physically changed to become the flesh of Christ. (Radbertus held that it did, Rastramnus that it did not.) The Fourth Lateran Council (1215) settled the matter on the side of "transubstantiation," declaring that the body and blood of Christ "are truly contained in the sacrament of the altar under the species of bread and wine" and that "the bread [is changed] into body and wine into blood through divine power." The Reformers did not accept this theological interpretation of the sacrament and came up with several other ways of constru-ing the use of the elements in communion, either as signs of Christ's presence or symbols of his saving acts.[27] Regardless of interpretation, the centrality of the Eucharist in worship is maintained by writers in each tradition. This continues to be the case today (again, excepting Quakers) in the most liberal of liturgical traditions. As noted above, the Pentecostal movement brought more innovation (speaking in tongues, dancing, being slain in the Spirit, prophesying) than any movement within the Christian church. Still, its worship is centered around the typical things, including the Lord's Supper: "Looking at the basic outline of the [Azusa Street] mission's worship life, it would be difficult to conclude that the services were anything other than ordinary Christian services. The mission . . . practiced Christian baptism by immersion in water using the traditional Trinitarian formula. It offered the Lord's Supper regularly, sometimes accom-

26. Ignatius, "Letters of Ignatius of Antioch: To the Ephesians," in Richardson, *Early Christian Fathers*, 93.

27. Luther held that Christ comes to the believer in communion "in, with, and under" the elements. This was explained in his 1520 treatise *The Babylonian Captivity of the Church*. Zwingli argued that the bread and wine were symbols that brought remembrance of Christ's saving acts (in *On the Lord's Supper* [1526], 195). Calvin found a middle ground (*via media*) whereby he identified Christ as spiritually present in the sacrament, though spatially the body of Christ is contained in heaven and cannot be elsewhere. This mystery he admits to in the fourth volume of his *Institutes of the Christian Religion* (1559).

Sidebar 3.2: Luther's Flood Prayer

Almighty Eternal God, who according to thy righteous judgment didst condemn the unbelieving world through the flood and in thy great mercy didst preserve believing Noah and his family, and who didst drown hardhearted Pharaoh with all his host in the Red Sea and didst lead thy people Israel through the same on dry ground, thereby prefiguring this bath of thy baptism, and who through the baptism of thy dear Child, our Lord Jesus Christ, hast consecrated and set apart the Jordan and all water as a salutary flood and a rich and full washing away of sins: We pray through the same thy groundless mercy that thou wilt graciously behold this [Name] and bless him with true faith in the Spirit so that by means of this saving flood all that has been born in him from Adam and which he himself has added thereto may be drowned in him and engulfed, and that he may be sundered from the number of unbelieving, preserved dry and secure in the holy ark of Christendom, serve thy name at all times fervent in spirit and joyful in hope, so that with all believers he may be made worthy to attain eternal life according to thy promise; through Jesus Christ our Lord. Amen.

"The Order of Baptism Newly Revised (1526)," in Luther's Works: Liturgy and Hymns, *trans. Ulrich S. Leupold, Helmut T. Lehmann, and Paul Zeller Strodach, vol. 53 (Philadelphia: Fortress, 1965), 107–8.*

---

panied by the washing of the 'saints'' feet in the manner of many Anabaptist and Wesleyan holiness congregations."[28]

Sending

Finally, the sending is also a biblical practice and mandate that is connected to the *missio Dei*.

Go therefore and make disciples of all nations. (Matt. 28:19)

As the Father has sent me, so I send you. (John 20:21)

Simeon took [the child Jesus] in his arms and praised God, saying, "Master, now you are dismissing your servant in peace." (Luke 2:28–29)

And [Jesus] said to the woman, "Your faith has saved you; go in peace." (Luke 7:50)

Again, Justin Martyr is the first of our elders to report the practice beyond the biblical period: "when we have finished the prayer, bread is brought, and

---

28. Robeck, *Azusa Street Mission and Revival*, 136.

wine and water, and the president similarly sends up prayers and thanksgivings to the best of his ability, and the congregation assents, saying the Amen; the distribution, and reception of the consecrated [elements] by each one, takes place and they are sent to the absent by the deacons."[29] Because the wisdom of being sent from the assembly is a matter of sense rather than doctrine, let the wisdom of the action be referenced by the bracketing comments of Justin (the first liturgical writer) and Marva Dawn (a living commentator). Her vision for sending returns us to our main task, to see the sending as the connection to mission:

> What would happen if everyone in our pews for worship on Sunday morning departed afterward with a deep understanding of all that Jesus meant by the sentences ["You did not choose me but I chose you. And I appointed you to go and bear fruit, fruit that will last . . ."]? For that to happen, our worship would have to be remarkably filled with the sense that we did not choose to come, that God has chosen us for his purposes, appointed us specifically for our various ministries in the world, and equipped us to bear lasting fruit, we would depart with a vision for being Church the rest of the week.[30]

Ordo Summary

The historic wisdom of the church at worship has given us this fourfold pattern by which to discuss the actions of worship, give theological focus to the central things around which we gather, and connect adoration and action. The four movements of worship are not something that can be prescribed universally for worship because God's people are creative and there are many ways of offering praise and prayer to God. This simple ordo is, nonetheless, a strong guide and pertains with greater or lesser detail to nearly every worship tradition, as we will demonstrate in the table below. Naturally, it will be used in different ways, according to the necessary particularities of each local context and the theological demands of differing faith traditions. The World Council of Churches recognized the need for this diversity of practice in its 1982 statement on *Baptism, Eucharist, and Ministry*: "The liturgical reform movement has brought the churches closer together in the manner of celebrating the Lord's Supper. However, a certain liturgical diversity compatible with our common eucharistic faith is recognized as a healthy and enriching fact. The affirmation of a common eucharistic faith does not imply uniformity in either liturgy or practice."[31] The principle achievement of this document is that it represents

29. Justin Martyr, *First Apology*, in Richardson, *Early Christian Fathers*, 287.

30. Dawn, "Worship to Form a Missional Community," in *A Royal "Waste" of Time*, 333.

31. *Baptism, Eucharist, and Ministry*, 16. The World Council of Churches (WCC) is made up of churches representing virtually every confessional tradition. (Currently, the membership is more than 340 churches or faith organizations, including a number of Orthodox bodies.)

a move toward Christian unity after centuries of division. The common use of the sacraments of baptism and the Lord's Supper by all churches is seen as a sign of this unity. Note how the shape of the ordo is presumed in the statement's description of our common practice of Eucharistic worship:

> In the celebration of the eucharist, *Christ gathers*, teaches and nourishes the Church. It is Christ who invites to the meal and who presides at it. He is the shepherd who leads the people of God, *the prophet who announces the Word of God*, the priest who celebrates the mystery of God. In most churches, this presidency is signified by an ordained minister. The one who presides at the eucharistic celebration in the name of Christ makes clear that the rite is not the assemblies' own creation or possession; *the eucharist is received as a gift from Christ living in his Church*. The minister of the eucharist is the ambassador who represents the divine initiative and expresses the connection of the local community with other local communities in the universal Church.[32]

From such gatherings, regardless of their denomination, tradition, shape, or setting, God's people are sent forth as the church in mission.

For the sake of unity, this statement recognizes but does not try to harmonize the diverse views on Christ's presence in the Lord's Supper, nor those between infant baptism and believer's baptism. It calls for respect of one another's perspectives and seeks to achieve such unity in faith as can be found when believers acknowledge that they have much in common with one another, even with regard to baptism and Holy Communion. This commonality can be expressed in a number of ways. For Tom Long, there is a stream that connects "Hippolytus and Willow Creek." It is represented by congregations that shape local worship that is attuned to culture, "but also fully congruent with the great worship tradition of the Christian church; a service that attracts young people and seekers and the curious and those who are hungry for a spiritual encounter, but that does so by beckoning people to the deep and refreshing pool of the gospel of Jesus Christ as it has been understood historically in the church."[33] Missional theologian Craig Nessan puts it this way: "When we worship using the historic liturgy, not only are we connected with Christians

---

Though the Roman Catholic Church is not a member of the council, this theological statement was developed by a commission that included Catholic theologians and those from other non-represented churches. While now over twenty-five years old, this "Lima Text" (so-called because it was adopted by the Faith and Order Commission of the WCC at its 1982 meeting in Lima, Peru) still stands as the council's view on baptism, Eucharist, and ministry. In subsequent years, the WCC has developed additional materials that add perspective to this statement or provide resources for ecumenical use. They include *So We Believe, So We Pray: Towards Koinonia in Worship* (1994), *Celebrations of the Eucharist in Ecumenical Contexts—A Proposal* (1995), *Becoming a Christian: The Ecumenical Implications of Our Common Baptism* (1997), and *One Baptism: Towards Mutual Recognition* (2006).

32. *Baptism, Eucharist, and Ministry*, 16; my italics.
33. Long, *Beyond the Worship Wars*, 12.

Sidebar 3.3: The Order of Worship and the Order of Human Fellowship

The historic wisdom that gave the church the fourfold ordo is not dissimilar to the wisdom of the common gathering of people for fellowship and a meal in the home. Any common dinner party will do by way of example, but consider Mark's telling of the Last Supper. Jesus *gathered* with the disciples to celebrate this event ("When it was evening, he came with the twelve," 14:17). Once assembled, they engaged in *words* and *table* fellowship, though the conversation on this evening was anything but festive ("And when they had taken their places and were eating, Jesus said, 'Truly I tell you, one of you will betray me,'" 14:18). At the conclusion of the meal, they *took their leave* ("They went to a place called Gethsemane," 14:32).

A more festive version of this fourfold pattern is known by those who host dinner parties: they greet their guests as they gather, offer them fellowship and conversation over a meal, and send them on their way as friends blessed by participation in the event. As in Christian liturgy, the same kinds of questions give shape to the occasion. Where do we gather? (Usually in a home or restaurant.) What do we gather around? (Words and food.) How do we conclude? (Guests are sent on their way with the host's blessing.)

over the ages, but we are immersed in an encounter with God in Christ that has been effective in preserving the faith for nearly two thousand years!"[34]

Growing Consensus on the Celebration and Remembrance of the Sacraments in Worship

Not every service of worship on the Lord's Day includes baptism or Holy Communion. While the Eucharist is observed daily in some traditions, it is celebrated monthly or quarterly in others. Baptisms are celebrated according to schedules that are hard to generalize. When newcomers have been trained in the faith and desire to publicly declare their faith commitment, or when families are prepared to bring infants or young children to be baptized, congregations will schedule baptismal rites as needed. The frequency and timing of sacraments in worship are a matter of local determination. Nevertheless, there is an increasing sense of agreement about these matters. Three points of growing consensus can be identified.

The first is mounting encouragement for more frequent, even weekly celebration of the Lord's Supper. This is not a surprise in traditions that inherited a weekly celebration of the Eucharist. Lutherans, for example, received the Roman practice of weekly communion.[35] This did not mean, necessarily, that

34. Nessan, *Beyond Maintenance to Mission*, 10.
35. "In our churches [the Reformers wrote] Mass is celebrated every Sunday and on other festivals, when the sacrament is offered to those who wish for it after they have been

an individual received the sacrament on a weekly basis. It was provided each Sunday so that worshipers could receive it when they desired. Unlike Catholics, who typically received the sacrament weekly, if not daily, Lutherans sometimes chose to receive the sacrament as few as several times per year. This was enough of a concern that in the introduction to the Small Catechism, Luther warned, "It is to be feared that anyone who does not desire to receive the sacrament at least three or four times a year despises the sacrament and is no Christian."[36] Today, many Lutheran congregations are returning to a weekly celebration of the Eucharist in which most congregants participate. Likewise, many other Protestants are following suit. James White reports that "the eucharist is now celebrated weekly as the main Sunday service in thousands of Episcopal and Lutheran churches and some United Methodist and Presbyterian congregations. Thousands of the latter two have moved to monthly celebrations."[37] The interest in more frequent communion is also being embraced by evangelical and free churches.[38] In making suggestions for worship renewal in these churches, Robert Webber calls for returning to a "full biblical witness" regarding the Eucharist, including more frequent celebrations.[39]

The second growing point of consensus about the sacraments is that baptism is to be celebrated as part of the corporate worship of a faith community. Every tradition understands baptism to be a sign of entry into the Christian faith. Yet many have allowed baptism to become a private ceremony or one removed from the regular worship of a congregation. Today there is a call to return baptism to corporate worship: "Since baptism is intimately connected with the corporate life and worship of the Church, it should normally be administered during public worship so that the members of the congregation may be reminded of their own baptism and may welcome into their fellowship those who are baptized and whom they are committed to nurture in the Christian faith."[40] (See sidebar 3.4 for an example of a creative pastoral way to deal with a family that insisted their child's baptism take place on a Thursday morning.)

A third point of consensus about the place of the sacraments in worship is that when they are not celebrated, the sacraments can be ritually remembered. This especially applies to baptism, which is often practiced less frequently

---

examined and absolved" ("Augsburg Confession," article 24, in Tappert, *The Book of Concord*, 249).

36. Martin Luther, "Small Catechism," in Tappert, *The Book of Concord*, 341.

37. White, *The Sacraments in Protestant Practice and Faith*, 142.

38. It is worth noting that one strand of the free church movement springing from frontier revival worship has maintained observance of weekly Eucharist from the outset. The Church of Christ, following the leading of Alexander Campbell (1788–1866) during the Second Great Awakening, employs only worship practices that are warranted in Scripture, including weekly celebration of the Eucharist. They are also committed to a cappella singing.

39. Webber, *Worship Old and New*, 249.

40. *Baptism, Eucharist, and Ministry*, 6–7.

Sidebar 3.4: A Baptismal Rite within a Little Assembly

Pastors are often confronted with the dilemma of a family's desire for baptisms to take place privately or at convenient times when, for example, grandparents happen to be in town. One pastor dealt with this problem in a creative way. Committed to the understanding that baptism is a rite of the church that needs to be celebrated within the corporate worship of the congregation, he nonetheless allowed for a baptism to be administered on a Thursday morning when the child's grandparents were in town. Whether they were truly unavailable on Sunday morning or the family simply used this claim as a lever to avoid what they thought of as an unnecessary public display was not certain. Regardless, the pastor found a way to satisfy both sets of needs. The baptism was held at 10:00 on a Thursday morning at the regular assembly for worship of the church's preschool. Fifty children, their teachers and aides, and the baptismal party gathered before the font in the chancel and attended to the baptism of the child. What might have been a confrontation between pastoral better judgment and parental insistence became both a time of corporate worship for the teachers and children that was enriched by participation in the sacrament and a time of learning for the children and the baptismal family alike. The children did their part, witnessing to the baptism and speaking their words of welcome and commitment for the newly baptized. The family learned that the congregation has a critical role in what they took to be a private matter.

---

than the Eucharist. Remembering our baptism in worship emphasizes that growth in faith begins with the sacrament but takes a lifetime of learning and maturing. Accordingly, churches are now including rites for sprinkling with water (holy water in Catholic practice), thanksgiving for baptism, affirmation of baptism, and renewal of baptismal vows. Being aware of the place of the sacraments in worship also allows for more intentional reflection on baptism and the Lord's Supper in preaching.

What these points of consensus mean for the ordering of Christian worship is that the sacraments are understood as integral to our assemblies. When corporate worship does not include baptismal or Eucharistic rites, it finds ways to remember that all Christians are united in faith through "one baptism" (Eph. 4:5) and "one loaf" (1 Cor. 10:17). In other words, if the liturgical movements in a given service of worship are gathering, Word, and sending, they can still be imbued with the memory of our sacramental identity.

The Fourfold Pattern in Various Traditions

I have been saying that we can recognize the fourfold pattern of worship in the liturgies of various traditions. The following table indicates the elements within each action, as currently represented by several worship traditions. For the sake

The Fourfold Pattern of Worship in Various Traditions

Roman Catholic, Episcopalian, Lutheran	Presbyterian	Baptist	Pentecostal*
Gathering			
Confession of sins and absolution Apostolic greeting Entrance song or psalm *Gloria in excelis* (Glory to God in the highest) or song of praise *Kyrie eleison* (Lord have mercy) Prayer of the day	Call to worship (Greeting and sentences of Scripture) Prayer of the day or opening prayer Hymn, song, or psalm of praise Confession of sins and declaration of pardon Sharing the peace Song, hymn, or psalm	Welcome and prayer Call to worship or invocation Opening hymns and songs Pastoral prayers (sometimes concluding with the Lord's Prayer)	Call to worship Praise and worship through song and hymn singing (for an indeterminate length of time) Pastoral welcome and prayer (Speaking in tongues and prophetic interpretation may happen at any time)
Word			
Old Testament reading Psalm Epistle reading Gospel acclamation Gospel reading Sermon Hymn or song of the day Nicene or Apostles' Creed Prayer and intercessions Sign of Peace	Prayer for illumination Old Testament reading Psalm for the day Epistle reading Anthem, hymn, psalm, or song Gospel reading Sermon Hymn or song Affirmation of faith (Nicene or Apostles' Creed) Prayers of the people	Scripture reading Anthem Sermon and invitation to faith Hymn or song of response Offering and prayer (sometimes placed after the Scripture reading)	Scripture reading Anthem Sermon Call to commitment or recommitment Offering of tithes
Lord's Supper			
Offering of tithes and communion elements Prayer over the gifts Eucharistic Prayer: Great Thanksgiving; preface; *Sanctus* (Holy, holy, holy, Lord); acclamations; institution narrative; the Lord's Prayer; *Agnus Dei* (Lamb of God) Breaking of bread and distribution *Nunc dimittus* (Simeon's song) or post-communion song	Offering of tithes Invitation to the Lord's Table Eucharistic Prayer: Great Thanksgiving; Holy, holy, holy, Lord; acclamations; institution narrative; the Lord's Prayer Breaking of bread and distribution Prayer after communion	Prayer of thanksgiving Words of institution Distribution Hymn or song	Words of institution Distribution (with singing, and/or prayer and dancing)
Sending			
Greeting Blessing or Benediction Dismissal Closing hymn or song	Hymn, song, or psalm Charge and blessing or benediction Final hymn or song	Benediction Parting hymn or song	Benediction Parting hymn or song

*The sources for assembling the shape of this generalized Pentecostal service are Robeck, *Azusa Street Mission and Revival* (esp. chap. 4, "Worship at the Azusa Street Mission"); and Work, "Pentecostal and Charismatic Worship," 576–85.

of concision, it has been necessary to make generalizations about these orders of worship, especially in the cases of the Baptist and Pentecostal services, where free church practice allows for flexibility.[41] The table indicates the typical parts of worship used within these traditions when the Lord's Supper is celebrated (see "The Fourfold Pattern of Worship in Various Traditions").

This table could also be drawn using other widely divergent worship forms. For example, it would not be difficult to separate the many ritual actions of a typical Orthodox liturgy into the four key movements of worship (see the appendix at the conclusion of part 2). Next to that, we might place the old frontier service, followed by a seeker-sensitive idiom of worship. Even the old Methodist "hymn sandwich" (hymn-prayer-hymn-reading-hymn-sermon-hymn) can be seen to fit into this structure when the Eucharist is included.

The Use of Liturgical Wisdom

What is the prudent use of this wisely wrought fourfold liturgical pattern today? Is it crucial that Christians all worship in the same way, as churches sought to do in the medieval Roman period, or as the Church of England's Book of Common Prayer attempted to regulate? Or is it better to embrace free-flowing innovation, with little regard for the shape or purpose of the actions within each rite? My purpose in this book is to identify the points of liturgical convergence that seem to be available to us today and to argue that by apprehending the historic wisdom of the church at worship, we can use the movements of the ordo to give shape and plot to worship as we craft liturgies for local use. This pattern can be used creatively and need not be used woodenly and rigidly. Ultimately, how this common pattern will be used is a matter of local theology. Chapter 6 will argue for the use of this pattern in such a way that the broad issues of context regulate its most proper local expression.

Form as Freedom

Some will argue that adherence to form stifles creativity and the free exercise of the imagination. Accordingly, they might prefer worship without any pre-scribed form over highly structured worship. On the surface, the worship of free churches seems to follow this line of reasoning. As we can see from the table and discussion above, however, nearly all worshiping traditions have pre-

41. Telford Work, in describing Pentecostal worship norms, says, "The variety of Pentecostal ceremonial forms makes description of 'the typical Pentecostal liturgy' all but impossible, but many features of its distinct liturgies are widespread across the tradition" ("Pentecostal and Charismatic Worship," in Tucker and Wainwright, *The Oxford History of Christian Liturgy*, 576).

ferred forms that they use out of congregational or denominational habit, and yet they find capacity for limitless expression within them. Even Pentecostal services have discernable patterns and do not tend to be completely free-form. Only Quakers wait solely on the free moving of the Spirit in the midst of the assembly, yet even they meet in a habitual place and sit in a customary fashion, with strong expectations as to what forms of communication are proper within the community.

The fact is that form is the friend of freedom. It releases creativity. Artists, especially, know this. "The enemy of art," said Orson Welles, "is the absence of limitations."[42] Ask an artist to create something and they will quickly make you aware of the necessity of form. Imagine that a church commissions a composer to write a new piece of music for its fiftieth anniversary celebration. The composer will have no place to begin until certain questions of form are settled: Is it a congregational song, a choral anthem, an instrumental, or orchestral piece? How long should it be? Where will it fit into the liturgy? What are the musical capacities of the person or group that will perform the piece? Until the form of the composition is settled, the composer has no scaffold from which to assemble musical ideas. Once these matters are established, the composer's imagination takes flight and he or she begins to envision how the piece will move and sound. Liturgical artist Catherine Kapikian admits that she is "empowered by the commissioning process" that some consider a restraint and "an obstacle to self-expression." The reason is that within the limiting constraints of a carefully defined commission, "unlimited expressive possibilities exist."[43] One might even go so far as to say that an artist's work does not even appear to the typical percipient *as* a work of art unless it is wed to some identifiable form. Perhaps the best known example of the truth of the dictum that form releases freedom is the music of J. S. Bach. It is well established that Bach did not create new musical forms or modes of expression. He simply received the musical conventions of his day and worked with and within them. In terms of form, he was not creative in the least. Yet he is held to be the most imaginative and successful composer of the Baroque era. So exhaustive was his musical creativity within these forms that the Baroque period is said to have come to its end upon the death of this musical giant.

The forms of worship, as a received historical gift, are available to Christians today. They can be used unimaginatively and with rote formality, or they can describe friendly limits that birth creativity and foster soaring expressions of praise and proclamation. (See sidebar 3.5 for the description of another historic form that is still useful in worship.) We cannot assume that traditional liturgies are necessarily boring or that free liturgies are automatically creative and inspired. Nor can we say that free worship is always

42. Quoted in Kapikian, *Art in Service of the Sacred*, 45.
43. Ibid., 46.

Sidebar 3.5: The Wisdom of the Collect

The *collect* (pronounced **coll**-ect) is an ancient pattern of prayer that is still useful today. It is used to gather the themes of worship or prayer and present them together in a unified address to God. The collect is a form that can foster tremendous creativity. The form has four parts: (1) we address God, (2) we state a brief attribute of God, (3) we tell God our needs and usually say why we are asking for them, and (4) we conclude with a statement of mediation (that is, through whom we pray). A shorthand for this has been developed by liturgical scholar Karen Westerfield Tucker: *You, Who, Do, Through*. Since the petition section (asking God to *do* something) often includes a second clause whereby we state our reason for the request ("give us this, so *that* we might . . ."), I like to add the word *that* to the formula: *You, Who, Do (That), Through*.

Thomas Cranmer made extensive use of the collect. Here is his prayer for Ash Wednesday:

[*You:*] Almighty and everlasting God, [*Who:*] which hatest nothing that thou hast made and dost forgive the sins of all them that be penitent; [*Do:*] Create and make in us new and contrite hearts, [*That:*] that we worthily lamenting our sins, and acknowledging our wretchedness may obtain of thee, the God of all mercy, perfect remission and forgiveness; [*Through:*] through Jesus Christ.

C. Frederick Busbee and Paul F. M. Zahl, The Collects of Thomas
Cranmer *(Grand Rapids: Eerdmans, 1999), 32.*

Two things can be kept in mind regarding the use of this formula. First, a prayer written in this form need not sound like a museum piece. Contemporary, even colloquial, language can be used to create prayers appropriate to local occasions. A formal sounding prayer might be composed for Sunday worship, a less formal prayer might be crafted for blessing a meal in the church's social hall, and a simply worded prayer might be said at a youth camp meeting. For example:

[*You:*] God of earth and sky, [*Who:*] you brought us into the woods today to see your wonderful creation and to enjoy it. [*Do:*] Give us a good day together, filled with laughter and friendship, [*That:*] so that we can grow together as Christian friends. [*Through:*] In Jesus's name we pray. Amen.

The second thing to remember in using the collect form is that language, especially with regard to addressing God, can be thoughtful and creative. It need not sound lofty or churchy. And it is best (that is, it draws people into the prayer most effectively) when it uses words and images that are fresh. There are many ways to address God and describe God's attributes. There are innumerable ways to speak of human needs. It is worth the prayer leader's time to think poetically in preparing these portions of the prayer. For the collect to be of use today, prayer leaders should employ the freedom that comes from understanding a form and using it to create something new and pertinent for local worship.

chaotic and lacking in structure. I have happily worshiped in places where traditional liturgies were filled with life and spontaneous engagement of the people. Similarly, I have been drawn to full participation in charismatic services that were well planned and executed with hospitality and excellence. But I have also seen leaders of traditional and free worship services press their leadership so heavily on the people that worship was stifled and cold. Our goal is to encourage the church in the creative use of common forms of worship that will find inspired expression articulated according to local necessities. Let us remember that the Holy Spirit guides congregations toward engagement in God's mission in the world and that the historic liturgy of the church has been inspired by the same Spirit as a vehicle for joining adoration to action.

Conclusion

As churches find common ground today for discussing worship and shaping liturgies according to simple forms that represent the historic wisdom of the church, they are helping to bring an end to warring over idioms of worship and music. Our divisions are old ones and have fostered amazing diversity in the church. As noted above, the World Council of Churches has a membership of over 340 denominations or church bodies, which does not include the Roman Catholic Church, the world's largest denomination. It is not hard to distinguish the things that divide Christians into these groupings. Yet neither is it difficult to demonstrate that there is much that unites us. All Christians assemble for worship. When we do so, we attend to God's Word and administer the sacraments in some orderly manner. From our assemblies we are sent forth to be the church in mission. We share these common practices. What I am urging is that a common apprehension of this four-part pattern gives us a shared platform from which to understand our diverse worship practices and liturgical theologies. It also provides us a common scaffold from which to assemble services of worship that are historically informed and locally balanced. To attend to these matters of common practice is to admit that there is wisdom available to us regarding worship, wisdom that can nudge us past our human impulses toward sectarian division and internecine conflict.

In this chapter I have been employing a water metaphor, speaking of streams of practice that are coming together in confluence or convergence. In the next chapter, as I consider the role of the arts in this coming together of thought and practice, a musical metaphor—the harmonization of diverse ways of thinking about and crafting liturgies—will stand in for the image of a current.

Through the examination of the wisdom behind the ordo in this chapter, we have encountered several theological and liturgical principles:

1. The Christian church is united in many ways, through the sacraments and reliance on God's Word, through the use of common prayers and creeds, through a common mission in the world, and through common means of praising God.
2. The fourfold pattern of worship is a biblical and historically tested means of ordering Christian liturgy.
3. Use of more than a single Scripture reading in worship expands our hearing of God's voice and more strongly connects us to the faith of our elders and those who worship with us on the Lord's Day around the globe.
4. The frequent celebration and remembrance of the sacraments in public worship represents biblical and historical wisdom.
5. Form and freedom are not contradictory qualities in worship; the first enables the second.

4

Worship and the Arts

There are three collaborating attributes [in worship]: the Word, beauty, and "a place set apart," where the Word and beauty can come together to enhance our focus on God. A place set apart could be an elaborate structure obviously intended for worship—a cathedral, a neighborhood church, a mosque, or a temple. Or it could be an informal setting—at home, or around a campfire. The Word and beauty likewise can be either elaborately or simply expressed. But each in its own way must be eloquent. Their combined effect can then evoke thought and emotion, thereby animating the Word and transforming the place set apart into a place of worship. . . . The worship experience ultimately depends on divine gifts. The Word itself is a gift, as is the ability of the speaker. And so is the beauty, whether created by nature (as in the sunset over the beach), or through the God-given talents of architects, speakers, and artists—using talents they have developed to interpret their faith.[1]

Bill and Dee Brehm

In the previous chapters I have been discussing the missional nature of worship and the ways in which there is a growing sense of liturgical convergence at work in many parts of the church today. In this chapter, I will look at the ways this convergence is occurring through the use of the arts in worship

1. Schmit, "The Word, Beauty, and a Place Set Apart," 18.

and the connection between the art of worship and mission. In the process, I will diversify the image of this coming together of thought and practice by using a metaphor more attuned to the material of this chapter. The idea of confluence can also be expressed as harmonization. Convergence has its value, especially because it is the term used by those who are mapping the terrain of the merging streams of worship forms and interests. But harmony supplies another value. Musical harmony occurs when separate musical elements come together to create a blend of sound that is both derivative and new. Each harmonic part retains its own shape and value. The new sound derives from the juxtaposition of the separate musical lines. I have been saying both that thoughts and attitudes about worship are coming together and that they need to be seen in light of particular local issues of context: commonality juxtaposed with particularity. The image of harmony captures the sense that as things flow together, they do not meld into one (as tributaries into rivers do) to become univocal (or unison), each losing its distinctiveness; rather, the image of harmony suggests that something discrete is maintained by each voice that converges. This is nearer to the center of the book's project, which celebrates diversity while apprehending what is held in common between traditions. What is hoped for is a church that worships harmoniously. While distinctive practices and theologies provide counterpoint for one another, we can nonetheless celebrate our unity in faith that is centered in a belief that "there is one body and one Spirit, just as you were called to the one hope of your calling, one Lord, one faith, one baptism, one God and Father of all, who is above all and through all and in all" (Eph. 4:4–6). In establishing such harmony, the arts play an important role.

The Place of the Arts in Worship

The use of art for devotional purposes has been with us from the beginning of our faith. The first chapter of the Bible is itself an elaborate poem on creation, likely used in worship. Throughout the Old Testament, there are references to songs offered in praise (as in Moses's song of praise at the deliverance of the Israelites from the Egyptian army at the Red Sea in Exod. 15), as well as to dancing (as Miriam did in the same episode) and to drawings and carvings (such as the gold cherubim on the ark of the covenant prescribed in Exod. 25:18–20 and the numerous art pieces in Solomon's temple that are described in 1 Kings 6). And certainly there is poetry, as can be found throughout Scripture and especially in the psalms. The temple of Solomon itself was an artistic masterpiece, one of the greatest architectural wonders of its time. The New Testament makes less reference to art in relation to worship, but it does not prohibit the use of art in worship. The chief art that is mentioned, though not frequently, is music. Calvin Stapert reminds us that "the New Testament begins and ends with outbursts of song"[2]; Luke records Mary's song, the Magnificat, and other songs relating to the birth of Jesus (chaps. 1 and 2), and John records the song to the Lamb in Revelation 5:8–13.

The references to the use of music and other worship arts in Scripture are sure indications that the incorporation of art in worship is a part of God's mission. Through the arts of architecture, sculpture, and furnishings, the Spirit engaged the gathered people of God in tabernacle, temple, synagogue, and home. Through the arts of poetry and song, the praise, prayers, and cares of God's people were borne heavenward. Through the arts of prose, poetry, and story, the Word of God was proclaimed as prophecy, parable, and good news. The New Testament stories of baptisms and celebrations of the Eucharist are part of the narrative structure of the gospel, and the Eucharistic meal could hardly occur without benefit of the folk art of pottery. And, using the arts of poetry and song (as in the Aaronic blessing, Num. 6:24–26, and Simeon's Song, Luke 2:28–32), God's people were blessed and sent out to serve God.

Art continues to be crucial to worship. Through it, humanity finds expression for things that cannot be said in other ways. As philosopher Susanne Langer put it, "art is the creation of forms symbolic of human feeling."[3] Because faith resides at the soul-deep level of human experience, we need art to give expression to those feelings that are too deep to express with ordinary language (see sidebar 4.1).

The arts thrived in Christian worship throughout the New Testament and early church periods and continued through the Middle Ages and the Renaissance to deepen the church's capacity to express prayer, praise, lament, and the proclamation of God's Word. During the Byzantine era, the arts were used resplendently in the Orthodox Church. The Orthodox developed the use of icons as a means to meditate into deeper realms. And they created splendid architecture with soaring ceilings and elaborate decorations to draw worshipers heavenward. When Russian emissaries of Prince Vladimir of Kiev returned from a visit to the Hagia Sophia in Constantinople in 988, they remarked, "We did not know whether we were in heaven or on earth. Such splendor and beauty are not found anywhere on earth: it is impossible to describe. We only know that God was there among the people."[4] In the West, the world's museums, cathedrals, and concert halls continue to be filled today with Christian art created for worship in previous centuries: statuary and carvings, paintings and tapestries, architectural features, stained glass windows, music of nearly every conceivable form, and so forth. So united have the arts been with worship that the history of the liturgy is parallel to and often coincident with the history of Western art and music.

2. Stapert, *A New Song for an Old World*, 14.
3. Langer, *Feeling and Form*, 40.
4. Quoted in Nes, *The Mystical Language of Icons*, 12.

Sidebar 4.1: Art and the Wellspring of Worship

God's people assemble for worship to enter into a communion and a communication [with God and with one another]. . . . By what measure can we determine whether this communication and encounter is effective? It would be impossible to invent an empirical means by which to measure the quality of such a highly subjective experience. But, we do know that when God speaks to us it is about matters of the soul. Worship is not concerned merely with our minds and moods. It is not about education or entertainment. We do not go to worship to learn math or science or how to spell Ecclesiastes. And we do not worship in order to be made to laugh or cry or be moved by music. God's people worship because we long for an encounter with the God of the universe. We seek a deep sense of meaning and belonging and to enter into a dialogue with the One who knows us better than we know ourselves. The communion of worship is no shallow stream, but a deep river into which our souls dive to find comfort and contentment. This cannot be measured, but it can be known and felt. . . .

Worship, when it is effective . . . , is about matters that are soul-deep. The psalmist knew this, who said, "As a deer longs for flowing streams, so my soul longs for you, O God. My soul thirsts for God, for the living God. . . . Deep calls to deep at the thunder of your waterfalls; all your waves and your billows have gone over me" (Ps. 42:1, 2, and 7). Worship is a wellspring from which we draw and dispense living water. . . .

Why do we need art in worship? Because faith resides on that soul-deep level of human experience. To reach that depth in human or divine communication, or to unleash the secrets of the heart in prayer, we need symbols that get us to that level. Mere words will not suffice. . . . In worship, we need art that has a purpose. Without it, we are mute. When we attend worship that does not work, we do not realize the failure empirically. It comes to us as an unkept promise. Something wells up that finds no expression: a volcano that cannot erupt; a stroke victim who has much to say but cannot find speech. That kind of worship is frustrating on the deepest level. What it needs is the art. Therein lies our voice, our fluency, our exclamation, our eruption of praise.

Clayton J. Schmit, "Art for Faith's Sake," in Worship at the Next Level, *ed. Tim A. Dearborn and Scott Coil (Grand Rapids: Baker Books, 2004), 159–61.*

Art continued to be crucial to worship even as the Reformation began. Luther was a lover of art and music and declared that he "would like to see all the arts, especially music, used in the service of Him who gave and made them."[5] But other Reformers were suspicious of art's usefulness for worship. Whereas Luther held that anything not expressly prohibited by Scripture was open for use in worship,

5. Martin Luther, "Preface to the Wittenberg Hymnal, 1524," in *Luther's Works: Liturgy and Hymns*, trans. Leupold, Lehmann, and Zeller Strodach, 53:316.

Calvin maintained the opposite perspective: only things expressly permitted by Scripture for worship should be used in prayer and praise. Accordingly, Calvin and those who followed in his wake placed restrictions on the use of the arts in worship, allowing principally for the singing of the Psalter. Otherwise, Reformed churches were kept stark and simple. Ulrich Zwingli held similar views. He maintained that believers should place nothing between themselves and God. When believers went to pray before the images filling the churches of his day, he felt they were betraying a trust in those images over their trust in God.[6]

The churches that followed the Reformed (Calvinist and Zwinglian) theological line continued their mistrust of art in worship. The Puritans, for example, sought a plain style in preaching and worship. The architecture of their simple meeting houses excluded anything that "would distract from the plain preaching of Scripture."[7] The result of this Reformed thinking was that "unlike the early periods of Christian history, art was seen as having little or no particular theological content; it certainly had no relationship to the worshiping life of the church."[8] Such thinking led Jonathan Edwards to conclude that the use of imagination and creativity are the playgrounds of the devil: "The imagination or fancy seems to be that wherein are formed all those delusions of Satan, which those are carried away with who are under the influence of false religion and counterfeit graces and affections. Here is the devil's grand lurking place, the very nest of foul and delusive spirits."[9]

This mistrust of art as a fitting vehicle for prayer, praise, and proclamation continued to the present century in many churches. While some never really lost their love of artistic expression (e.g., Bach followed Luther, helping to establish a strong Lutheran connection between worship and the arts), others began to turn away from even the most basic symbols in an attempt to draw new people to the faith.[10] This was the approach adopted by the church growth movement of the past several decades.[11] It fostered the development of worship spaces that looked more like auditoriums, warehouses, and corporate office buildings on the assumption that seekers would be more comfortable in spaces that did not palpably smack of religion. This can be seen when visiting megachurches such as Willow Creek Community Church near Chicago, whose

6. Dyrness, *Visual Faith*, 58.

7. Ibid.

8. Ibid., 59.

9. Edwards, *Religious Affections*, 213–14, quoted in ibid.

10. It should be noted that some Protestant writers on worship tend to focus on the Reformed side of the aesthetic equation, thereby overlooking the fact that certain Protestant traditions, especially Lutherans, Anglicans, and Episcopalians, have historically embraced the use of the arts in worship. As an example, Robert Webber has lamented that until the twentieth century "the Protestant church had not exercised its calling in the arts and now had to recover from four hundred years of neglect" (*Worship Old and New*, 211).

11. See Plantinga and Rozeboom, *Discerning the Spirits*, esp. chap. 2, "Costa Mesa, South Barrington, and Rome: The Rise of Contemporary Worship."

aesthetic sensitivities bear the fingerprints of Reformed teaching[12] and whose worship is modeled after that of the frontier camp and revival meetings.[13]

The simplified worship of seeker services seems to have worked for those "who thought the church had gotten stuck in 1950."[14] It was especially fitting, it seems, for those disgruntled baby boomers who were dragged to church as children by their parents but later sought a connection to the faith that was more culturally accommodating.

Today, however, this trend away from the use of art and symbol in the worship of churches influenced by revivalist practices and Reformed theology is reversing. A sign of this reversal is that the Willow Creek Association (an offshoot ministry of the Willow Creek church) is a leading advocate for the use of arts in worship. It offers an annual conference that provides worship leadership workshops on instrumental and vocal music, drama, technical arts, dance, and creative arts leadership. Another sign of the renewed embrace of the arts in worship is that Calvin College in Grand Rapids, Michigan, has established the Calvin Institute for Christian Worship. This multifaceted institute is providing leadership and training in worship for a multidenominational constituency. Its annual January symposium regularly draws 1,500 to 1,800 participants to the upper Midwest in the coldest part of the year. Through this conference and others provided throughout the year, the Calvin Institute offers classical music concerts, workshops, and lectures in such areas as the use of the psalms in worship, beauty and theology, the use of drama in worship, liturgical art, film and theology, leading congregational song from the organ and with a band, the poetic use of language in preaching and prayer, choral music, and so forth. In addition, the institute provides grants to congregations throughout America for the local renewal of worship, often through the use of the arts. What seems at the same time remarkable and refreshing is that both Willow Creek and the Calvin Institute follow the teaching of the Reformed theologians who first drove a Protestant wedge between art and worship.[15]

12. The founding pastor of Willow Creek Community Church was trained at Trinity Evangelical Divinity School, operated by the Evangelical Free Church of America, a denomination with roots in the Reformed tradition. The church has built a worship auditorium (finished in 2005) that has been described as the largest single-purpose theater in America. It seats 7,200 people on the main floor and in its stadium-style stacked balconies.

13. Senn identifies the frontier roots of seeker services in his chapter "Liturgical Revision and Renewal," in *Christian Liturgy*: "In spite of the use of high-tech media, the typical 'seeker service' is really a form of the old frontier or revival pattern of worship with a gathering including songs, testimonies, concerns, and prayers, followed by the reading of Scripture and preaching, and a response to the word" (688).

14. Crouch, "A Humbling Experience," in Dearborn and Coil, *Worship at the Next Level*, 132.

15. Another strong example of the Reformed turn to an appreciation of the arts in worship is the establishment of the Brehm Center for Worship, Theology, and the Arts at Fuller Theological Seminary in Pasadena, CA. The seminary has roots in Calvinist theology (Charles E. Fuller was ordained as a ruling elder of a Presbyterian congregation in 1916), and the leadership

Perhaps we should not be so surprised at the Calvinist turn toward the arts today, for embedded in Calvin's own thinking is at least a seed for a Reformed theology of the arts:

> We know the most perfect way of seeking God, and the most suitable order, is not for us to attempt with bold curiosity to penetrate to the investigation of God's essence, which we ought more to adore than meticulously to search out, but for us to contemplate God in his works whereby he renders himself near and familiar to us, and in some manner communicates himself. The apostle was referring to this when he said that we need not seek God far away, seeing that he dwells by his very present power in each of us. For this reason, David, having first confessed God's unspeakable greatness, afterward proceeds to mention God's works and professes that he will declare God's greatness. It is also fitting, therefore, for us to pursue this particular search for God, which may so hold our mental powers suspended in wonderment as at the same time to stir us deeply. And as Augustine teaches elsewhere, because, disheartened by God's greatness, we cannot grasp God, we ought to gaze upon God's works, that we may be restored by his goodness.[16]

While God certainly communicates to us today in many ways, our clearest communication of God and God's works comes through Scripture. There, God is revealed in the numerous artistic ways we have been discussing. David, in his attempt to articulate God's unspeakable greatness, used a nondiscursive manner of speech known as poetry. Poetry means more than it says. It is multivalent and in its symbolic openness points us toward the awe-invoking greatness of God that cannot be fully known or expressed. The poetry of David's psalms give us one means by which to apprehend God's greatness. Scripture tells us of numerous others, namely, the arts used in worship and in fulfilling God's mission. Calvin has it exactly right: "our mental powers are suspended in wonderment" when we attempt to search God out. At the same time, we are "stirred deeply."

As we have seen, the arts enter worship precisely for these reasons. Only by nondiscursive means are we able to express our adoration; only through art are we capable of singing or saying or praying about the things that stir us deeply. If we are to be restored by gazing on God's works, how else can we see them unless we are provided with images that we *can* perceive. God's greatness is too vast to know or behold. We need the windows of art and the perspectives of artists to provide us a glimpse of God and a means by which to respond to God's goodness. The arts are like Moses's veil (Exod.

---

of the Brehm Center is largely from churches in the Reformed tradition. The center is home for institutes in film and theology, visual art and architecture, preaching, dramatic arts, the emerging church, and music. It also has interests and activities in the areas of literature, dance, ethnomusicology, and sculpture.

16. Calvin, *Institutes of the Christian Religion*, 1.5.9.

34:33–35). They shield us from the full glory of God that shined so brightly that it seared Moses's face with its brilliance. Yet they give us a look—one that our eyes can manage. Or, to put it another way, the creative works of the creatures-made-in-God's-image are extensions of God's own works, rendered on a scale that is accessible. When we look at art, we see what donkeys and dogs cannot, for they cannot behold the glory of human creativity, just as we cannot attain to God's full glory. Thus, we might say or sing, "In our *arts*, Lord, be glorified today." And when we return our praise, we use art again because when we are stirred deeply nothing else will contain the unspeakable response.

From this current theological perspective on the arts, embraced by Catholics, Orthodox believers, and most Protestants,[17] John Calvin is on the right track here. If Calvin had not been famously suspicious about the use of the arts in worship, we would not be surprised if this passage in the *Institutes* would have concluded this way: "because, disheartened by God's greatness, we cannot grasp God, we ought to gaze upon God's works, that we may be restored by his goodness. *For this reason, we employ the arts in worship in order to have a means by which to apprehend something of God's greatness.*" Calvin, of course, could not have said this. But the many Reformed churches that are embracing the arts today can at least look to their forebear for a kernel of a theology of art today.[18]

What are the causes for this renewed interest in the use of art in worship? It is occurring for at least two reasons. The first is the result of over a hundred years of liturgical renewal. The second is the postmodern embrace of symbol and art.

The Liturgical Renewal Movement and the Arts

Patrick Keifert traces the origins of liturgical renewal to the early nineteenth century. This ecumenical movement began with church leaders in Europe who "struggled to restore the vibrance of Christian liturgy and its central place in the life of the church."[19] It involved the Oxford and Cambridge movements in England as well as efforts by Roman Catholic and Lutheran theologians in Germany and Denmark. It also had an influence on the German Lutheran churches in North America.[20] A second wave of liturgical renewal began

17. Robert Wuthnow has done a survey on the place of the arts in American ecumenical Christianity and has concluded that worship is being revitalized specifically through attention to the place of art in worship (*All in Sync*, see esp. chap. 5, "The Joy of Worship," 134–82).

18. For a careful look at Calvin's theology vis-à-vis the arts, see Dyrness, *Reformed Theology and Visual Culture*, esp. chap. 4.

19. Keifert, *Welcoming the Stranger*, 39.

20. Ibid., 39, 43–50.

early in the twentieth century with the Benedictine monk Lambert Beaudin, "the first of many Benedictines who later joined pastors and academics of other traditions."[21] The focus of the second wave of renewal efforts can be summarized as an attempt to refocus Christian worship based on these core principles: the biblical concept of the church as the people of God, a reverence for the worship practices of earlier periods, an emphasis on baptism as the initiation into faith, a stress on the corporate nature of public worship (liturgy is the work of the people), the involvement of laity in worship leadership, an emphasis on biblical preaching, a renewed emphasis on celebration of the Eucharist, and an appreciation for ritual, gesture, symbol, and art in worship. A key sign of the success of this movement came about with the worship reforms issued by the Roman Catholic Church in the Second Vatican Council, as articulated in the document *Constitution on the Sacred Liturgy* (1963).

Among the reforms indicated in the *Constitution* (which includes the introduction of the vernacular Mass) was a renewed emphasis on the place of the arts in faith and worship. The document states,

> Very rightly the fine arts are considered to rank among the noblest activities of man's genius, and this applies especially to religious art and to its highest achievement, which is sacred art. These arts, by their very nature, are oriented toward the infinite beauty of God which they attempt in some way to portray by the work of human hands; they achieve their purpose of redounding to God's praise and glory in proportion as they are directed the more exclusively to the single aim of turning men's minds devoutly toward God.[22]

The interest in sacred art has always been high in the Catholic Church, but the relationship between the church and artists has often been strained. This was a relationship that Pope Paul VI sought to strengthen through the Vatican II reforms.[23]

As the liturgical renewal movement restored the Catholic Church's interests in the arts and artists, its influence even more strongly rejuvenated the use of the arts in Protestant churches, especially those, as noted above, that have historically denied the value of art for liturgical expression.

21. Ibid., 39–40.

22. *Constitution on the Sacred Liturgy: Sacrosanctum Concilium* (1963), chap. 7, sec. 122, http://www.vatican.va/archive/hist_councils/ii_vatican_council/documents/vat-ii_const_19631204_sacrosanctum-concilium_en.html.

23. The straining of this relationship was admitted by Pope Paul VI in his "Allocution to Italian Artists in Sistine Chapel at the Artists' Mass, May 7, 1964," *The Pope Speaks*, 9:390–95, quoted in Kapikian, *Art in Service of the Sacred*, 20. While he blamed the artists in part ("you have gone far afield to drink at other fountains seeking to express other things"), he admitted the part that the Catholic Church played in imposing "as a first canon that of conventional imitation—on you who are creators, vivacious people, alive with new ideas and innovations."

Sidebar 4.2: The Biblical Nature of Pentecostal Dance

Many people at Azusa Street responded to God's presence in much the same way that David did when he brought the ark of the covenant back to Jerusalem (2 Sam. 6:12–23; 1 Chron. 15:25–29). David led Israel's worship with sacrifices, accompanied by an orchestra of lyres, harps, bronze cymbals, tambourines, trumpets, and castanets. He did not respond to the presence of God in a silent, "reverent," meditative, awe-filled, intellectual mode such as could be found at Los Angeles's First Methodist, or First Presbyterian, or First Congregational Church. David's worship of his Lord was not simply or even primarily cerebral. The expression of worship, the response to the Lord's presence that came from David as he "danced before the Lord with all his might," rose from his very soul. It was primal! It was passionate! It was exuberant! It was filled with emotion and feeling! It touched his whole body, from head to toe. It was not limited only to his mind. Indeed, it was quite like the worship that many African American slaves enjoyed when left to themselves, with dance and shout, rhythm and song, possession and falling.*

Cecil M. Robeck Jr., The Azusa Street Mission and Revival: The Birth of the Global Pentecostal Movement *(Nashville: Nelson, 2006), 132–33.*

* Friends Bob Kaul and Moses Pulei have reminded me that in Swahili the term for "white man" literally means "those who stand still while singing."

Postmodern Interest in Symbol, Art, and Ritual

A second reason for the renewed use of the arts in worship is what I take to be a gift to the church from the postmodern ethos prevalent today. While it remains impossible to categorically state what postmodernism is,[24] one aspect of its culture is clear: the arts and artists are trusted as purveyors of truth, even as others are not. "Our age has more regard for the artist than the orator," reports Eddie Gibbs.[25] This is no surprise in a culture that distrusts dehumanizing institutions and their spokespersons (churches and their preachers are often included here). Words, which are losing their meaning through overuse and misuse, are being replaced by silence and by nondiscursive means of expression. It's not that there is necessarily more art today than in the modern period. It is rather that, because speakers using words are less trusted, art

24. There are many signs of the difficulty in identifying what postmodernism is. One tongue-in-cheek definition, which comes as close as any to capturing the mercurial essence of the philosophy, comes from the writers of the cartoon program *The Simpsons*. *Po-mo* is defined for Homer by Moe the bartender as "You know, weird, for the sake of being weird." ("Homer the Moe," *The Simpsons*, written by Dana Gould, directed by Jen Kamerman (Gracie Films in association with 20th Century Fox Television, 2001).
25. Gibbs, *Church Next*, 26.

assumes greater responsibility for speaking to the heart of matters. This is, as noted above, what art is particularly able to do. It gives expression to those ineffable qualities of human existence that are difficult to capture through the use of discursive symbols. Unlike words, which are symbols with assigned and discrete meanings, the symbols of art allow for multivalence. They mean many things, depending on who perceives them or when they are being perceived.

Artistic symbols may not provide particular meanings that can be agreed on by all percipients, but they provide multiple meanings that, though perhaps different from one person to another, are not wrong. What Michelangelo's *David* means to one observer will be different from what it means to another, yet neither meaning has to predominate since both are valid. Artistic symbols are roomy. They are also connective: they create resonance between the artist and those that participate in the art, whether as performers or as observers. Art allows for mystery to take shape or form or sound, given through particular symbolic articulation, yet does not force it to be strictly defined. Art allows mystery to speak, yet always to remain mysterious.

The arts are being welcomed in worship with renewed vigor. Some churches familiar with the power of art for liturgical expression are embracing artists in stronger relationships. Some are admitting artistic expression in worship for the first time. Emerging churches are employing the diversity of post-modern art to speak of the juxtapositions of life and faith in a disjointed existence.[26] Some emerging church leaders even see their worship planning entirely in artistic terms, whereby they serve as "a framer, . . . a curator of worship."[27] The result of this is that the use of art in worship is part of the liturgical harmonization taking shape today. Churches once suspicious of art are now embracing it and moving more toward a sense of liturgical and sacramental awareness.

The synchronization apparent in this movement can be expressed by logical extension: those who love art are comfortable in the world of symbol; those at home with symbol are open to mystery; those open to mystery in worship are dancing on the edge of sacrament where God meets God's people. To put the conclusion another way, there is a liturgical resonance between Christians who meditate on Orthodox icons, those who kneel before a Christ-laden crucifix, those who hear proclamation in Bach's St. Matthew Passion, those who pray through Taizé chants, those who embody charismatic worship with dance, those who raise hands in praise while singing, those who are drawn to deep communication by the poetry of prayer, and those who baptize and commune in house churches.

26. Dan Kimball reports that in emerging worship gatherings, "we now see art being brought into worship, the use of visuals, the practice of ancient disciplines, the design of the gathering being more participatory than passive-spectator" (*Emerging Worship*, 5).

27. Riddell, Pierson, and Kirkpatrick, "New Approaches to Worship," in Dearborn and Coil, *Worship at the Next Level*, 138.

Art in Service of Worship

Art may serve many purposes. Up until the modern period, Western art usually served public institutions. Art proclaimed biblical stories to illiterate believers, recounted historic battles (usually emphasizing nationalistic causes), captured likenesses of social or cultural heroes, and so forth. For a while, artists rebelled and created art for its own sake.[28] Today, art is still made for many purposes: marketing, entertainment, self-expression, illustration, community beautification, career establishment, and more. Even Christian artists sometimes create work that is not intended to be used for worship or devotional purposes. But many Christian artists do feel called to create art for use in worship. For them, art is not only in "service of the sacred,"[29] in the general sense of exercising a God-given talent, but is also specifically in service of those who gather for worship.[30] The art of worship gives expression to those things about the life of faith that are too deep or complex for people to put into words (Rom. 8:26). It draws people together in the shared experience of song, poetry, and movement. It generates layers of connectivity as worshipers are given access to the expressions of faith communities in other places and from other times. Art plays the crucial role of giving embodied response to people's encounter with God in worship.

Because such art serves worship and worshipers, there are aesthetic values that should be considered by people who use art in crafting liturgies. Here are twelve considerations for worship leaders and planners to keep in mind regarding the nature of art in relation to worship.

1. *The rituals of worship are art.* Rituals take many shapes. Some are simple actions performed routinely by individuals (e.g., one's morning ritual for grooming) or family patterns enacted regularly to give shape to life and a sense of belonging to family members (e.g., bedtime or mealtime prayer rituals). Public rituals take on increased symbolic function. They do what art does: give expression to human experience through the use of forms and symbols. This is true whether the ritual is singing "Take Me Out to the Ballgame" during the seventh inning stretch at a baseball game or reciting the Pledge of Allegiance before a public meeting. This is certainly true of the rituals of worship.

Rituals function as art in worship. They employ forms of action and expression that provide means by which to articulate the experience of faith. Thus, we have gathering rites that employ song, prayer, and other forms in the task of establishing worshiping individuals as a worshiping community. And we have sending rites that move worshipers from adoration into the worship

28. See Schmit, "Art for Faith's Sake," in Dearborn and Coil, *Worship at the Next Level*, 156–62.

29. This phrase, coined by Catherine Kapikian, is used as the title of her book on the use of art in worship: *Art in Service of the Sacred*.

30. Schmit, "Art for Faith's Sake," in Dearborn and Coil, *Worship at the Next Level*, 161.

of action. In between, we have rites for proclamation and sacraments that center and unite us as people of faith. These ritual movements give us the opportunity to be in God's presence and to communicate with God in diverse ways. We speak and listen, we sing and observe, we eat and drink, we sit and stand and move.

The rituals of worship are forms of art that require the participation of all people. They do not exist if they are indicated in a service bulletin or on a projection screen but fail to enlist people in their activities. There is no gathering if no one comes. There is no baptism if no one is bathed. There is no communion if the table is set and no one is fed. Our participation in these rituals is crucial to their completion. The vitality of worship depends on full involvement in its rituals. When people give themselves wholly to them, worship is alive. Accordingly, we as worshipers should be encouraged to abandon ourselves so that with mind and voice and body we can use the symbols of ritual to express our faith and our response to God's initiatives. (More will be said of the communicative power of ritual in chap. 5.) Here are two points of common interest that we can teach one another. Charismatic and Pentecostal worshipers can grow in appreciation of the power of ritual forms to speak and give shape to the articulation of things that are too deep for words. Spirit-borne sighs and angelic exclamations can be creative expressions released by ritual movements. More traditional worshipers can learn to express themselves by using rituals creatively (as do charismatic and Pentecostal worshipers), being open to the moving of the Spirit within them and to holistic ways of praying and praising that use heart, soul, mind, and body.

2. *Worship is an art.* Certainly worship is made up of many art forms: ritual, for one, but also music, poetry, drama, literature, visual art, and so forth. But worship is also an art form in itself. It can be compared to opera, a grand form of art that is also made up of many other art forms. The opera analogy should not be taken too far, lest it hint that worship must also be grand, formal, and spectacular. Some liturgies do have such qualities and are sometimes seen as show pieces that do not engage people with heart, mind, and body. Still, worship is an art because, like its constituent rituals, it does what art does. It consists of forms that provide conveyance for deeply held things. We gather for worship so that through its various forms we can articulate the adoration that wells within us. Through worship, we say what is otherwise difficult to communicate as we use the accumulated wisdom of the church that has given us forms new and old: hymns and songs, texts and prayers, rituals and movements that give voice and shape to our praise.

Because worship is an art, and because all who are assembled need to participate in order for worship to reach its full vitality, we need to remember that there are no observers in worship. The typical way of describing this idea is to place God as the only audience in worship. All others are on stage, performing their roles, even if from the pew. For example, Robert Webber, following a famous image from Søren Kierkegaard, has said, "Worship is a drama played out before God by all the people. The worship leaders are the prompters, the people are the players, and God is in the audience."[31] This image brings us halfway to a complete understanding of the work done in worship. What is missing are the crucial and central roles that God plays in worship. The Holy Spirit calls the church and gathers it for adoration. God speaks through the Word read and proclaimed, making Christ present. God moves in baptism and the Eucharist, and the Spirit sends us forth in action. Clearly, God is not an idle auditor in worship but its chief agent. "God has a share in the activity of worship. Which share? The lion's share."[32] A better image than the theater, in which performers are playing to some audience, is a music session in which all attendees are performers. The musicians do not gather to perform for an audience but assemble to "jam" with one another. God, of course, is like the composer in this image, present and active, giving life and direction to the playing. Whoever shows up is expected to be occupied in the music making, even if they need to sit idle for a while until they learn a part and how to contribute. Worship is like this. God institutes and guides the event, calling, gathering, centering, and sending. People contribute by assembling, hearing and responding, partaking, and going forth in mission. Everyone has a part, from the newest convert to the most mature believer, from the littlest child to the eldest saint. Each has a unique gift to bring to the ensemble, a voice, a body, a perspective, an insight. Each plays along as he or she is able. Leaders invite participation and plan for veterans as well as newcomers to find a part.

Because worship is an art, a final issue must be made clear. Performance is not to be avoided but embraced. Certainly not performance in the sense of one person performing for the mere entertainment of another. Rather, performance in the sense that bringing the artistic forms of worship to life requires

- knowledge: of texts, music, movement, and the performance space
- development of proper habits: for reading, oration, crafting language, vocal production, gesture, and even for singing from the pew
- rehearsal: especially for the few who lead at any given service, but also for many who need to learn texts and songs in order to participate
- abandonment: the capacity to give heart, mind, soul, and body to the moment of performing together

There is another aspect of performance that is necessary to note: performance does not occur only as worshipers play their individual parts during the hours of adoration. It also takes place as believers go forth to enact their roles of

31. Webber, *Worship Old and New*, 213.
32. Schmit, *Too Deep for Words*, 32.

mission when they are sent forth in action. This, too, is a kind of performance. "Performance can refer to the manner in which the whole community embodies the biblical text," says Richard Lischer. "The community's interpretation of specific passages dealing with prayer, mission, or hospitality will not be written down but enacted in its daily existence." He reminds us that "Bonhoeffer has been dubbed a performer of Scripture not because of any one sermon he preached but by the manner in which he lived and died."[33] Performing the Word in daily life is the living liturgy of discipleship. This work of God's people is their ongoing performance of the Christian life. If all of life is worship, then all of life is gospel performance, whether in the arena of adoration or in the sphere of action.

3. *The arts enrich adoration.* Utilizing the artistic aspects of worship and using them richly creates the opportunity for deep engagement by worshipers. Not all will respond to every form of art used in worship, and clearly not all will respond in the same way. Yet a rich use of arts does the opposite of what Marva Dawn has called "dumbing down" worship.[34] British theologians Carolyn Headley and Mark Earey suggest that a generous view of liturgy has the effect of "riching up" worship by "displaying all the riches of the Christian gospel." This is done even with worship visitors in mind,

> not in the expectation that all visitors will immediately understand or engage with every bit of it, but in the hope that they will apprehend something of the enormity of what is happening. No one ever rehearses a football chant, and no one suggests omitting the singing of "Happy Birthday to You" when young children are present, in case they will not know what to do. In these contexts, as in so many others in life, understanding does not precede participation; we only understand by beginning to take part. This is the theory behind enriching the liturgy rather than slimming it down.[35]

Headley and Earey also remind us that those who are decidedly postmodern in outlook, especially young people today, are highly interested in ritual and seek greater access into mystery through it. Consequently,

> [they] respond better to worship that leads them to experience and know something of the otherness of God. In our postmodern world we cannot assume that people do not want a taste of the mystery and majesty of God that more liturgical forms of worship can express, as well as the sense of his accessibility and intimacy that we value as part of the gospel. So worship must be accessible, but not ordinary. . . . A simplistic response of stripping it of all traditional

33. Lischer, *The End of Words*, 81.

34. See Dawn, *Reaching Out without Dumbing Down.*

35. Headley and Earey are referring to the baptismal liturgy of the Anglican service of Common Worship here, one rich with ritual and opportunity for use of the arts (*Mission and Liturgical Worship*, 8).

elements may be a counterproductive move that also strips it of its depth and attractiveness to outsiders and church members alike.[36]

4. *Ritual art is incarnational.* Rituals do not live unless they are enacted. Until they are brought to life by living persons, they are merely texts and rubrics, descriptions of things that people might say and do. They come alive when words and actions are embodied by participants. "Whatever we think liturgy is, it is always an embodied practice," observes Michael Aune.[37] For this reason, those engaged in the rituals of worship need to be encouraged in the free use of voice and body to allow worship to engage us fully as human beings. Let us remember that ritual provides the form, but within it we are free to create full-bodied means of participation. When people abandon themselves to the activity at hand, ritual cannot be rote or cold. It captures the vibrancy of lived experience through movement and sound. This does not mean that all worship needs to be loud or boisterous. Some rituals call for quiet, even silence. Some call for dancing and others for kneeling. What we can encourage in our worship leaders and in worshipers alike is the freedom to give the appropriate fully incarnated response to what God is doing among us in worship.

5. *Art serves worship.* Too often, we find the artistic elements of worship employed with the implication that we gather in service of art. If the choir has rehearsed a winning anthem, it seems only fitting that worshipers attend to it with admiration and gratitude, even supplying applause afterward as a sign of our appreciation. Choirs and other musical performers exist in worship, however, to serve the assembly. The same can be said of visual art (such as banners, tapestries, and architectural features), liturgical dance, drama, media technology, even preaching. A key question to ask with regard to the use of any form of expression in worship is this: what does it serve? Anything that is used in service of an artist, a performer (including the preacher), a leader, or a technician is gratuitous. Anything used in service of the gospel or those gathered to hear it will find a suitable home in worship.

6. *Worship art is honest.* Because worship is the genuine encounter of God's people with their Creator, full disclosure is mandatory. If we attempt to meet the God-who-knows-us-better-than-we-know-ourselves with anything but honesty, we are deluding only ourselves. The term for self-delusion is denial. We should seek art in worship and artistic language in preaching and prayer that does not deny the stark reality that faith has to do with weakness, suffering, persecution, and death. These are profound matters and dealing with them requires profound reflection through metaphor and symbol. Some art cannot do this because it is sentimental. It may fail in the artist's imagina-

36. Ibid., 22.
37. Aune, "Ritual Practice," in Schattauer, *Inside Out*, 154. This chapter is especially informative regarding the relationship between ritual theory and the missional characteristics of worship.

Sidebar 4.3: Peter Storey on Faith and Honesty

Peter Storey, former president of the Methodist Church of South Africa and of the South African Council of Churches, was a key leader in that country's struggle against apartheid. His ministry was necessarily honest about evil and about God's love for the poor and oppressed. He has a number of things to say about being truthful:

> I am little interested in the "sweet by and by," and have no time for a God who cannot affect life here and now. I refuse to waste time with a God who cannot trump the evil forces at work in the world today.
>
> People often are persuaded to ask Jesus into their hearts. But, when they do so, Jesus asks, "Can I bring my friends, the poor, the despised, the hungry, the dirty, the powerless?" People often respond, "Well, Jesus, it is really only you we wanted." And Jesus replies, "Love me, love my friends."
>
> We need to be up-front with people about the nature of faith. It can require us to take an uncomfortable stand, to fight for justice, speak out when it may endanger us. It is not fair to proclaim the gospel and draw people into the faith without first telling them what is at stake.

From remarks given in a homiletics class at Fuller Theological Seminary, Pasadena, CA, April 30, 2001.

---

tion or articulation to create deep resonance with the stuff of human life (as always, preaching is to be included here). A sign of sentimental art is that it is nostalgic. It recalls only part of the human experience, usually, the most pleasant or romantic part, and implicitly denies the rest. Honest art evokes the fullness of human experience: its negative aspects, such as pain, fear, uncertainty, doubt, longing, anger, hatred, and resentment, as well as its positive qualities, including joy, peace, hope, and gratitude. Sermons that fail to speak accurately of listeners' circumstances will fail to pertain to them. Such sermons, even if well crafted or performed, will leave listeners asking the question, "What difference does it make?"[38]

Likewise, songs and hymns that express only what is ideal will fail to serve as proper prayer, praise, or lament. Hymns that point only to the sweet by and by do little but give our spirits the equivalent of an endorphin push. And songs that place on our lips the immodest claim of how "I" can praise God naturally or eternally fail in describing how things really are with us. Life is far more complex than these sentiments allow. Worship cannot be about what I can do; it needs to be about what God will do with me and through me. Better by far

---

38. This insightful question came from the lips of one of my preaching students who, in commenting on an otherwise well-developed sermon of a colleague, was concerned that its technical merits did not make up for its failure to address her life.

are songs that hold an honest tension between who we are in all our sin and frailty and who God is in all God's grace and power. The best model for such art is the Psalter. It captures nearly every conceivable human emotion and often juxtaposes the greatest despair with the most hopeful flights of gratitude. In terms of introducing honest art in worship, most churches would do well to make fuller use of the psalms.[39]

7. *Worship artists must be honest.* Certainly, faithful worship leaders will not desire to be dishonest in the execution of their roles. Nevertheless, there are mistakes commonly made that, at their core, are matters of integrity. The most obvious example is the misuse of copyrighted material in worship without receiving permission. A choir director might make a few bootleg copies of a choral anthem if there aren't enough purchased copies to go around. A media technician may borrow images from an online source without regard for their ownership or legal use. A preacher may use portions of another's sermon and palm the work off as original. A movie clip may be shown during worship without permission. If we desire to worship in spirit and truth, as Jesus demands in his conversation with the Samaritan woman by the well ("God is spirit, and those who worship him must worship in spirit and truth," John 4:24), we will do all we can to maintain integrity with regard to artistic use. While we expect worship to be inspired by the Holy Spirit, we know that the Spirit will not participate in a lie.

A more complex example is what happens when those charged with central leadership roles make a mistake but blame others. Here are two egregious instances: I have seen a microphone failure occur during the sermon. The preacher, instead of handling the issue graciously, began to make frustrated gestures to the youth who happened to be staffing the sound board. Finally, he said something about the situation, placing blame on the kids who were quietly serving as well as they could. The problem in this situation is that it was the preacher's responsibility to make sure the electronic amplification of the sermon was working adequately. While such an issue could be the fault of a media technician, in this case the young people running the sound board were doing their best and certainly had no power to insist that the preacher do a suitable sound check before worship began. It is a lie to shirk one's responsibility and imply that the fault lies with another. What is especially disturbing in this case—and this applies whether it is an experienced technician or young trainees—is that those who staff sound boards are people who desire to serve invisibly. When the equipment functions properly, the technicians are unnoticed. They are only apparent when things malfunction. Media technicians, like altar servers and those that toil in the kitchens of our churches,

39. To encourage all churches (traditional as well as "evangelical, free church, low-church, contemporary and/or emerging" churches) in greater appropriation of the psalms in worship, John D. Witvliet has written *The Biblical Psalms in Worship*; see p. xvii.

are humble servants who avoid the spotlight. To single them out for notice in worship because of a leader's mistake is a grave error.

The second instance is like the first. A musical leader regularly switched the sequence of verses and choruses while leading the congregation in praise songs. Meanwhile, the media technicians attempted in vain to keep up with the changes and often had words on the screen that the leader was not singing. They were following the planned sequence while the leader insisted he was "following the moving of the Spirit." In discussing the problem later, the leader argued that his will could not be impeded by sticking to a prepared sequence. From the perspective of the congregation, the leader appeared to be inspired, caught up in the moment of worship. The media technicians, on the other hand, appeared to be clumsy and ineffective as they put up one wrong slide after another. Again, a mistake was made, and by implication, blame for it was heaped on the silent and powerless people behind the scenes.

Art and artistry in worship need to be honest so that worship may be fully inspired. When mistakes are made, they should be briefly, graciously, and honestly acknowledged by the presiding minister, with whom the buck stops. Mistakes are sure to happen because God chooses a few ordinary people to lead others in worship. Mistakes are not a sign that we are failing to worship in spirit or truth, but denying them or blaming others for our own failures is sure to create a barrier between the Spirit's full participation and our worship.

8. *Worship art can be local and transitory*. While we seek art that is honest, it need not all be high art or even durable art. Some helpful things grow out of the soil of the local context, have honest value for a moment, and can be happily consigned to memory. Think, for example, of a trumpet fanfare played as prelude to events on Easter Sunday morning. The first thing heard ringing throughout the sanctuary and nave is the joyous heralding of the resurrection. For a moment, the brilliant sound provides worshipers with a visceral connection to the event they have come to celebrate. Then it is gone, lost in the air, carried forward only in memory. Its purpose is not to be recorded for later visitation of the moment, but to be an eruption of momentary praise, an infusion of sound that lifts every worshiper's voice to new heights.

Or think of the art provided by a congregation's children. What could be more honest than the offerings of our youngest worshipers? Their banners may be simple in conception, even cheap in construction, yet they are the real stuff of praise from those who have yet to be tempted to feign greater sophistication. Perhaps the final resting place for such work is the cardboard box that stores childhood keepsakes like cards drawn for Mother's Day and plaster handprints. Their great value occurs in the moment of presentation. Afterward, they go to the memory box to make way for new art from other children.

Adult worshipers can learn from the children. They too might create worship art that is impermanent or ever-shifting. Sacred artist Catherine Kapikian advocates "the creation of temporary, evolving (an addition each week building incrementally), or changing work for worship" that "offers insightful breakthroughs of meaning."[40]

Even musical compositions can be created for temporary use. Some preachers write new hymn stanzas to accompany their weekly sermon themes. Youth can compose psalm antiphons or short choruses that will provide double value: they will be the earnest expressions of young worshipers given as a gift to a congregation, and the use of them gives honor and place to those who are often overlooked as leaders. Some music may be composed for use within a given congregation and never go any farther. If it fails to be published for use by others, it has not failed in its purpose to be a vehicle of praise in the setting it was created for. Congregations should encourage the musicians and other artists God has placed in their midst—even, or perhaps especially, the budding artists—to exercise their gifts in the process of adoration. The local congregation is the place for people of all ages to experiment with forms, learning what is possible and what is appropriate. Those who make temporary works should take comfort in knowing that Bach wrote more than three hundred cantatas, two-fifths of which are lost. Or they might find solidarity with their preachers who typically spend hours each week creating sermons that have freshness and immediate pertinence but that are usually never heard again.

9. *Folk art is appropriate for worship*. Erik Routley, the renowned British hymnologist of the last century, had strong opinions about what kind of music is appropriate for Christian worship. Much classical music, he argued, is simply too plush for use in worship because it "distracts from the church's true conversation."[41] He argues, instructively, for church music to be *folk music*, music prepared for the people of faith because composers who write hymns and songs for worship are writing for a largely unmusical community. While great composers may desire to write music that is interesting, they should remember to write congregational songs that ordinary people can sing. This amounts to composing a hymn or song tune that is "about 10 per cent original and 90 per cent traditional." Such songs "cannot be composed by people who do not positively like the people who sing them." For the great composer, writing music for congregational use is a matter of humility: "It is not only a question of writing less music than one would otherwise write, nor is it a matter of rebelliously accepting the limitations of the unmusical community. It is a matter of liking the people

40. Kapikian, *Art in Service of the Sacred*, 60.

41. Routley, *Church Music and the Christian Faith*, 90. The stubbornness of Routley's opinions sometimes yields humorous insights, such as when he criticizes the sacred music of the great British composer Arthur Sullivan (1841–1900). Of his *Te Deum*, Routley says it contains material "which for sheer flatulent pretentiousness is even in that age hard to beat. (When this great composer wrote bad music, he wrote it to professional standards.)" Of a Sullivan choral piece, he opines, "It needs no argument; it is one long butter-slide" (92).

who are going to sing the hymns [and songs], and that means 'welcoming the duty' in a truly Gospel sense."[42]

Routley's case for worship music to be "of the people" is equally applicable to other types of art employed in worship. It is in keeping with our last point that worship art can be of local creation and temporary use. This is especially true for the art of preaching, as Leonora Tubbs Tisdale demonstrates in *Preaching as Local Theology and Folk Art*. In this book she argues for preaching that is derived from local theology, created out of the midst of a community of faith and attuned to the needs and values of the local context.[43] Such preaching is folk art that searches "for the expression of local theology through symbols, forms, and movements that are capable of capturing and transforming the imaginations of a particular local community of faith."[44]

Another important quality of folk art is that, like ritual, it is incarnational. Because it comes from the people, it is accessible to everyone and can be embodied (sung, performed, or observed) by God's ordinary people. Like a plant grown in the garden, folk art has a little dust on it. It is not sterile or distant but organic, wholesome, and available.

The argument for the appropriateness of folk art in worship is not meant to suggest that great works of art are *in*appropriate in worship. Rather, it is to acknowledge that they have their place and purpose. As liturgically fitting as Bach's cantatas are for the church year, they do not represent the kind of art that most worshipers today find immediately accessible. Certainly great choral works can be used in worship and produce the effect of enlarging the musical and theological awareness of worshipers exposed to them. The same can be said, as Kapikian does, of visual art that is not immediately accessible to the untrained eye. Such art "communicates through nuance and suggestion, its power to endure arising from its obliqueness. The imagination is awakened in such an encounter of meaning-making possibility. Our capacity to see needs thoughtful reinvigoration, for it is now disoriented by the rampant plethora of trivial, depersonalized, and often degrading images emerging from technological culture."[45] It is not the first purpose of worship to reorient the eyes and ears of people to art and song that are not trivial and degrading. But, this goal will likely be met when we use art in worship that is honest, wholesome, derived from local theology, and capable of awakening worshipers to new insights.

10. *Worship art that derives from other cultures is appropriate in worship.* If the worship of the church is a two-thousand-year-old hymn to which each new generation and culture adds its stanza (as I mention in the introduction), then our use of art from other cultures and eras broadens and enriches our

---

42. Ibid., 90–91.
43. Tisdale, *Preaching as Local Theology and Folk Art*, 31–55.
44. Ibid., 124.
45. Kapikian, *Art in Service of the Sacred*, 41.

understanding of the faith. The universally appealing example is the use of African American spirituals and their offspring, the black gospel songs. Spirituals, ever since they were taken out of the fields and onto the road, have been widely embraced and adored. When the Jubilee Singers of Fisk University first performed the spirituals (beginning in 1871), the songs were met with acclaim by concertgoers and heads of state in America and Europe. Those once held captive in slavery held their audiences captive with the haunting beauty of their singing. The songs were true folk music that grew out of the profound suffering of the slaves. Even today, singing the spirituals in worship summons a deep respect for the circumstances that gave them birth and a resonance with the authentic lament of this oppressed population. The spirituals work in worship because in them (as in the psalms) all people find a voice for their darkest fears and their greatest hopes.

Similarly, there is a folk quality in black gospel songs that draws cultures together. Chorally, they are usually best sung by gospel choirs, for the performance values of black gospel music are different from those of European-based musicality. Still, whether listening to a gospel choir in worship, hearing traditional choirs perform the music, or singing the songs corporately, the innate joy and hope of the music gives vibrancy and voice to the gospel good news that has near universal appeal. Those not personally acquainted with the African American experience are awakened to an awareness of this culture's faith through music that resounds with hope even when born of pain.

Likewise, we can employ music and art from the world church in our local congregations, in what might be called "liturgical plurality."[46] While we seek to maintain the distinctive qualities of our own situations, our worship—not to mention our theology—is enriched when we borrow wisely from others to gain access to wider perspectives on the faith. Borrowing *wisely* is key to our practice, lest we slip into what ethnomusicologist and theologian Michael Hawn calls "meaningless eclecticism." By this he means three things: "liturgical ethno-tourism," singing global songs as congregational recreation; displacing one's own heritage in favor of someone else's; and attempting to synthesize global idioms into one "universal" form of worship music. An informed eclecticism, on the other hand, seeks to juxtapose borrowed and local forms of music alongside one another in a way that "causes them to influence one another." Doing this, Hawn suggests, has several positive values: it makes liturgy a countercultural expression of faith that can "stem cultural captivity that would lead to the idolatry of a single cultural perspective"; it "celebrates the incarnation as a cross-cultural manifestation of God's presence among us"; it makes us aware of Christians who are invisible to us; and it gives us an eschatological taste of the future kingdom of heaven and its vast plurality.[47]

46. Hawn, *Gather into One*, 15–16.
47. Ibid.

11. *Not all worship art can be held to the same standards.* Professional church musicians and hired or commissioned artists can be held to high standards. Their training and experience allow worshipers to trust that they are in capable hands as professionals lead and give shape to worship environments. Folk art, especially that made by the ordinary people of a congregation or faith community, needs to be assessed differently. Because it is highly incarnational, it can be expected that imperfections will occur. Even as amateurs and volunteers practice and do their best, they operate within limitations and should not be overly concerned if things do not go as planned. Aidan Kavanagh gives helpful advice to those who are concerned over making mistakes: "To be consumed with worry over making a liturgical mistake is the greatest mistake of all. Reverence is a virtue, not a neurosis, and God can take care of himself."[48]

It must be added that while folk art holds to different standards than professional art, it is not without standards. We make worship art or perform our roles in worship as well as we can. We strive for excellence so that we get ourselves out of the way in order that the symbols of ritual and art have their own say. We are not perfect and cannot do everything flawlessly.[49] And when we include the artistic participation of budding artists, we naturally adjust our expectations for excellence. A strong adult gospel choir with years of experience will surely sing more beautifully than a hastily assembled Sunday school choir singing for an annual Christmas pageant. Folk art in worship allows for some failure, some cracking, some looseness, some faultiness, not because it has no qualitative benchmark but because it is human.

Graham Hughes has given us a means by which to capture this sense that different standards apply for various forms of art and artistry in worship. He borrows the term *best account* from Charles Taylor, who uses it to make allowances for human finitude and inability to achieve our highest ideals. Hughes stretches the use of the term to apply to the way we perceive signs in worship. We cannot obtain full knowledge of God or indicate things of God in absolute ways. We can hardly even know ourselves absolutely, let alone the world in which we live, so we give a best account so that people can make the best sense they can of God, themselves, their neighbors, and the cosmos.[50] I would like to stretch Taylor's image of best account one step further, hoping it is elastic enough to meet the need.

The theory of best account is useful for us here because it provides a means by which to make appropriate allowance for the levels of art and artistry we employ in worship. While we may desire professional standards in all aspects of ministry, that is unrealistic. The professional musicians, architects, and technicians we hire are human and will present imperfect work; our amateurs

---

48. Kavanagh, *Elements of Rite*, 31.

49. For a description of "the hallmarks of excellence" in worship leadership and a warning that "excellence is not perfectionism," see Schmit, *Too Deep for Words*, 63–79.

50. Hughes, *Worship as Meaning*, 195–96.

and volunteers, and our children and youth, will offer gifts to worship that are even further removed from perfection of form or expression. Because the professionally trained artists are able to do more, we expect them to give their own best account of themselves through their art. From others with less training and greater limitations we also expect the best account of what they have to offer. While what is best from our finest artists is vastly different from that of our amateur and budding artists, we can hold the best account standard to all their work. This allows us to uphold high standards for excellence in worship while giving us room to make allowance for different capacities and levels of spiritual giftedness.

12. *Spiritual gifts are part of God's creativity in worship.* Whether traditionally liturgical or charismatic or somewhere in between, all worshiping communities desire and expect that the Holy Spirit will be present to inspire worship. Measuring the Spirit's presence is an impossible task. Often what is perceived as the moving of the Spirit (as in the music leader anecdote above) is merely an emotion. Having a religious feeling, being moved to tears, or feeling led in a certain way are not guarantees of God's presence or moving among us. Moods are fickle and can be played on.[51] Proof of this is readily available: consider the ways our emotions are regularly manipulated through advertising. The surest sign of God's presence in worship is that God has promised to be with us when we gather.

One of the scriptural promises is that God will provide the church with spiritual gifts. Every community of faith is blessed with them, even if the community is small. When the gifts of the people are employed in leading worship or providing artistic expression in worship, it is a clear sign that God is enlivening our gatherings through the things that God has created. The New Testament lists of spiritual gifts (1 Cor. 12:1–11; Eph. 4:11–13) cannot be taken as complete, for the Spirit's gifts of creativity are not indicated. But they are clearly all around us. Some have the gift of bringing Scripture readings to life through oral interpretation. Others are able to make quilts, banners, vestments, and paraments to adorn our worship spaces. Some have gifts for drama to make proclamation come alive. Visual artists can create images that resonate with our experiences of life. Clearly, musicians abound in the church and allow worship to sing and breathe through their gifts.

In order for churches to draw richly on the Spirit's power in worship, they need to tap into the Spirit's gifts within the community. The artists are usually pleased to receive the opportunity to do in worship what they know God has privileged them to do as artists in life. This is especially true of our children, who are the most natural artists among us. "Our children communicate

---

51. Tom Long is helpful here: "If one desires an intimate encounter with the holy at every service, then go to the Temple of Baal. Yahweh, the true and living God, sometimes withdraws from present experience. In sum, God does not always move us, and everything that moves us is not God" (*Beyond the Worship Wars*, 32).

Sidebar 4.4: We Are All Artists

How might all churches help worship participants know that in response to God we are all called to the "work" of worshiping God and of being church for the sake of the world? In other words, how might our churches help worship participants know that in response to the splendor of God, we are all artists? . . . Wouldn't it be wonderful if all who worship would realize that what they did in worship—the music they make, their attention to the sermon and prayers, and the way they live in response to the God they have encountered in worship—has cosmic significance? Furthermore, if we all recognize that what we do in worship is art, then we would recognize that all musical forms and styles must be chosen carefully for their music and textual and spiritual merit, that they must be sung or played as excellently as possible, and that they must be offered to God as the best we can craft. . . . The art of worship belongs to the church. It is the means by which the people of God live, work, remember, learn to be the church, and enjoy being God's.

Marva Dawn, A Royal "Waste" of Time: The Splendor of Worshiping God and Being Church for the World *(Grand Rapids: Eerdmans, 1999), 238–39.*

---

naturally through the nonverbal vocabulary of the visual (in fact they express themselves exuberantly until they are acculturated out of this capacity)."[52] To open worship to the creativity of children is a way to accomplish many fine goals. Their sincere and humble offerings are a model for everyone. Using their gifts brings honor to them and honors the One who created them. Allowing the use of children's art is a way to offer them full participation in worship and provides a reason for them to be included in the entire gathering rather than being sent away. In addition, employing children's voices, bodies, ideas, and imaginations in worship most certainly adds a layer of vitality that is natural and contagious. Whether they are children, youth, or adults, drawing on the gifts of our local artists is a way to connect the worship of a congregation to the mission of God in the world.

The Special Role of Music in Worship

Music has always had a special place among the arts used in worship. No one has captured the sense of this better than Luther, who lauded Dame Music:

> But thanks be first to God, our Lord,
> Who created her by his Word
> To be his own beloved songstress

52. Kapikian, *Art in Service of the Sacred*, 60.

In praise of him the whole day long;
To him I give my melody
And thanks in all eternity.[53]

Albert Blackwell is convinced that "music serves and manifests the sacred in ways that cannot be specified and articulated."[54] It would be impossible to compile all of music's effects in worship or the ways music speaks to and through us. Only generalities can be drawn. Accordingly, we can identify at least three general reasons for music's predominant place among the worship arts. First, music is highly participatory. While other arts are readily observed or attended to by those gathered for worship, singing allows for the most accessible embodied participation. Singing with others lets each voice have its place, yet to blend in concert and unity with others. The joined voices of worshipers are the distinct voice of the body of Christ. Second, music has the capacity to surround us with its effect. It is nondirectional. The eyes see visual art and dance only if it is in our line of sight. But the ears hear music whenever it is near. Accordingly, worshipers can close their eyes in prayer, meditation, or weariness, and still participate in music as an auditor or a player/singer. Third, music accompanies. It goes with words to add layers of meaning and connectivity. It goes with movement to give it rhythm and to set a tone. When it goes with visual art, drama, film, and dance, it is not only value added, it is value changed. The only thing music fails to accompany is silence. But that can be a kind of music too. It is the melody of stillness, what is heard when nothing stirs. We have all heard those pin-drop moments during a story or a sermon. What we are hearing is a greater silence than when people stop moving so as to hear. It is the silence heard when people stop *breathing*. There are times when the music of silence is required in worship; it is too infrequently provided. Sometimes we need to be surrounded by an aural vacuum so that it can be filled with silent prayer and so that, through it, we can perceive that still small voice. Too often, the voice of the Spirit is masked by heavier sounds.

Conclusion

As we consider—and advocate—the use of the arts and the employment of artists in worship, we are drawn to a necessary conclusion. Churches need to embrace the artists in their communities and enlist their help in creating worshipful expressions that will give voice, shape, and movement to people's response to God's love. Implied in this embrace is a renewed relationship between the church and the artists. Just as Pope Paul VI sought to do, Protestant

53. Martin Luther, "A Preface for All Good Hymnals, 1538," in *Luther's Works: Liturgy and Hymns*, trans. Leupold, Lehmann, and Zeller Strodach, 53:320.
54. Blackwell, *The Sacred in Music*, 11.

churches need to improve relationships with artists. Their gifts must be seen as gifts of the Spirit that are equal to the gifts of preaching, prophesying, teaching, and administration. The church surely needs these spiritual gifts as well as the others.

Two other key ideas are implied in such a renewed relationship: First, the church needs to be the place where the arts are encouraged, fostered, and taught. As public schools are cutting music and arts programs, the church needs to take up the slack and give young people training and public opportunity for artistic expression. Local congregations might even pay for the music and art lessons of talented young people who might grow into those who will replace aging and retiring organists, poets, choir directors, and dancers. Second, a sign of this renewed relationship between church and artists will be that congregations will pay decently for the work of artists. In most churches, preachers and administrators are paid enough to avoid "tent-making" ministries. Artists, however, are rarely paid enough to avoid having other jobs to support themselves. Churches can value art and artists, pay them appropriately, commission new work from established artists, and hire professional musicians, actors, and dancers as needed to bring special emphases to worship when called for.

In considering the place of the arts in worship, I have identified twelve points that worship planners and leaders should keep in mind as they seek to craft liturgies that deal honestly and concretely with the circumstances of life and faith. In addition, several theological principles have been noted.

1. The arts are means by which God communicates to us.
2. The incorporation of art in worship is part of God's mission.
3. Art provides a means by which to express things too deep for words.
4. Artistic expression is an echo of God's own creativity.
5. The arts are a means of experiencing and expressing unity in faith.
6. The arts of worship are incarnational.
7. Any form used in worship should serve the gospel or those assembled to hear it.
8. Spiritual gifts include the talents of artists; nearly everyone has some creative giftedness.

5

Worship Is Communication

A Christian liturgy will bespeak its *logos* of meaning in a style
that strains to embrace and articulate not just words but the
whole of creation—in fire and water, dust and ashes, oil and
perfume, bread and wine, soaring sounds and tender gestures; in
times of joy and bereavement, at times crucial in nature's course
as well as in the course of individuals and whole societies; in
social categories, in poems of violence and hymns of peace, in
silence as well as in noisy jubilation; with living plants and ani-
mals as well as with dead wood and lifeless stone; in movement
and in stillness, laugher and tears, by speaking and listening
and keeping quiet; by celibacy for some and sexual activity for
others and chastity for all; in tombs and bath houses and din-
ing rooms, wherever people meet to transact reality. Christian
liturgy must do all this because the *logos* it increments under
grace is just this all-encompassing. Its meaning fills all things,
in time and beyond.[1]

Aidan Kavanagh, *Elements of Rite*

I f worship and the mission of God are intricately connected, how do we
communicate the essence of *missio Dei* in our time of adoration? How is
our action as disciples in the world anticipated and animated by the things we
say and do when we gather as God's people to be centered and sent? We rely

1. Kavanagh, *Elements of Rite*, 90–91.

on the few who plan for these gatherings to understand that communicating these postures and powers is their responsibility.

Worship always communicates, but not always in obvious ways and not always felicitously. The meaning of liturgical texts can be betrayed by the way a speaker gestures or by a lack of presence or interest. We may fill our rituals with empty language used to cover its gaps with explanations or nervous chatter, reducing their capacity to have broad and deep meaning. We may attempt to communicate a certain theological idea with a physical movement but perform it in such a way as to present an entirely different meaning to the observers. What is needed in worship leadership is for leaders to know what they intend to communicate and then to speak or act in ways that accomplish their intentions. We are searching for congruence between the way we embody worship rituals and what we hope those rituals will accomplish and signify. In this chapter I will explore the ways that worship forms communicate and the responsibility of worship leaders and worshipers to propose and accept appropriate meanings.[2]

Three Modes of Signification in Worship

In his penetrating study *Worship as Meaning*, Graham Hughes presents three ways that signs function in worship. He terms them the *iconicity* of worship, the *indexicality* of worship, and the *symbolic* dimension of worship.[3] Exploring these categories briefly will provide us with a taxonomy for our discussion of the ways that we communicate (or fail to communicate as intended) in worship.

Iconicity

Iconicity has to do with the way signs function on "some sort of boundary or frontier" of perception. In worship we are constantly confronted by our inability to reach toward the mystery of God (remember Calvin's observation in the previous chapter about our incapacity to penetrate God's essence). So much of faith is beyond us, incomprehensible, unfathomable. Iconicity "has to do with the degree that we can manage to generate a *likeness* or *similarity* between what we do on the known side of this frontier and how we imagine things might be on its far side."[4] Iconic signs, says Hughes, "invite us to

2. The notion that worship leaders *propose* meanings that are *accepted* by worshipers has been developed by Hughes in *Worship as Meaning*. We will rely on Hughes for this and other insights as to how worship communicates.

3. These ways of looking at signs Hughes takes from the work of late nineteenth and early twentieth century philosopher and semiotician Charles Sanders Peirce. For his introduction to Peirce's thought, see Hughes, *Worship as Meaning*, 6.

4. Ibid., 148–49; italics in the original.

imagine how things are in the presence of God!"[5] When people come away from worship with the sense that they have had a meaningful encounter with the One who made them, it means the signs within our rituals and aesthetic forms have enabled them to negotiate the "human/divine frontier." Too often, the opposite happens: "In this case we shall say that an iconic dimension in the liturgy's signification was either deficient or absent; the transaction (of worship) seemed mostly continuous with everyday events (the sermon was scarcely distinguishable from other exhortations to altruism; and the 'fellowship' could have been replicated in any social gathering)."[6]

The proper functioning of iconic signs in worship gives a sense of satisfaction that God's transcendence was made approachable. This power of sign is clearly at work in the use of Orthodox icons. When worshipers gaze on the figures (painted two-dimensionally to avoid the implication of three-dimensional idols) their perceptions are drawn to and through them to the mystery that lies beyond them. The icons are windows at the frontier between what we can know and perceive about God and what we must only hypothesize. In this sense, they have a sacramental character, giving "a physical sign of divine presence."[7] The Lord's Supper functions in a similar way for most Christians. Regardless of one's Eucharistic theology, Holy Communion is understood to be an event in which believers come face to face with God's promise in the meal. We cannot penetrate beyond the bread and the wine to see a physical Jesus or to know the nature of his presence. We can physically come only to the material boundary represented by the elements. Eating and drinking allows us a certain embodied approach to the frontier, but only our imaginations penetrate further. "The Word comes to the element; and so there is a sacrament, that is, a sort of visible word,"[8] said Augustine. By this he meant to draw a distinction between what can be seen (the bread and wine) and what cannot be seen, "God's own knowledge and intention of himself and his works, the inner reality of all that truth which God knows and is."[9] The meal is iconic because it brings us close, whether in remembering Christ, following Zwingli's view, or in drawing near to his invisible presence.[10]

The iconic quality of signs means that they are "heavily impregnated not just with spatial, temporal and movement *imagery* . . . but with *actual, physical* movement and directionality."[11] In other words, the way we enter into God's presence, how we are centered, and the way we are sent forth come to

5. Ibid., 151.
6. Ibid.
7. Nes, *The Mystical Language of Icons*, 16.
8. Augustine, *In Johannem* 80.3, quoted in Jenson, *Visible Words*, 9.
9. Jenson, *Visible Words*, 10.
10. The iconic quality of Holy Communion, applicable irrespective of one's Eucharistic theology, will be discussed later in this chapter.
11. Hughes, *Worship as Meaning*, 153; italics in the original.

expression in the ways that we speak, move, invite, guide, intend, and present. Each of these modes of communication matter, and it is the responsibility of presiding and assisting ministers to signal things properly for the iconic function of worship forms to be achieved.

Iconicity in worship is easily and frequently squelched. For example, when a prayer leader begins to address worshipers in the midst of a prayer that is intended to be addressed to God on their behalf, a boundary is obscured. We might forgive the leader for making a common mistake, but we, in the process of being addressed rather than being invited to address God with our cares and yearnings, find that the barrier at the border has been raised. What remains is not the sense of being on the extraordinary frontier between human life and God. We are left with the ordinary sense that someone is talking to, even interrupting us.[12] We encounter a similar problem when we fill our worship with chatter. Not only does over-speaking ritual reduce its meaning (once we define it, it means that much and nothing more) but it also becomes an ordinary thing, incapable of transporting us to the frontier of perception from which we imagine further. Likewise, the iconic function of worship space is lost when it is designed to be homey, sociable, and familiar. Such space "silently yet powerfully corroborates the notion that 'nothing special' is expected of the people who enter it, nor perhaps of what will happen within it."[13] This is why the return of art to worship is a *riching-up* of liturgy. We need art to make space iconic. As the words of the epigraph from the previous chapter put it, the arts, through "their combined effect can then evoke thought and emotion, thereby animating the Word and transforming the place set apart into a place of worship."[14] Even when worshiping in a gymnasium or a home, art can be, and usually is, used to create the sense of a place set apart from its common function.

We cannot leave Hughes's explanation of the iconic power of signs without including his apt description of how it works at the conclusion of worship. His description of the final blessing perfectly captures the sense that the sending is the key point in worship where adoration is connected to mission and the sense that the presider needs to speak and act so as to inaugurate the action that follows:

Pretty well the last responsibility of the presiding minister in any given worship service is to *bless* the people (invoke over them benediction!) as they prepare

12. "Is it all that important? Does it matter whether people think the actions/language are addressed to them or to God? . . . For both leaders and people to be unclear about the 'direction' in which the liturgy is oriented at any given moment is to allow the meanings of worship to be, or to become, indistinguishable from those of any other public event in which speeches are made, songs are sung and symbolic acts are undertaken" (ibid., 163).

13. Ibid., 156.

14. Schmit, "The Word, Beauty, and a Place Set Apart," 18.

to leave the space and time of the liturgy. That is, the blessing requires to have about it an iconic quality such that it enables the people to *go back* from the encounter with the "other" who is God, carrying within and about them the sense of promise, of absolution, of the empowerment and the blessing which belongs in and flows from this encounter.[15]

Indexicality

Indexicality in worship has to do with congruence between what is intended and what is done. It is "'truthfulness' or 'authenticity' in the words and actions of worship, an integrity between 'form' and 'performance', or what the Second Vatican Council's *Constitution on the Sacred Liturgy* calls 'thoughts matching words.'"[16]

The term *indexicality* refers to the way that signs point, like a finger, to some object or particular meaning. The signs in worship can accurately or successfully point to what is intended or they can fail to do so. The failure occurs, for example, when a worship leader intends to indicate one attitude but ultimately indicates something else. Hughes gives a typical example drawn from the pages of his worship journal:

> The minister leading worship today—an elderly man, retired I would say—sought to communicate a light hearted, welcoming, personable style. But he managed it in such a way that it seemed (to this worshipper, at least) that this was an effect he desired rather than a fact he could assume. The actual communication seemed (to me), conversely, to be avuncular, saccharine, condescending; forms which attempted informality but which rather betrayed professional ineptitude, a style which attempted to make us present but which itself lacked "presence."[17]

The lack of congruence between what is intended and what is communicated in worship leadership is so common a problem that examples are limitless. (Sidebar 5.1 gives two such examples, one from a traditional liturgical context and the other from a free church setting.)

Instances of failed indexing occur when the words or actions of worship leaders belie a community's theology. This is often entirely accidental, the accomplishment of leaders who either are unfamiliar with the community's operating liturgical theology or unaware of the ways in which their performance betrays the intended meaning of the ritual form. Regularly, we see examples such as the following:

- gathering songs are selected that focus on personal or individualistic faith encounters, instead of songs that draw us together as one

15. Hughes, *Worship as Meaning*, 160; italics in the original.
16. Ibid., 148.
17. Ibid., 115.

Sidebar 5.1: Saying One Thing, Doing Another

I have frequently seen Protestant pastors make the following error while presiding over the Lord's Supper. During recitation of the words of institution ("In the night in which he was betrayed, our Lord Jesus took bread, . . .") a small, crisp wafer (which passes for bread in many settings) is taken from the paten (plate). As the words, "took bread and broke it" are uttered, the presider actually uses two hands to raise the wafer and snap it in half, making an audible click. The communication here seems to be that the *formula* confects communion. A small, convenient form of bread is used. Never mind that it lacks any resemblance to actual bread, just so long as it is *technically* bread. The words are recited as indicated in the worship book. The bread is broken precisely at the right moment in the text. The observer is left with the unmistakable impression that communion happens because all words and actions are done precisely as prescribed. Hocus pocus,* Christ is rendered present. This may be seen by some as merely a dramatic reenactment of the text. But that is precisely the problem. Enacting the narrative suggests that it is the enactment itself that is required for the sacrament to be efficacious.

The problem here is that there is no operant theology that suggests that Christ is confected in the bread by virtue of prescriptive action. Christ is present in the Lord's Supper because of the promise of God that declares "this is my body." The only purpose for breaking bread in communion is to enable a loaf to be distributed. In liturgies where the Fraction is indicated (e.g., Anglican and Roman practice) it is designated for this purpose: to break the bread for distribution. Since a single wafer is not intended to be divided for distribution, snapping it (especially as the relative words are voiced) can only suggest that it is done in order to necessitate Christ's appearance. When I describe this action to my worship class in seminary, they usually chuckle. I then tell them they have just performed the proper liturgical response to the action: indeed, it is silly.

The second example was observed by Todd Johnson:

I was in attendance at a large evangelical church on baby dedication Sunday. The pastor of family ministry was presiding over this part of the service, and invited over a dozen couples to come forward to the front of this church with their infant children. The families stood in a semi-circle facing the minister. He explained how this rite [brought] no spiritual blessing or benefit to the children in any way, but instead was an opportunity for the parents to dedicate themselves to the raising of these children. The pastor never held nor touched the children at any time lest they be seen as receiving some sort of blessing. He reiterated that this rite has nothing to do with salvation. The pastor then began to pray, "Bless, O Lord, these children that they might come to know Jesus Christ as their savior."

Todd E. Johnson, "Liturgical Links: Toward a Theology of Free Church Worship," unpublished address at the installation of Todd E. Johnson in the Brehm Chair for Worship, Theology, and the Arts at Fuller Theological Seminary, Pasadena, CA, May 22, 2007.

* This phrase, used by magicians since the seventeenth century, is thought to have originated from "*hoc est corpus meum*," Latin for "this is my body." John Tillotson, archbishop of Canterbury in 1694, made this observation drawing on the idea that Catholic priests would turn bread and wine magically into Christ by the "trick of transubstantiation." The *Oxford English Dictionary* includes this line as the first known use of the phrase: "1687 R. L'Estrange *Answ. Diss.* 18, I never lov'd the Hocus-Pocussing of *Hoc est Corpus Meum*" (*The Compact Edition of the Oxford English Dictionary* [Oxford: Oxford University Press, 1971]: 320).

- a song leader attempts to lead a congregational song in such a popular, idiosyncratic style that worshipers are discouraged from participation
- a church with a high theology of Word allows preaching that is not based on biblical texts
- a song of praise is rendered lifeless by an inappropriate tempo or too loud an accompaniment (whether by organ or band)
- the "prayer of the people" is subverted by a leader's language that is personal and privatistic
- the anamnetic (remembrance) aspect of the Lord's Supper is blurred when the communion liturgy fails to give account of God's saving acts for which we give thanks (as in the Eucharistic prayer)

Congruence between "saying what we believe" and "believing what we say" is a pastoral issue that needs "constant pastoral monitoring and careful theological reflection."[18] This kind of care is especially needed, as I have been suggesting, in the sending portion of our liturgies if our churches are to be missionally oriented. If our theology is outwardly focused, then worship needs to anticipate and empower the liturgy of discipleship as we send people out into action.

One of the chief complaints about worship that is liturgically traditional is that it can be cold, rote, overly formal, routine. This complaint does not come only from expected critics, such as those on the free church or charismatic end of the liturgical spectrum. Note this comment from one of the most seminal thinkers in the area of liturgical theology, Edward Schillebeeckx: "'What's the use?' I heard a twelve-year-old girl say in the United States after a Sunday mass, which struck me, too, as pretty well meaningless, with its accompanying banal talk on video tape. Even though it was all conducted precisely and punctiliously according to the official precepts, there was no bond with the communicants, no inspiration, just a vacuous routine."[19] The failure noted here is an index problem. The leaders of worship went through the apparently proper motions, but did not present themselves or their words and actions with clarity or vitality. The rituals of the Mass can point to life in Christ, joy in being gathered, honest human experiences that are addressed in prayer, the certitude of Christ's presence in the Eucharist (Catholic interpretation), and so forth. The Mass is about the real stuff of life and our genuine encounter with the God of the universe. How could any of these things be uninteresting?[20] When rituals are fully incorporated—that is, fully voiced and embodied—they cannot be rote or routine. They are a living enactment of incarnation. Yet too

18. Johnson, "Liturgical Links."
19. Schillebeeckx, "Towards a Rediscovery of the Christian Sacraments," in Lange and Vogel, *Ordo*, 8.
20. We pray with William Willimon, who once offered this petition: "Lord, forgive us for making the gospel boring!"

often we perceive a sense that liturgy consists of nothing more than mechanical recitation of texts and repetitions of actions mandated by rubrics.[21] This indexical problem is described by Hughes (borrowing from Max Weber):

> There are doubtless many factors which contribute to actions being formal signs, the "meaning" of which has been betrayed or evacuated by the fact that such signs were not "meant". The most prevalent of these . . . is what Max Weber described as "routinization": this is when religious forms, forged in charisma, "[become] either traditionalized or rationalized or a combination of both." . . . In religious devotion "the rites [are] symbols of the divine"; but "once it [devotion] is missing, only the bare and formal . . . ritualism remains."[22]

It need not be that way, and what I am advocating in this book is the revitalization of forms that come to us as historical wisdom for worship. While we won't all worship according to the rubrics of the Roman Mass, we can use rituals appropriate to our own tradition and location that are alive with incarnation. Or, to put it again in Hughes's terms, the signs of word and action in worship are "indices of a presence or absence of the person's spirit *in* the liturgical actions he or she is undertaking."[23] The way to ensure lively enactments is to remember this: "in order to lead worship, leaders *must themselves be worshippers*."[24] When this occurs, there can be surprising results. Hughes's worship journal also includes this entry describing a visit to King's College Chapel in Cambridge, England:

> One presumes, given the illustrious reputation of the place, that every aspect of the liturgy will have been meticulously rehearsed. I was therefore struck during the prayers of intercession, by the noticeably "prayerful" quality of the prayers, and, on glancing up, realized that the chaplain, though he had manifestly prepared the topics of prayer, was in fact praying "extempore". The aesthetic experience moved through to a more exactly worshipful experience.[25]

Symbolic Signs

The third category of sign in worship is symbol. While semiotics gives us many ways to define *symbol*, Hughes says that symbols are signs that articulate things to us through the interpretation and discipline of tradition. Symbols are signs with meanings assigned by laws (of grammar, say, or the

---

21. To put it bluntly, and somewhat painfully, we might borrow a phrase often voiced by liturgical theologian Michael Aune, who says that such thinking assumes that liturgy is merely "one damned thing after another" (Aune, unpublished lecture).

22. Hughes, *Worship as Meaning*, 173.

23. Ibid., 174.

24. Ibid., 175; italics in the original.

25. Ibid., 115.

literal laws governing driving on a road) or by custom or convention. In this sense, symbols mean certain things according to the tradition or community within which they are used.

A clear example of this comes from right outside my door. The community I currently live in was established in 1926. The streets are lined with tall green streetlamps. These are figured ornamentally, and among the figures near the bottom of each lamppost is a row of an ancient symbol that has been known by many cultures and by many names. The Chinese call it *wan*; in England it used to be called the *fylfot*; in Greece, it is known as the *tetraskelion*; in Germany, it is the *Hakenkreuz*. But today it is best known by its Indian (Sanskrit) name: *swastika*. The community these lamps were placed in does not predate the Nazi era and its use of the *Hakenkreuz* as its central symbol. Yet in 1926 there was no local tradition or convention that the *fylfot* not be used. Hitler adopted the use of the symbol as the central point of the Nazi flag in 1920. For the rest of the world at the time, the symbol tended to carry a positive meaning (the Sanskrit meaning was literally "to be good"). Today, passersby are struck by the absurdity of street lamps in America that display the swastika.

Our most obvious example of Hughes's use of symbol is that we assign meanings to words by convention. When we take three letters (note that letters themselves are symbols with certain agreed upon referents—that is, a *t* can be used in English, French, or Spanish to denote the same sound), such as *c*, *a*, and *t*, we have the English convention that in this order the letters spell the word *cat*, which means a small, furry, domestic animal. In another order, *act* means something else.

How does this view of symbol play out in worship? It reminds us that our interpretation of Christian symbols and the actions and texts of worship are understood on the basis of community interpretation. For example, the cross is typically bare in Protestant tradition. In Catholic use, it usually has the slain Christ depicted on it (the crucifix).[26] In Hungary, the country's largely Reformed Christian population does not place crosses in or on its churches because they were used during the counter-Reformation as a symbol for torture. Hughes gives this example of sign functioning symbolically in worship: "When the presiding minister stands before the people and summons them to worship, perhaps in words of Scripture or with the ancient greeting, 'The Lord be with you', these words, these gestures *are already—instantaneously in fact—deeply imbued with meaning for the people.*"[27] The communal meaning that inheres in such symbols is not something that can be precisely indicated.

26. Richard Mouw tells the humorous anecdote of a Benedictine friend who once removed his monastic robes in order to attend a niece's graduation. On his drive to the event, the monk stopped by a religious bookstore to purchase a gift for the occasion. He asked if they had crosses for sale. The clerk assured him of a wide array of choices, asking, "Do you want a plain one, or one with a guy on it?"

27. Hughes, *Worship as Meaning*, 179; italics in the original.

Nor can it be limited, for symbolic meaning is always multivalent. If we were to ask worshipers to write an essay on the meaning of the cross, we would have as many answers as there were respondents. Each answer would provide an accurate measure of one person's sense of the symbol. There would be overlap and coincidence between the answers, but they would not be identical, and none of them would be wrong.

As with the iconic and indexical ways that signs function in worship, the symbolic function of sign can be undermined and communication can become blurred. A common example is available in many churches. The American flag represents many conventional ideas to American people and sometimes contrary things to people of other countries. Placing it within our worship spaces, often very near the front and center of our chancels, blurs both the meaning of the flag and the meaning of our space set apart. The flag is not a Christian symbol nor a sign useful for worship—at least not according to historical Christian convention—yet by such placement, we apply Christian value and meaning to it that betrays the American constitution (which forbids the establishment of any particular religion), and we apply meaning to worship that is eccentric. The symbols central to Christian worship are the cross, the Word, the table, and the font or pool. It is these symbols around which worshipers gather. When we gather around the American flag, it is another type of assembly that we create. Assemblies that gather around the flag (such as community meetings, political rallies, public school functions, even American sporting events) have their own conventions, and often the presence of a Christian cross in such settings is seen as an unwelcome religious intrusion.

Signs and the Mission of God

How can worship communicate its connection to the mission of God? It does so in the three ways that Hughes describes. Through iconicity, we engage signs that take us to the threshold of divine presence. Ritual, art, Word, sacrament: these take us as far as we can humanly go. Only our thoughts and imaginations reach further into the mystery that we dance with but never comprehend. We cannot fully know God's mission for us as a church, a congregation, or a disciple, but we are brought close to God in worship and allow in this encounter for God to reach the rest of the way. Remember I said at the outset that worship is made pertinent by the way we shape and perform it, but only God can make it relevant. The iconical measure of worship brings us to a place where God condescends to us and touches us in sacramental ways, and speaks to us of God's will for our lives. To achieve the iconic quality of worship signs, we rely on the nondiscursive quality of aesthetic expression.

The indexical qualities of worship signs call us to establish congruity between *what we believe* and *what we say we believe* through word and action.

Because church traditions have differing theologies, there ought to be some variety, some local particularity or local theology evident in worship that aligns with who we say we are. Yet there ought also to be something about the way we present ourselves as leaders and worshipers that anticipates that we are only engaged in part of worship during the hour of adoration. We ought to show in our spirits that we are available for more: to be empowered to be disciples in living liturgy within and without the church doors. Worship leaders especially need to present the sense that *missio Dei* is *missio noster*, our own mission in the world. If we believe that worship is both adoration and action, then let us prepare and execute the hour of adoration so that, in all its ritual and aesthetic expressiveness, it points toward action.

Through understanding the symbolic nature of the signs in worship, we are able to draw on the shared conventions of interpretation that make our central symbols and actions meaningful for us as worshipers. The historic wisdom of the church at worship has established the core meanings for our worship rites. At the same time, those meanings are large and fluid, capable of shared interpretation while open to the nuances of local and individual interpretation. These central symbols give shape to our liturgies. Our gathering rites establish us as one in Christ, assembled from various locations of action and discipleship. The Word centers us and connects God's promises to our lives of service in the world. The water and the wine unite us in the fellowship of faith and compel us out to share friendship and bread with those we meet in daily life. Our sending rites are pivotal, providing a final blessing during the hour of adoration, propelling us out into a week of action.

The Responsibility for Communication in Worship

The responsibility for communicating accurately and richly in worship falls principally to the few who plan for and lead the gathering. While Hughes maintains that it is up to the people assembled to accept the proposed meanings offered by worship leaders, it is up to the leaders themselves to know the direction and intent of word and gesture. For a worship leader to be unaware of such proposals is to make certain that what is accepted will be vague or misleading. Taking responsibility for communication in worship means that worship planners and leaders will attend to the following eight issues:

1. *Worship is a dialogue.* The conversation of worship is between God and God's people. The role of leaders is to facilitate this dialogue and not to interrupt or subvert it. This means that the most important voice to be heard in worship is God's. This comes through Scripture readings, preaching, and stillness.

When humans are called on to serve God's speech, they must do so not only with humility but also with the conviction that they are called to an important task.[28] Accordingly, they should prepare as carefully as possible and pray that God will use them in the way that God requires.

The second important voice in worship is that of God's people. When individual believers gather as one body in Christ, it is their voice that needs to be enlivened in the dialogue of worship. Sometimes this happens when the people are invited to sing or speak for themselves in response to what God has said or done. At other times, the leader speaks on behalf of the people who accept the words and gestures proposed for them.

2. *There are three directions of communication in worship.* God speaks to God's people. People speak to God. People speak to people. The leader's role is to know which direction of speech is operating at given points in worship and to allow that communication to succeed. The people cannot make this happen but can only follow. Leaders learn to speak for God when called to do so (reading the Word well, preaching with the composure that is born of humility and the confidence that the preacher speaks with God's authority). They learn gesture and movement that gracefully invite people to participate. They also learn to phrase prayers that allow people to accept the leader's words as their own prayer. Such things take preparation, thoughtful selection of words and actions, rehearsal of movements, knowledge of the people and their concerns, familiarity with the worship space, and so forth. Worship leaders are performers whose goal is not to entertain (although that may happen) but to facilitate the dialogue of worship. When worship leaders speak directly to the people, or invite participation in the horizontal communication within the community, they need to speak and act so as to facilitate the voice of the body of Christ, rather than impose themselves as a central agent. Worship is never about worship leaders. It is about God and God's people.

3. *Music has three communicative purposes in worship.* Music can serve many purposes in worship (such as to accompany liturgical texts and actions, to cover movement, to set a tone or heighten a mood, etc.). But, within these functions, music communicates in three ways. The first is to proclaim. As in reading Scripture or preaching, music selected for worship can teach the biblical narrative or provide commentary on it. Choral anthems, hymns, and songs can proclaim scriptural texts in dimensions that reach beyond the denotive power of the words.

The second communicative purpose for music in worship is to facilitate the voice of the people. Choirs, bands, and song leaders have the primary duty of inviting people to sing. Any other duty is secondary. This means that:

- Congregational songs will be accessible, and taught in advance, if necessary, to enable participation.

28. Charles L. Bartow thoroughly addresses the place of the human voice as an instrument of God's self-performance in *God's Human Speech*.

- Songs are best led by human voices; they have the greatest potential to encourage worshipers to sing.
- Instrumental accompaniments will support congregational singing and not overwhelm it.
- Songs will be led in a corporate manner and will not be stylistically self-conscious. Leaders' voices should summon people to sing; showmanship should not impede their participation.
- Acoustic space in worship should be designed or tuned to allow for the congregational voice to resound. When the space is acoustically absorbent, individuals will hear only themselves, or will hear only those whose voices are amplified. The voice of the body of Christ is an ensemble voice, never a solo voice.
- Amplified voices should only serve to lead the corporate voice, not replace it.
- Musical flourishes during congregational singing (introductions, choral descants, instrumental interludes, modulations, obligatos, fanfares, etc.) invite and lift participation, so as to "give worshipers a voice they never knew they had to sing praise and offer prayer to God."[29]
- The songs for congregational use are chosen to facilitate the liturgical moment. Praise has a different quality than lament. Thanksgiving is expressed differently than supplication.

Music in worship has a third communicative purpose. There are times when a song of praise or lament needs to be sung for us. Like the sighing of the Spirit who prays for us when we are unable, the choir, ensemble, or soloist can be our voice, saying what we need to say but cannot. Like the leader who crafts poetic language that draws us into prayer, musicians provide expression for our soul-deep sentiments. In such cases, the congregation's part is to listen, to receive the proposed prayer or praise, to allow it to resonate within, and to let the music serve the iconic function that allows people to send their imaginations past the frontiers of sound to all that lies beyond.

4. *The test for the appropriateness of any mode of communication in worship is to ask what it serves.* This is an indexical question: what do the words, actions, or artistic elements point to? Because worship is an encounter between God and God's people, all aspects of worship should be designed to point to God or to serve those gathered to hear God's Word. It is not uncommon to find aspects of worship serving other purposes. Here are a few examples:

29. Witvliet, "Beyond Style," in Johnson, *The Conviction of Things Not Seen*, 75.

- A sermon or song may serve the ego needs of a preacher or musician.
- A projected visual presentation may serve the congregation's expectation that it be culturally relevant.
- The presence of a national flag in the chancel may serve people's sense of patriotism.
- Cushions and carpet in the worship space might serve the worshipers' comfort.
- Announcements might serve the church's program.
- A joke might serve a speaker's need to be seen as friendly.
- Clothing worn by leaders may serve their desire to be stylish or to be seen as likeable or approachable.

These concerns abound in worship because cues as to what or who is being served can be subtle. The first purpose of an excellent sermon or song might be betrayed only by a lack of humility in the performer. The projection of visual art may serve the people especially *because* its use is a cultural commonplace. A humorous story might serve worshipers by drawing listeners to the character of the speaker, through which they hear the message. Let worship leaders, preachers, artists, and technicians attend to the key question, the one we asked previously about the use of art in worship. Who or what does this aspect of worship serve? If the answer is not God or God's people, it does not deserve a place in worship.

This leads to two related issues. The first is entertainment. Clearly, things that are entertaining can serve such purposes as humor, distraction, nostalgia, and so forth. This is not necessarily bad or wrong, for a deeper purpose may be proposed. They might serve a rhetorical purpose that achieves the ultimate goal of drawing people more deeply into the encounter between God and God's people. But if the use of humor, distraction, and nostalgia serve *only* to entertain, they are gratuitous and out of place. A simple example makes the point: people respond more fully to a sermon that is interesting. To make it interesting, the preacher may employ creative language, humor, story, plot, drama, or music. When used wisely, these tools have rhetorical purpose. They create a hearing for the gospel by virtue of their capacity to engage the audience. Thoughtful worship leaders will learn to employ things that create interest in ways and for reasons that serve the body of Christ. They will avoid entertainments that are gratuitous.

The second issue relating to the question of what is being served has to do with God's prerogative. It is always up to God to make better use of something than we might have planned. Even if we choose to use art or entertainment for its own sake, the Holy Spirit may find a means by which to use it for God's purpose. This effect is known by every worshiper who sees through the ego of a preacher or performer and finds the message coming through in spite of its prideful presentation. Still, this does not give preachers, presiders, technicians, and artists the right to presume that God will redeem any manner of presentation. It should go without saying that those who lead in worship do so with an attitude of servanthood. There is no other biblical model for leadership than service.

5. *Worship leaders should strive for a sense of liturgical presence.* This idea stems from the world of theater, where performers seek to have "stage presence." This involves poise, posture, graceful movement, and the power to command attention at the right times. The sense of a performer's presence points the audience toward the proper thing: the play and its drama. Liturgical presence is similar. Speakers, leaders, and musicians strive to perform with dignity and poise, moving gracefully, speaking with clarity, and exhibiting a sense of hospitality. Liturgical presence, whether it occurs in free or high liturgical settings, points toward adoration. In addition, it provides worshipers with a sense of assurance that they are in good hands as they are led to negotiate their way through it. Worshipers will always mirror the presence of a leader. If he or she is nervous or ill at ease, the congregation will be anxious for them. If the leaders are relaxed and poised, worshipers will have confidence in them and will settle comfortably into the activities of worship.

6. *The symbols of worship should be simple and uncluttered.* Because we gather around central symbols and because they are filled with meaning, their power to communicate is amplified when they have space to speak. Having five crosses in the chancel does not make the cross five times as meaningful. Let there be a single, large cross that stands *iconically* at the frontier between our need for salvation and God's satisfaction of that need on such an instrument of death. And let a single, visible cross stand *symbolically* as a magnet for shared and expanding perceptions of God's grace.

The proliferation of a symbol does not add to its capacity to create meaning. Neither does cluttering the symbol. The table on which the communion elements are placed stands (symbolically) for more than can be expressed by worshipers about the ways we meet and remember Christ in the sacrament. Placing books, the Bible, offering baskets, and other things on it creates an index problem. The table points to the Lord's Supper, until it is used as a horizontal catchall, in which case it points to nothing in particular.

While proliferation of a symbol is not useful, its abundant use is. Let bread for communion be clearly bread; a large loaf can be seen best by all in the assembly. It can hardly point to God's promises if it cannot be seen. Likewise, water in baptism can be used abundantly. Even in communities where the baptized are merely sprinkled, more water than is necessary to dampen a brow can be used so that all in attendance may obtain the symbol and the meaning it points to. (Sidebar 5.2 gives an example of how water can be used abundantly, even when architecture dictates against it.) The liberal use of water in baptism is, in fact, one of the things that can be borrowed from free church practice by traditionally liturgical churches. Baptist churches, for example, typically

Sidebar 5.2: The Sound of Water as a Sign in Baptism

The first congregation I served as a pastor had a large baptismal font made of stone. It was placed at the entrance to the worship space (nave) by architects who had a sense of iconicity. The font stood at the entrance as a sign that we enter faith through baptism. While this is a fitting theological interpretation in a Lutheran church, the placement of the font created an index problem. When baptisms were performed, the congregation would turn in their pews to face the font. But since they were all on the same level, only the people in the nearest pews could see what was happening during the baptism. The majority of worshipers attended to the baptism through sound only as the presider's microphone allowed them to hear what was being said.

Since there was no possibility of moving the font to a more visible place, I made a point when presiding over baptisms to bend over the water and reach into it with both hands. I would lift up as much water from the font as I could and let it cascade back into the font before sprinkling a few drops on the head of the baptized. When I did this, my lapel microphone clearly picked up the sound of the falling water and filled the nave with the lively sound of a sign that pointed toward the action taking place. Three times I would lift water from the font and place it on the head of the baptized: in the name of the Father, and of the Son, and of the Holy Spirit. That my worship robe became drenched from wrist to elbow only served to amplify the sense that water is the sign God chose to accomplish this means of grace.

have a baptismal pool rather than a font. The baptized are fully immersed in the water by a presider who stands with them in the pool. There can be no mistaking the indexical quality of water as sign in such baptisms.

7. *The communicative power of ritual speaks for itself.* Rites, like all symbols, are filled with meaning—with many meanings, in fact. Each person will find his or her own way of gathering meaning from ritual activities. The temptation for worship leaders is to provide explanations for the rites as they unfold. They presumably do this to make them *more* meaningful and to allow people to enter into them with greater volition. In fact, the opposite occurs. Explaining the meaning of rituals violates all three ways that signs function. Iconically, explaining the meaning or power of a rite reduces its capacity to suggest meanings beyond the frontier of the human/divine encounter. The rite is used particularly because things beyond the border are too mysterious and complex to explain. We use the rite, in all its own inherent mystery, to approach the border and imagine what lies beyond. Indexically, explanations of rituals assert that the rites point in precise and finite directions, specifically, those indicated by the leader's words. When words are given as concrete pointers, ritual is no longer indexical. It is dampened and deadened, reduced to rote enactments of the actions described. Aidan Kavanagh put it bluntly:

If a poet must explain the poem before it is recited, there is something wrong with the poem. If a liturgy must be explained before it is done, there is something wrong with the liturgy. . . . This is not to say that preparation is never needed. It is only to say that lengthy explanations are always abnormal and should never occur as an immediate prelude to the act itself. . . . When it comes to liturgy, precision can be bought at too high a price, and some things cannot be said.[30]

Symbolically, explaining rites reduces their symbolic meanings. Once we tell people what a symbol means, our *stated* meaning crowds out or masks any other meanings that might otherwise occur to the participant.

Another problem with speaking too much during rituals is that the leader's speech inserts the host's voice between the two chief conversationalists. The vertical dimension of worship's dialogue is between God and God's people. The rituals of worship facilitate this conversation in discursive and nondiscursive ways. For the host to break into this lively engagement is to interrupt the conversation. Garrison Keillor, writer and humorist, put the matter in blunt terms: "When a minister stands in front of people he is interrupting what the people have come to church for. He had better have a good reason for doing that. . . . We go to look at the mysteries, and all the substitutes for communion with God are not worth anyone's time."[31]

Sometimes, what the leader interrupts in over-speaking ritual is silence. While many speakers are uncomfortable with silence during orations or rituals, listeners and participants are not uncomfortable with it unless the silence is longer than expected. In sermons and other speeches, listeners employ silence meaningfully. They use it to reflect on what has been said or to prepare for a change in the speech's tone or direction. Public speakers can learn to embrace the silence as part of the oration's essential vocabulary. In ritual, silence can function in similar ways, or it can allow aural space for people to enter into the rite and allow it to engage them. The quietness of ritual is one of the elements that enables it to function iconically. Mystery has its own volume. The journey beyond the human/divine border is one to be made with bare feet and whispers, not boots and shouts.

8. *A key role of worship leaders is hospitality.* Because the dialogue of worship is primarily between God and God's people, leaders need to remember their own place in the conversation. It is merely to facilitate the primary dialogue. Like hosts at a dinner party, their role is to draw others into conversation. Learning to serve in this manner means that leaders have to overcome certain necessary obstacles.

We usually place our worship leaders in locations that seem elevated in one sense or another. They may stand on a raised platform. They may wear robes or other special clothing. They have the privilege of using microphones to am-

---

30. Kavanagh, *Elements of Rite*, 101–2.
31. Keillor, "In Search of Lake Wobegon," 108.

plify their voices. Culturally, these accommodations imply that the persons so designated as leaders are the most important persons in a given event. This is not the intention in worship that is properly focused on bringing God's people into an encounter with their Creator. Given that our worship architecture, voice amplification, clerical dress, and furnishings (e.g., pulpit, lectern) regularly propose to the assembly that the leaders have heightened roles in worship, it is up to presiding and assisting ministers and other leaders to perform their roles with an aptitude for and an attitude of hospitality. They are to act in ways that demonstrate that raised platforms, distinct dress, and voice amplification are not matters of leadership privilege, but essentials that allow for leaders to be seen, heard, and identified by all participants in a gathering. They are also to act with discretion, moving or speaking when necessary, with adequate grace and purpose.

The temptation for leaders is to crowd the conversation, inserting commentary, instruction, and chatter where they are not needed and not helpful. Thoughtful leaders will be attentive to how much explanation is needed in order to facilitate the primary dialogue of worship. There should be a balance between saying what is needed so that people can follow and respond with vitality and being silent so as to allow the rites of worship to achieve their iconic, indexical, and symbolic potential.

Two additional aspects of leadership hospitality are friendliness and humility. These traits serve together. People will be drawn to worship when it is clear that the few who have anticipated their arrival are delighted that they have come. Leaders welcome them with sincerity, ease their way through the rituals of worship, match the tone of their own speech and actions to the mood of the ritual moment, and invite the people into full participation. Too often, leaders assume a parental or hortatory tone in their speech. It sounds unfriendly for someone to say: "You may be seated." For a host in a home to use such language would seem condescending. More fitting in home and in church is the invitation: "Please be seated." Similarly, an effective leader will invite people to prayer rather than adjure them or instruct them in how to pray with sincerity. An invitation to prayer is proper (e.g., "let us pray" or "please join me in prayer"). Giving directions on how one ought to pray is not. (We often hear, for instance, "open your hearts, now, to worship the Lord. He deserves your praise. Don't be afraid to raise your hands and move your bodies.") Such instructions assume the voice of parent: do this, don't do that, do as I say, and so on. The hospitable leader speaks humbly. However earnest the exhortation to pray in a prescribed manner may be, it presents an attitude of hubris rather than humility. This borders on idolatry because, in this conversation, God is the parent and we are all the children. Let God exhort through Scripture or sermon. Let the hosts invite, accommodate, facilitate. Let them not impose demands or pressure people to act in certain ways.

Conclusion

Worship is communication. Its primary function is to draw people into an encounter with God. The adoration that occurs in Sunday worship requires speech and silence, ritual and symbol, music and poetry and other artistic expression. Worship leaders each have a role in facilitating the tri-directional dialogue of worship. And, like good hosts, they have a need to know when to speak and when to remain silent, when to step in to be helpful and when to retire for the sake of the gathering's success. For worshipers to see the connection between the adoration of Sunday and the action of the week, worship leaders have a responsibility to see that worship communicates as it intends. Accordingly, we have considered eight issues for which worship leaders can take responsibility to ensure that worship communicates in the intended ways. We have also uncovered a number of liturgical and theological principles relating to the way that adoration and action are articulated.

1. Worship is made up of speech, silence, art, and ritual; each of these has the capacity to signify in multiple ways: to engage the imagination, to point to particular meanings, and to symbolize things that are difficult to articulate discursively.
2. It is the quality of worship as indexical sign that points the moment of adoration toward Christian action.
3. Worship leaders, whatever their particular roles, have the responsibility to establish clear and congruent communication, whether from God to people, people to God, or people to people.
4. Worshipers gain an awareness of the connection between worship and the mission of God when *missio Dei* is imbedded as expectation and anticipation in the hour of adoration.
5. Additionally, worship communicates what God wants to do in the world when faithful action bursts forth from the lively dialogue that takes place between God and God's people in Sunday worship. Performing Christian action is performing the gospel.

6

Extraordinary Worship

> And Sunday after Sunday, we nourish a hope, faint and often unfulfilled, that our worship will take us to places of beauty and meaning we do not normally inhabit, places we have helped to create, places we will return from, refreshed and whole. . . . We come to this setting to hear the sacred story and pray the great prayer with sisters and brothers, hoping to feel enlarged, expansive, full of praise, better than we are, knowing this is the way God sees us in Christ Jesus.[1]
>
> Virginia Sloyan

This chapter concludes the first portion of this book and provides the last theological building block for our consideration of the ways that worship and mission are related. I have been asserting that worship is both adoration of God in worship assemblies and active performance of the gospel message in the world. In the first chapter, I considered the common ecumenical order for worship—gathering, Word, sacraments, and sending—and acknowledged the missionary state of the church in the world. In chapter 2, I reviewed the ways in which the adoration of God and enacting the mission of God are elements of the same worshipful activity. In chapter 3, I identified strands of the present-day liturgical convergence and recognized the ecumenical fourfold pattern of worship as an expression of the historic wisdom of the church at

1. Virginia Sloyan, as quoted in Huck, *A Sourcebook about Liturgy*, 155.

worship. I discussed another expression of liturgical harmonization in chapter 4, the revitalized use of the arts in churches, even those that have historically eschewed the arts as fitting modes of liturgical expression. In the previous chapter I attended to the ways in which worship communicates and the responsibility of worship leaders to plan, speak, and act in ways that are congruent with their intentions, especially those relating to worship as mission.

In this chapter I take up the matter of contextual theology and its relationship to the missional church. I seek to demonstrate how an understanding of the historic wisdom of the church that is brought alongside local traditions, issues, and opportunities will enable worship to be properly particularized for local celebration. To begin, let's consider what is at stake when worshiping communities misapprehend the distinctive qualities that give them shape, coherence, and theological footing.

Throwing the Baby Out with the Baptismal Water

There is a temptation among congregations to attempt worship renewal at the expense of those things that provide their core identity. A famous example occurred, for instance, in San Francisco's most well-known congregation, Glide Memorial United Methodist Church. Under the leadership of Pastor Cecil Williams, the church determined in 1967 to do away with the symbol of the cross in the congregation's worship space. The pastor's rationale, as the church's own history relates, was for the congregation to "celebrate life and living."[2] That move resulted in a mass exodus of the congregation's traditional Methodist members. When this central symbol of the faith was removed, also jettisoned was what many saw as the congregation's theological birthright. Soon thereafter, the church shortened its name to Glide Memorial Church. (Today, the church has returned crosses to its worship space and reclaimed "United Methodist" as part of its name.)

Attempts at renewal in Christian churches are a commendable practice—indeed, it is the aim of this book to encourage them—yet renewal must be done with an awareness of each congregation's core identity lest changes in worship and congregational life have unintended negative consequences. A renewal practice occasionally employed in my own Lutheran denomination will demonstrate what is at stake when renewal is undertaken without regard for those things that provide core identity.[3]

2. Available at the church Web site, www.glide.org/Timeline.aspx.
3. Those seeking additional examples of this trend among Lutheran churches to accommodate themselves to cultural and megachurch influences will find an analysis of them in Stephen Ellingson's *The Megachurch and the Mainline*, in which he does a case study on nine Lutheran congregations in the San Francisco Bay area, several of which have elected to abandon distinctive Lutheran tenets for the sake of being culturally attuned. A telling comment made by a pastor

One of the distinctive qualities of Lutheranism is its carefully articulated view of baptism as the entry point for faith. Luther argued strongly that baptism, whether infant or adult, is the vehicle by which God draws persons into the community of faith.

> Thus we see what a splendid thing baptism is, which rescues us from the very jaws of the devil, makes us God's own children, overcomes and takes away sin, daily strengthens the new [person] in us, and always continues with us until, snatched from the misery of the present, we shall have attained to the eternal glory beyond. Accordingly, everyone should treat baptism as a garment for everyday use. Every day [one] should be found in faith and amid its fruits; . . . when, therefore, we have once received in baptism the forgiveness of sin, it remains with us day by day as long as we live.[4]

It is not mere water that accomplishes these things, but "the Word and our trust in this Word, which is with, in, and among the water, and faith, which trusts this Word of God in the water."[5] Luther considered baptism to be a once-and-for-all event (thus, there would never be a need to rebaptize a person who chose to move into the Lutheran fold) but one that has daily significance. Baptism calls for daily reflection and renewal in the life of the believer. Accordingly, Lutheran worship celebrates baptisms communally and remembers the place of baptism frequently in preaching and liturgy. The newest Lutheran hymnal, *Evangelical Lutheran Worship*, includes a rite of "Thanksgiving for Baptism" that can be celebrated at any service that does not contain the actual celebration of the sacrament.

Because baptismal theology is central to Lutheran theological identity, it would be a loss for Lutheran worshiping communities to dispense with the baptismal focus in life and worship. Still, in accommodation to the church growth movement of the late twentieth century and its strategy to remove "churchy" things from worship in order to appeal to baby boomers,[6] some Lutheran congregations adopted worship practices that were more aligned with seeker services and their frontier meeting roots.[7] They built worship spaces

---

from one such church bears witness to the trend: "What keeps me going as a pastor? The minister's edition of *The Lutheran Book of Worship*? [*long pause*] No, that won't help." His quip, Ellingson notes, was met with peals of laughter (2).

4. Luther, *Luther's Large Catechism*, trans. Lenker, 137.

5. Luther, "Small Catechism," in *The Book of Concord*, trans. and ed. Theodore G. Tappert (Philadelphia: Fortress, 1959), 337–56.

6. For a description of the preference for minimizing Christian symbols in megachurches, see Johnson, "Disconnected Rituals," in Johnson, *The Conviction of Things Not Seen*, 53–66. Especially striking is this quotation from a guide at Willow Creek Community Church: "In fact, you will see no Christian symbolism here at all. The metaphor or image we are trying to project here is corporate or business, not traditional church. Now, we do have a cross. We bring it out for special occasions, . . . we think of the cross as a prop" (63–64).

7. See Senn, *Christian Liturgy*, 688.

that bore resemblance to auditoriums and hotel banquet halls. They displaced the strong symbols of worship and supplanted the tradition of Lutheran hymns and chorales with songs reminiscent of the idioms of popular music. Baptismal fonts, usually located in prominent places in Lutheran churches, were removed, along with other theological symbols. Such churches sought to meet the marketing needs of baby boomers in worship music and worship idiom as well as in congregational programming. This created congregations of people who, as Frank Senn has observed, had "a great deal of confidence" that nevertheless needed to be shored up through self-help support groups and therapeutic preaching.[8]

The problem encountered in these churches was that they established worship practices and church programming that ran counter to a theology that places Christian identity in God's call for sinners to be baptized and washed daily in the waters of regeneration. Lutheran theology holds that only through God's ongoing grace, initiated in baptism, can the believer find his or her true identity. In trying to reach out, the Lutherans in these congregations lost out. In throwing out the traditions of Lutheran liturgy, worship architecture, and congregational life they correspondingly jettisoned much of the theology that has historically identified Lutheran Christians. These churches effectively threw the baby out with the baptismal water. When Lutherans cease to be identifiable by such theological distinctives as baptismal identity, they run the risk of losing not only their traditional worship practices but also their theological character.

Since the turn of this century, there has been a renewed interest among Lutheran worshiping communities, including those that sought to avoid being overtly Lutheran, in missional theology.[9] They are asking, what is God doing in the world and how can we align our ministry with God's projects in the world? With a renewed emphasis on *missio Dei*, worship in these Lutheran congregations has become less concerned about appearing to be *too* Lutheran. There is decreasing interest in setting aside the use of signs and symbols that have the indexical capacity to point to distinct theological ideas. Lutheran worship, as evidenced by the constellation of worship materials that is currently being produced by the leadership of the Evangelical Lutheran Church in America, is shaped by the distinctive theological qualities that identify Lutheran Christians. Missionally focused Lutherans seem not to be embarrassed by such things but instead embrace the baptized baby (and adult) and the baptismal water as welcome and familiar signs, rich with shared meaning.

8. Ibid.
9. An example of this reversing trend is Community Church of Joy, a church of the Evangelical Lutheran Church in America. In its literature, it recounts that as it began in 1974, it sought to be "a church that was relevant for real people in the real world." By the turn of the century, the church reordered its focus: "With the new millennium came the call to focus on making disciples of Jesus and serving the community as a dynamic missions center." See the church's Web site, www.joyonline.org/our_stories.php.

These two examples from mainline Methodist and Lutheran churches demonstrate a principle that is applicable to every worshiping community. Proper worship renewal cannot be achieved at the expense of a tradition's theological birthright.[10] One can just as easily imagine the loss that would be felt by traditional Baptists or Pentecostals if they found their churches drifting toward a highly articulated and formalized liturgy. The purpose behind seminary training for pastors in denominational theology and polity is to safeguard congregations from capitulating to theological, liturgical, or cultural whimsy.

At the same time, it is necessary for every worshiping community to embrace the particularities of their context in such a way that the idioms of their worship reflect a balance between their core theological identity and local culture.

Balancing Constants with Particularities

Missional worship, while it can wisely be built on a fourfold ecumenical order that can give it shape, focus, plot, and direction, should at the same time be particularized to express the distinctive qualities of a given worshiping community. Some of those particularities derive from a community's denominational or historical tradition. Others relate to the local, geographical, social, and cultural circumstances in which each congregation is set. What God is doing in the life of a given congregation has much to do with what is going on in local communities. Worship that is fitting within these communities will represent and reflect the local particularities. To hold the things that are constant for a tradition in tension with things that are local suggests that it would be inappropriate for Lutherans, Methodists, and Baptists in Kenya to worship identically as Lutherans, Methodists, and Baptists in Kansas. There ought to be some commonality between Baptists in one part of the world and those in another. But those commonalities are harmonized with contextual particularities in order to create worship in a given community that demonstrates both constancy and diversity. The tension between these two forces has been helpfully described by Pedrito Maynard-Reid:

> What *are* the constants? . . . It seems fair to deduce that the ageless, universal, common and core factors in worship are (1) an assembling or gathering of the people of God to experience the numinous (or divine presence) in encounter with their neighbors, (2) a celebration of festivals and sacraments, (3) the presentation of the Word in Scripture readings, study and sermon, and (4) prayer. . . . These, I believe, must remain constant if we are not to degenerate into what has been called "particularization," resulting in a narrow religious provincialism that

10. While this opinion may sound strictly subjective, I will build a case for what is *proper* for worship in any given setting in the rest of this chapter.

would cause us to lose a sense of the church's catholicity. Yet particularity used appropriately is essential to the mixture of constancy and diversity.[11]

Successfully striking a balance between constants and particularities in worship calls for doing local theology.

Local Theology

There is a significant and growing literature in what is variously described as contextualized, localized, or folk theology.[12] Local theology derives from an array of disciplines. Cultural anthropology provides tools for interpretation of cultures and their ways of expression, ritualizing, and meaning making. Semiotics gives guidance as to how symbols and signs can be understood within communities as cultural codes. Dealing with the differences between people groups and subcultures within them draws on the resources of ethnography. The particular makeup of a given context requires demographic research. The theological dimensions relating to these social considerations are added through the study and practice of missiology and ecclesiology. Missional theologian Mark Lau Branson demonstrates how these disciplines relate when he says "meanings and practices are to cohere to a local on-the-ground church that is called and sent by God; and the word 'church' in the New Testament is primarily a reference to such local groups."[13] In this brief statement alone, we see the interplay and implication of semiotics, anthropology, ecclesiology, missiology, and biblical hermeneutics.

Local theology, in its richly interdisciplinary approach to theology, holds several principles as central to informing our understanding of worship that is missional in character. Leonora Tubbs Tisdale, a teacher of preaching who argues that sermons need to be expressions of local theology, summarizes three core anthropological assumptions behind local theology: "Cultural anthropologists tell us that people are, in certain respects, (1) *like all others* (sharing certain universals with the whole human race); (2) *like no others* (having distinctive traits that mark them as individuals); and (3) *like some others* (sharing cultural traits with a particular group of people)."[14]

From the field of missiology and the foundational work of Lesslie Newbigin (who follows Karl Barth) comes a trinitarian emphasis on missional theology where "the focus is on the sending work of God: God's sending the Son into

---

11. Maynard-Reid, *Diverse Worship*, 43–44; italics in the original.

12. See, for example, Tisdale, *Preaching as Local Theology*; Bevans, *Models of Contextual Theology*; Sedmak, *Doing Local Theology*; and Schreiter, *The New Catholicity*.

13. Branson, "Ecclesiology and Leadership for the Missional Church," in Van Gelder, *The Missional Church in Context*, 102.

14. Tisdale, *Preaching as Local Theology*, 11; italics in the original.

Sidebar 6.1: What Is a Congregational Idiom?

"Idiom"... incorporates all the symbolic forms by which a congregation communicates its own peculiar identity. It includes verbal symbols (such as stories and jokes, sermons, favorite hymns, oral and written histories, and church publications) and nonverbal symbols (such as ritual acts, architecture, gestures, and visual arts). All are significant components of the symbolic language through which communities of faith give meaning and order to their lives.

Leonora Tubbs Tisdale, Preaching as Local Theology and Folk Art *(Minneapolis: Fortress, 1997), 15.*

---

the world to accomplish redemption, and the Father and Son's sending the Spirit into the world to create the church and lead it into participation in God's mission."[15] Additionally, Craig Van Gelder has observed that the gospel is inherently translatable to every culture: "Jesus took on the particularity of his context as the incarnate good news. But even in his particularity, he retained his universal relevance. This is part of the mystery of the good news of Jesus Christ." Thus the gospel "is inherently translatable into every particular cultural context" and is "the good news to *everyone, everywhere.*"[16] This means, further, that the church and its ministries are translatable into every context and "able to find expression *everywhere.*"[17]

Given the similarities and differences between people and people groups, as with preaching, worship needs to be contextualized so as to make the universal practices for Christian assembly appropriate to local communities. This means that each congregation or worshiping community will have its own appropriate balance between constancy and diversity in shaping its gatherings. Accordingly, each community will develop its own idiomatic approach to worship.

A semiotic view of such balanced gatherings would reveal that the signs, symbols, rituals, and language of each could be understood on three levels. First, there would be elements common to Christians of all times and places (people are like all others). These would typically include the centrality of the Word and sacraments; the use of the cross, table, font, and pulpit as the central symbols around which people gather; the use of prayer and music in some form; and so forth. Second, there would be elements of worship that derive from denomination or tradition (people are like some others). A Pentecostal church in any location, for example, would likely be marked by the use of invocations of the Spirit, speaking in tongues, and prophetic interpretations. These would properly stand alongside the universal things

15. Van Gelder, *The Missional Church in Context*, 29.
16. Ibid., 33–34; italics in the original.
17. Ibid., 34; italics in the original.

(preaching, baptisms, etc.). Third, there would be those things best known, valued, or understood by people gathered from a given neighborhood or community (people are like no others). I attended, for instance, a Lutheran service of worship in a village in Tanzania. Much of the worship, though performed in Swahili, I was able to apprehend because of the constants: there were hymns and songs, reading and preaching of the Word, signs of baptism and communion even though neither were celebrated on that occasion. As a Lutheran, I could also identify many elements of worship that represented our distinct theological and liturgical identity: the use of vestments, seasonal banners and paraments (decorative pulpit and altar cloths), presentation of a series of lectionary readings, strong attention to the preached Word, use of hymnbooks, recitation of the Apostles' Creed and the Lord's Prayer, a recognizably Lutheran order of worship, a mix of male and female clergy and lay leadership, and so forth. There were also those signs and gestures that were best or only understood by the local worshipers: the mixed Western/African architecture, the use of a drum as the main accompaniment to singing, the unison bowing dance that choir members all performed at precise moments during the singing of an anthem, songs that emerged within the context of the East African church, references to local congregational ministries, and the length of the sermon (forty-five minutes, where in most American Lutheran settings twenty-five minutes would be the norm). There was one element of local theology we might all wish were a universal quality of worship: my companions and I attended one of two Sunday services that were so crowded that people gathered in the church's doorway and in the outside courtyard in order to participate in the weekly adoration of God.

One might legitimately argue at this point that the observations drawn above are hardly new ideas. They are merely common assumptions made about worship that is properly inculturated. Such a conclusion would be accurate. Yet one regularly finds worshiping communities that fail to understand that the most appropriate local expressions for their adoration of God are those that are rich mixtures of broad (universal and traditional) and narrow (local) contextual expressions. One can easily find churches in Africa, South America, and Asia following megachurch worship practices that were developed in the frontier regions of eighteenth-century North America and given contemporary expression through use of worship songs and choruses that reflect Western and Northern cultural patterns and philosophies (emphasizing, e.g., the individualism of American culture). Equally, one can find churches in North America that have lost their traditional and cultural distinction because in attempting to draw more people in, they have simply adapted worship practices from those that seem to be working for churches across town, or from a church that holds a worship conference to peddle its own unique brand of culturally relevant worship.

It should be no surprise that such wholesale absorption of another community's worship practices regularly results in the loss of identity within a local congregation and a failure of experimental worship idioms to take deep hold or adequately express the faith of communities of persons that are rich with local character. The failure of such worship renewal experiments would be expected by a semiotician. It is understood as a first principle of semiotics that human communities resist losing a sense of their tribal identity.[18] If that tribe is a Presbyterian church of one hundred in a small town in Nebraska, there will be natural resistance when its leaders attempt to impose models for worship developed in a suburban Southern California charismatic congregation of five thousand members. Such a failure will also be no surprise to those who know that missional theology has a strong local component that seeks appropriate expressions to address what God is uniquely doing in particular neighborhoods.

Missional Theology and Contextual Worship

In order to see the direct connections between contextualized worship and missional theology, we turn to the following seven-point description of missional methodology offered by Craig Van Gelder. He explains that missional congregations have these aptitudes. They have the capacity to (1) read their context, (2) anticipate new insights into the gospel, (3) anticipate reciprocity, (4) understand that they are contextual, thus also particular, (5) understand that their ministry is contextual, thus also practical, (6) understand that doing theology is always contextual, thus also perspectival, and (7) understand that organization is always contextual, thus also provisional.[19] Of these seven aptitudes, five are especially pertinent to our understanding of the connection between missional theology and contextualized worship (passing over Van Gelder's second and third points as less material to the present discussion).

1. *Mission and worship that can read context.* "It is critical," says Van Gelder, "that congregations develop the ability to read a context."[20] The reason here is self-evident. To align one's church with what God is doing in the world means that a congregation needs to be aware of what God is doing locally. This anticipates both "what God is doing" and "what God wants to do" in a given setting. Regarding worship, the expectation here is that missional worship is attuned both to the expressions of a local culture for giving adoration to God as well as to the unique opportunities for serving God in the community. The capacity for exegeting a congregation, which Tisdale demands for preaching,[21]

18. Danesi, *Of Cigarettes, High Heels, and Other Interesting Things,* 19.
19. Van Gelder, *The Missional Church in Context,* 38–41.
20. Ibid., 38.
21. See Tisdale, *Preaching as Local Theology,* esp. chap. 3, "Exegeting a Congregation," 56–90.

is critical for discovering the ways in which a community of faith can shape its assemblies for worship and send its people out into the action of its local mission and ministry.

2. *Mission and worship as particular.* Van Gelder asserts that to speak of local congregations presupposes that they are catholic, "bearing the full marks of the church universal and the historic Christian faith." They are at the same time necessarily congregations of persons in a particular time and place. "This means that there is always a certain provisional character to the church as it lives within a context. As contexts change, the church should expect to change. . . . In reality, there can be no model congregations. While there can be illustrative examples of contextualized congregations that might help inform others, no congregation can function as a model for others."[22]

Similarly, contextualized worship bears the marks of the universal church (constancy) as well as those of its location (diversity). It adapts as the community of faith changes yet resists capitulation to model theologies and liturgies that are disconnected from the historic wisdom of the church universal and the particularities of tradition and location. Its provisional nature takes into account that God is constantly bringing new opportunities for adoration and action into each worshiping place and that to seek alignment with what God is doing locally is at the core of the church's mission. "It is important to remember," Van Gelder strongly advises, "that it is the work of the Spirit to lead a congregation to contextualize itself within its particular location."[23]

3. *Mission and worship as practical.* Van Gelder emphasizes that all forms of ministry within a given setting have to "bear the patterns and shape of the culture" in which the ministry occurs. Because the gathering of a community for worship is one of the key and central ministries of a congregation, this aspect of missional methodology is particularly applicable to worship. Worship also represents a key aspect of a congregation's program; accordingly, Van Gelder's further explanation applies: "While a basic programmatic framework may inform the development of ministry, each congregation is best served by thinking carefully about how such a program might need to be adapted to fit its particular ministry and the context it serves."[24] Likewise, a basic worship framework can inform a congregation's adoration, but it too may need to be adapted to accommodate the local particularities of a given community of faith.

4. *Mission and worship as perspectival.* Here, Van Gelder is referencing the universal aspects of Christian theology, noting that they have been shaped by historical perspectives that "have embedded within them elements of the culture and context in which they were formulated." The argument here is

22. Van Gelder, *The Missional Church in Context*, 40–41.
23. Ibid., 41.
24. Ibid.

for theological and confessional statements to be interpreted and translated when "moving from one context to another."[25] For the application here to extend to liturgies is elementary. The historic wisdom of the church at worship provides shape and continuity for localized liturgies. At the same time, it requires discernment, or local wisdom, to determine how those patterns can be translated and articulated appropriately for each place of worship.

5. *Mission and worship as provisional.* "The challenge," reports Van Gelder, "is for the church to bring the gospel into diverse contexts as it allows the leading of the Spirit to give birth to approaches that are informed by the historic Christian faith, while it also reflects the realities of the context in which congregations are now planted." These approaches will be provisional, that is, "adaptive and flexible," rather than standardized and prescribed.[26] His concern here is for congregational organization. But the principle bears immediately on the shaping of worship assemblies. They, too, can be adaptive and flexible. One of the frustrations people express relative to traditional liturgical services is that they can be inflexible, rote, and impersonal. Free church worship, on the other hand, can be seen as too flexible, chaotic, and lacking in form. A provisional perspective urges that liturgies of any idiom can be lively and suited to a people and place and moment. Formal liturgies can be animated incarnations of prayer and praise, as they are shaped according to the leading of the Spirit. This takes into account that God's Spirit is not merely a passing force but a source of inspiration as worship is planned and rehearsed, as sermons are researched and written, as music is selected and practiced, and as a congregation draws on the rich gifts of local artists. Free church worship can also be enriched by operating within an understanding that whatever its formal structure, it is a liturgy that God seeks to inhabit. Through it, the Spirit may move freely and spontaneously; but the Spirit also moves through the work of those who plan carefully and execute their roles with care. Furthermore, the Spirit provides provisional gifts for worship: folk expressions and ways of speaking, music of a local culture or setting, the artistry of a community's children and other creative people, and so forth.

One of the key provisional aspects pertaining to worship is that the context of worship is constantly shifting. On a local level, for example, people are moving into and out of a neighborhood, crises develop that give rise to opportunities for worshipful action, and seasons change and bring with them special needs for worship both within and beyond the church walls. Likewise, within a congregation, situations are always in flux. There is a different group of people at the early service than at the late service. Events occur during Sunday morning that may bear on the hour of adoration. Week by week, special challenges and opportunities arise that need to be taken into

25. Ibid., 41–42.
26. Ibid., 42.

account. It is a matter for local worship committees and/or teams to think carefully and weekly about shifts in the context and make accommodation to what God is doing moment by moment in a congregation and within the larger community.

The Global Context of Worship

I have been arguing for a contextual view of worship that takes into account what God is doing in each worshiping location. Adoration and action ought to reflect localized theology. At the risk of sounding contradictory, I want to add a final consideration to the discussion of contextual theology. Today it is clear that awareness of the entire planet enters into local discussion and contextual consideration. At the moment of this writing, the world has been made aware that a cyclone has devastated the country of Myanmar and over a hundred thousand people have perished. Suddenly, this important piece of information is news in every nation, and response to the disaster has become the responsibility of people around the globe. Not only have nations rushed supplies to meet the crushing needs, local communities of faith have begun to respond as quickly and effectively as they can. This is just one example of how things are for us in an age of information and worldwide networking. The point is that while we attempt to balance adoration and action between universals and particularities, there can be no discontinuity between one local community and another, no matter how distant. World disasters and other major events are part of the context of a local congregation. Responding to world needs is part of the local action undertaken by faithful worshipers in every setting. For worship and mission to be contextual, then, requires knowledge of a broad network of communities starting with persons in neighborhoods, and reach-

---

Sidebar 6.2: The Diminishing World

When I was a child, this common household circumstance occurred: When a youngster did not finish his or her peas, a parent would say, "Eat your peas—there are children starving in China." The child would usually consider it high humor to reply, "Okay, then send my peas to China." This common exchange applied to life in North America fifty years ago. It no longer applies, because the world has changed so dramatically that there can be a strong expectation that the food we cannot eat should be brought to places of great need. This is a lively paradox: what we do locally is a response both to community and world needs; and what we do globally is our local calling. Perhaps a fitting parental response today would be, "Eat your peas so that you are strong enough to help the people in the world who don't have the opportunity for good nutrition that you do."

ing to villages, towns, and cities within regions, states, and districts within nations, countries within continents, and hemispheres within the globe.

How can local worship recognize and express these aspects of the global context without trying to be something or somewhere they are not? How can they relate to global issues with integrity? Here are a number of practices (since contextual worship is practical) that have served congregations well:

- ministry trips sponsored by local congregations
- choir and other tours made by congregational groups (see sidebar 6.3)
- expanding a congregation's song repertoire to include global music in worship (see sidebar 6.4)
- invitations to musicians and groups from other communities and nations beyond a congregation's usual reach
- hosting international speakers to give truthful witness to the state of the church in other places
- asking members of specific ethnicities within a congregation to host a meal for the congregation during which aspects of culture are taught
- holding international fairs or picnics at which cultural foods, games, and stories are shared

Ordinaries, Propers, and Contextualized Worship

In establishing the terms employed in this book in chapter 1, I indicated that I would take a new look at an old set of liturgical categories that have helped to give shape and propriety to Christian worship through the centuries. The terms *ordinary* and *proper* derive from the classic shape of the Roman Catholic Mass. Ordinaries are those elements established as invariable elements of the Roman ordo. They consist of the following parts: (1) *Kyrie eleison* (Lord have mercy), an introductory prayer; (2) *Gloria in excelsis* (Glory to God in the highest), a song of praise that begins with the angel's words from Luke 2:14; (3) *Credo* (creed); (4) *Sanctus* (holy, holy, holy), a Eucharistic hymn that is based on Isaiah 6:3 and contained within the Eucharistic prayer; (5) *Benedictus* (Blessed is he), part of the Eucharistic prayer response that comes from Jewish tradition; and (6) *Agnus Dei* (Lamb of God), a sung prayer that follows the Eucharistic prayer. The regular use of these elements of worship gave rise to composers creating musical settings of the ordinary texts. While originally used for worship, many of these settings have emerged from worship as concert pieces, and the texts continue to inspire composers to write new settings that are prepared exclusively for concert audiences. Today the term *ordinary* is used in a derivative sense, especially among Protestants. It refers to those elements of Sunday worship that are used regularly within a given worship

Sidebar 6.3: The Touring Choir

Choir tours are one way for local worshiping communities to gain a sense of the global context of worship today. The following excerpts, adapted from an article encouraging congregations to sponsor tours of its choirs, indicate the benefits of such a ministry.

There are many reasons for people to travel: adventure, curiosity, to visit friends, to see historically important sights, and so on. . . . But there is one predominant reason for church choirs to visit Christians of other cultures: to fulfill a sense of Christian mission. This is what makes a choir tour different than an ordinary vacation. It is important for choirs to understand that the tour is not simply a trip to an interesting place but that they are going to share the gospel with fellow Christians, to participate jointly in worship and communion, and to learn of the faith experiences and struggles of others.

Having such a mission in mind will help a choir determine where to visit. Touring companies will take your choir anywhere in the world it wishes to go. It is up to the choir to determine the nature of its mission and then to discover the geographic regions that would allow for its accomplishment. It is then important to share this information with the prospective participants. . . . Understanding the mission will help them to realize that touring in less-traveled areas may provide the greatest opportunity for ministry. . . .

It is recommended that the choir . . . establish a mission statement [that] will give focus to the preparations made for a trip. . . . The statement should be brief, direct, and should give a clear statement of the expected ministry results.

Becoming involved in a choir tour also creates benefits for the choir's congregation. The congregation will be asked to support the mission of the choir both financially and through prayer and encouragement. As preparations unfold before the tour and as experiences are shared following the tour, the congregation learns of the needs, concerns, and struggles of the Christians visited by the choir. In some circumstances, the tour may open doors for an ongoing relationship with the churches visited by the choir, and the mission begun by the choir can be expanded to be a continuing ministry of the congregation.

Why not encourage your congregation to embark upon a ministry that will involve its choir and other members in being instruments of peace and unity? Once you have entered into this kind of communion, your prayers will never be the same. The faces, struggles, and situations of Christian sisters and brothers around the world will forever be a part of your experience. The nameless multitudes for which you may once have prayed will become people with names and faces, and you will know firsthand that you share a faith that binds you together.

Adapted from Clayton J. Schmit, "The Touring Church Choir: Sharing the Gospel through Song," in Cross Accent *no. 5 (July 1995): 40–46.*

Sidebar 6.4: Singing Globally in Local Congregations

There can be good reasons for singing music from the world church in local assemblies. While noting again C. Michael Hawn's cautions offered against "meaningless eclecticism" and "liturgical ethno-tourism" in chapter 4, we can learn from Madeleine Forell Marshall who offers insights into the values of singing global prayers.

> The Christian world is a large and diverse community and it behooves modern Christians to learn as much about the Christian experience of people unlike themselves as possible. We have many good motives for such education: We may be motivated by love and concern, by brotherhood and sisterhood, or by the simple, human fascination with what's different. Or we may be motivated by the need to hear the Gospel, to be preached to. Certainly the profound faith of Bishop Desmond Tutu or of Bishop Romero inspires and moves us. Or we may know our need to be led out of our own parochialism, our little private world of Christian people just like us. We may realize how we tend, without such consciousness, to take possession of Christianity, to define and limit it to our own culture. Most of us want to resist the sort of Christian colonialism that has marred too much mission effort in the past.
>
> Contemporary Third-World and liberation hymnody in our churches seems intended, in the first instance, to widen our horizons, to break us out of parochialism. It is, further, something of a political act. The motives we scanned above are largely political. They imply that we need liberation from our own white, powerful, colonial perspective. They imply that we can somehow express our solidarity with Mandela and Bishop Tutu and the victims of oppression in Central America when we sing African and Hispanic hymnody. Hymnody can raise our consciousness. Besides, solidarity feels good!
>
> *Madeleine Forell Marshall,* Common Hymnsense
> *(Chicago: GIA Publications, 1995), 161–62.*

---

setting. In some settings (especially Anglican, Episcopalian, and Lutheran) the *Kyrie, Gloria, Credo, Sanctus, Benedictus,* and *Agnus Dei* are still used as the ordinaries that shape Eucharistic services. In less traditionally bound settings, the ordinaries might include invariable elements such as a creed, the Lord's Prayer, and the Aaronic blessing.

Propers, in relation to the Roman Mass, are those variable elements selected to pertain specifically to the liturgical day or season of worship. They have historically included the introit (entrance chant), psalmody, the gospel acclamation (or alleluia verse), an offertory chant, and so forth. Derivatively, the term can be used to refer to any element of worship that varies according to the day or season (readings, sermon, prayers, songs and hymns, etc.).

The foregoing paragraphs indicate the established uses of these terms. For purposes of encouraging worship celebrations that are well balanced between the constants of Christian practice and the particularities of local context, I propose that these terms can be given additional nuance. To state that an hour of adoration is ordinary does more than suggest reference to its invariable qualities. It implies that it is mundane, without interest, uninspired. To suggest that worship is proper implies that there is some elite liturgical perspective that passes judgment on the correctness or incorrectness of liturgical form. Neither of these implications is constructive.

I propose that we understand these terms in the following way: Ordinary worship is that which, in connection with the church's historical wisdom and denominational traditions, embraces certain key constancies, including assembling as the body of Christ, gathering around the Word along with central signs and sacramental celebrations (and remembrances), and utilizing those words and gestures that ground our response to the Word in catholic (universally Christian) practices. The expression of these ordinary elements of worship can and should be enriched in each worship event by calling on the rich array of possibilities available to the local worshiping assembly so that what is ordinarily executed can be done with extraordinary grace and impact. Chief among the local possibilities is the presence of the Holy Spirit to inspire the most ordinary modes of praise and prayer to be expressions that are highly connective among and deeply resonant within the hearts of those assembled to worship.

Proper worship, I propose, consists of a rich and regular balance of ordinary things (constancies) with things appropriate to a particular worshiping community (particularities). They may include such things as denominational theology and liturgy, historical particularities associated with each tradition, judicatory requirements or points of reference, congregational distinctives, demographic considerations, global and local issues that deserve attention and reflection, the range of spiritual gifts (including the arts and artists) available to or within a community, financial resources, human tastes and expectations, awareness of shared public symbols,[27] issues relating to architecture and technology, language and translation considerations, and various issues relating to music. It is, again, the balance of such a range of local possibilities with the universal aspects of worship that allow for it to be entirely appropriate yet extraordinarily rich and refreshingly different each time and in each place that God's people gather. In other words, the hour of adoration will always be *ordinary* in certain aspects, but it can also, and at the same time, be refreshingly *extra*ordinary when it is appropriately (that is, *proper*ly) articulated.

27. Following Carl Jung, Lawrence Hoffman draws a distinction between symbols (which bring things to mind) and signs (which can be identified in terms of what they mean). He notes, "a group's ritual symbol is an item that directs its participants immediately and with absolutely no commentary or explanation to an awareness of an experience or value that they hold in common . . . even though they cannot explain or even agree on the reason why" (*The Art of Public Prayer*, 20–21).

Appropriate Music

Music deserves special attention because it has been at the center of the so-called worship wars for several decades. Musical idiom is only one element in determining what is appropriate in worship, but it largely determines people's perception of worship idioms. For example, a traditional liturgy in the Methodist tradition will appear to be *contemporary worship* when it primarily employs recently written praise choruses. Free worship appears to be traditional if it employs hymns predominantly. But what music is appropriate? Two answers present themselves. The first has to do with music that is generally appropriate for use during Christian adoration. The second has to do with the local issues that suggest how a congregation can weigh its musical choices to be most appropriate for local prayer and praise.

First, general considerations. Music (along with song texts) that is appropriate for Christian worship does the following:

- gives predominance to the voice of the gathered assembly (instead of leaders, choirs, or vocal and instrumental ensembles)
- provides a balanced palette of trinitarian references
- expands our metaphoric and imagistic understanding about God and God's relationship to humanity
- emphasizes God's actions over human capacities or accomplishments
- honestly represents the range of emotions that adoration expresses (praise, lament, anger, distress, despair, joy, etc.)
- broadens the worshiping community's sense of the church and represents expressions of faith from those beyond immediate awareness
- enlarges a community's scope of musical propriety and taste
- teaches the tenets of faith and proclaims the gospel
- is executed with excellence according to a best account standard
- allows for ready assent to the prayers, praise, and proclamation of the people

These general musical parameters immediately suggest a number of things that ought to be avoided:

- musical leadership that calls attention to itself through poor preparation, egoistic showmanship, overly stylized or idiosyncratic expression, playing too loudly (whether organs or drums), and so forth
- trying to make up for poor worship space acoustics by turning up the volume on amplified music (which fails to increase the sound of the congregation's voice)

- melodies that are too difficult or pitched too high to sing
- use of song texts that emphasize our human capacity for prayer, praise, love
- overuse of song texts that use the first person singular ("I will love You forever")
- overuse of song texts that emphasize a single person of the Trinity
- use of songs that are sentimental (that is, nostalgic, recalling only positive or romantic notions)
- careless use of musical idioms that are highly associated with secular culture (one can imagine, e.g., settings in which the use of country music, hip-hop, or jazz would seem inappropriate)
- physical placement of musicians and instruments in locations that obscure or eclipse the central symbols of the gathering space (e.g., a drum set in front of the altar—an all too common practice)

Second, what are the local considerations that can assist a worshiping community in making appropriate musical choices? Here are a few:

- the use of local musicians on every level (professional, amateur, youth, and children), expecting them to give their best account in performances and presentations
- encouragement for musicians to create new songs for a day, a season, or a place
- knowledge of a community's social and ethnic cultures and the musical idioms that represent them
- awareness of a community's canon of hymns and songs
- capacity for choirs and ensembles to learn and present complex music as a means by which to expand a congregation's interests and enrich people's perceptions
- awareness of a congregation's ability to read music and learn new songs
- assessment of a congregation's ability to sing and capacity to teach them to sing more strongly
- awareness of the acoustic architecture within a worship space
- ability to address acoustic issues structurally and technologically
- capacity to rearrange music to take advantage of local artists (e.g., adding a flute descant to a song or having a high school brass quartet accompany Easter hymns)
- encouragement for church musicians at all levels to attend conferences and training events (and for the congregation to pay for the training)

Sidebar 6.5: The Place of the Choir in Worship

One of the musical questions being asked by churches today is what the role of the choir in the worship music program is. The following insights are offered by Ed Willmington, a choral director and composer with a lifetime of wisdom relative to the choral art.

One dilemma, it seems, in the traditionally based church is how to avoid stagnation of worship style and language while not throwing everything out and starting over. Some have started over, either by initiating a service in a different style, planting a separate church, or eliminating the traditional service entirely. These choices, of course, break the body into parts in one manner or another. This dilemma often involves the role of the choir in the corporate worship experience. Choirs provide many wonderful benefits to a congregation but are in danger of extinction unless their function in the worship setting is reshaped.

Here are a three suggestions allowing for a fresh look at the role of the choir in corporate worship.

- Take time to educate choir members regarding their role as spiritual, corporate worship leaders. Use biblical and devotional materials to help them understand their high calling to serve God and the church community in this holy privilege. Pray together often.
- To further assist with this shift in thinking, utilize choral material that allows the choir to function with the congregation, therefore breaking down any "us vs. them" mentality that may exist between the platform and the people. The congregation will love being a part of the choir!
- Use the choir in creative ways in the service beyond singing the anthem. These may include musical things such as descants, processionals, and sung prayers. It may also include nonmusical roles that serve the community such as greeting, ushering, Scripture reading, and praying with people during the service.

Edwin Willmington, director of the Fred Bock Music Institute at the Brehm Center for Worship, Theology, and the Arts, Pasadena, CA (personal communication).

- awareness of the budding musicians in the community and encouragement for congregations to pay for their music lessons (especially given the declining place of the arts in public education)

Extraordinary Worship

I have argued above for worship to follow the forms of each community's tradition with the enrichment of local gifts to make it pertinent for a given gathering at a particular time. The ordinary practices of a worshiping community do not need to be executed in an ordinary fashion. It is, in fact, incorporation of the particular gifts of each unique community of faith that allows for worship to be more than ordinary each time the assembly gathers in adoration. The proper thing for a congregation to do is embrace the constants and enlarge them by applying layers of locally available gifts. For example, a simple prayer can be written and spoken by a leader. It can also be sung by a vocal group, sung responsively with the congregation, musically embellished with layers of accompaniment, repeated as a reprise during a period of prayer, accompanied differently at each iteration, sung by a children's choir, performed by multiple music ensembles to add variety and texture, and so forth. What is more, this range of possibilities occurs each time the ordinary prayer is offered. A simple, ordinary element of worship offers countless opportunities for congregations that seek to make every worship experience a rich and highly participatory event. The execution of an ordinary blessing in Asia will be different than in Africa and America, due to the differences in language, culture, custom, music, and local congregational giftedness. The first use of a form in each location can be different than the second, the twenty-second, and the ninety-second due to the extraordinary capacity for creative expression available within each worship setting. With limitless possibilities before us, how could we ever settle for worship that is rote, mundane, wooden, and uninspired?

The first objection to come to the mind of a reader who seeks to make ordinary worship extraordinary every Sunday is likely to be, Yes, but congregations hate change. The kind of enrichment of worship that I am advocating here employs change that may be welcome. No worshiper will prefer worship to remain dull or uninspired. All faithful believers seek worship that resonates deeply. The changes I am suggesting are small ones: making greater use of lay leadership, using the talents of local artists and children, and using familiar worship patterns and forms but executing them in ways that draw people more fully into participation. Who could object, for example, to church banners being made by talented local artists who produce not cheap felt articles but richly textured quilts? Who would not welcome a change that makes public reading of Scripture lively and intelligible? Who does not desire preaching that is pertinent and filled with hope? How could there be objection to the intentional connection of worship with the concerns and opportunities of the local community? What congregation would fail to rejoice if the music for worship involved talented young people playing along tastefully with hymns or songs? Who could oppose an international member of a congregation teaching a worship song from her homeland? Something new, something different, something local can be done each Sunday, even within the ordinary format of a congregation's customary idiom of worship. Extraordinary worship does not mean throwing out the old but enriching the familiar with the gifts of the community.

Sidebar 6.6: An Extraordinary Example

Stephen Ellingson has recently undertaken a penetrating study of how churches change in the face of cultural shifts. He gives this account of one Lutheran congregation in the San Francisco area that achieved the balance between tradition and change in an ordination service for a new pastor on her way to serve a church in South Africa. The service also demonstrates how local issues (a congregation ordaining one of its own for ministry) and global issues (the new pastor serving in South Africa) can become part of a balanced service of worship. Tradition, mission, local issues, global concerns, and the immediacy of the ordination celebration seem to have been brought together effectively by creative worship planners.

I attended the ordination service of a new pastor at Grace Lutheran Church in the Oakland suburbs. I entered the sanctuary to the sound of drumming. Eight young people were sitting in one of the four front rows pounding away on a variety of large African drums. The service began with a dozen robed clergy processing into the pastel-painted sanctuary arranged as a partial theater-in-the-round, singing a song from the contemporary Lutheran hymnal. The senior pastor of Grace welcomed us by using a traditional South African greeting . . . and then asked us to greet one another in the same manner. All the men said, "Nda," and the women responded, "Ah" (making a glissando from high to low). We then followed one of the three regularly sung liturgies in the hymnal of the Evangelical Lutheran Church in America (ELCA). For the Scripture-reading rite, a young woman sang the Shema for the Old Testament lesson, and a Roman Catholic priest and two faculty members from the local Lutheran seminary read a number of texts from the New Testament, all of which emphasized God's love, inclusivity, and justice.

The senior pastor read the Gospel lesson, from the fourth chapter of Luke in which Jesus delivers his first sermon and identifies his own calling to be one with which he will bring good news to the poor, set the prisoners free, and make the blind see. The pastor's sermon drew parallels between Jesus' call and the new pastor's call. "Like Jesus," he said, "you are called to speak the good news: light, joy, FREEDOM!!" Next he reminded her and all of us about Luther's understanding of the call to be a Christian by quoting from two of Luther's most remembered writings, "The Freedom of the Christian" and his alleged speech in front of the Diet of Worms in which he ended his critique of Catholicism with the words, "Here I stand, I can do no other." He finished by applying Luther's ideas and the Gospel lesson to the soon to be ordained pastor's call. . . . The bishop then led the official ELCA ordination service. We ended the service with a lively South African hymn, for which the newly ordained pastor taught us the words and hand motions and the senior pastor taught us a short line dance that involved a lot of foot stomping. Within minutes, the entire congregation was dancing and singing along with the incessant beat of the African drums.

Stephen Ellingson, The Megachurch and the Mainline: Remaking Religious Tradition in the Twenty-first Century *(Chicago: University of Chicago Press, 2007), 2–3.*

Extraordinary worship also suggests that a worshiping assembly will be open to surprise. The chief agent of surprise is the Holy Spirit at work in the creative minds of preachers, song writers, song leaders, musical groups, worship planners, visual and graphic artists, and children. The Spirit might even surprise a worshiper in ways that worship leaders did not plan.[28] Extraordinary worship is inspired worship, adoration that takes full advantage of the spiritual gifts that are God's contribution to the life of prayer in each community. God does not demand that worship be a spectacle. But God does provide the body of Christ with the limbs and organs necessary for its life. Full use of these gifts is not a spectacular achievement; it is merely the exercise of a healthy body. Yet, the body itself is extraordinary.

Conclusion

This final chapter of part 1 has attempted to relate contextual theology to the missional church and to demonstrate how issues of context can inform the way a congregation gathers for adoration of the Creator. I have argued that worship is always ordinary, in that it ordinarily employs familiar forms (regardless of their being high or low liturgy forms), but that it can also always be extraordinary by utilizing aspects of a congregation's context that make worship especially appropriate to its time and place.

In the pages that follow, I will present manual suggestions or rubrics for the design and implementation of worship that is missionally oriented. Here, the various principles that have been drawn out as chapter conclusions will inform the practice of those who seek to relate adoration and action in one worshipful activity.

In this chapter, a number of theological and liturgical principles have become apparent:

1. The core identity (theologically, denominationally, contextually) of a congregation is something to be embraced and ought not be overlooked or abandoned in the process of worship renewal.
2. Worship always draws on certain constant or ordinarily used patterns and forms (ordinaries), regardless of a community's liturgical frame of reference.
3. Worship within a given community should be properly inculturated, that is, it should take into account the particularities (propers) of local context.

28. Preachers, for example, regularly hear surprising things from listeners who have heard things in the sermon that the preacher did not intend. It is sometimes difficult to know whether to attribute a hearer's creative insight to imagination or inspiration.

4. The mission of the church in the world is related to the local adoration and action of congregations.
5. Adoration of God is best a balance of constants and particularities that yield extraordinary opportunities for worship.

Two

A Worship Manual
for the Missional Church

In the first part of this book, I identified a number of principles relating to Christian worship and the missional church. These now will form the basis of a set of rubrics or manual suggestions for churches seeking to design and execute services of corporate worship that are consistent with a missional theological identity and ministry. Among them is the understanding that missionally focused theology and worship draws on the particular and distinctive qualities and opportunities of each local community. One of the evident aspects of what God is doing in a community is represented by the spiritual gifts God places within each faith community. Missional worship will draw richly on the talents of local persons as well as the local culture, and it will be aware of local opportunities for service. In this age of information, it will also show an awareness of global issues and cultures.

A central thrust of this book has been that the *sending* of the church into the active mission of God is a pivotal moment in worship when we turn from adoration to action ("sending is mission," say the missional theologians). Accordingly, I will continue the contrary pattern here of speaking first about this concluding moment of the worship service. From there, we will consider suggestions for designing and executing the other portions of worship: the *gathering*, attending and responding to the *Word*, and celebrating or remembering the *sacraments*.

In most worship manuals, the rubrics are precise statements offered as directions for proper execution of liturgical rites. They imply that there are right ways and wrong ways to perform a particular rite. Traditionally, the rubrics are written in red print (hence *rubric*, from Latin for the color red). This is to distinguish the rules of execution from the *negrics* (words in black print), which generally follow the rubrics and contain the actual texts to be spoken. Typically, the rubrics are offered in two categories: *may* and *shall*. In instances where the celebrant is free to choose whether or not to include a particular action or text, the protocol allows a *may* rubric. For example, the rubric might read, "The minister may offer the following prayer." The *shall* rubrics give firmer instructions, indeed, prescriptions as to what is to happen: "The minister shall say . . ."

In this manual of worship for missional churches, the rubrics are neither *may* nor *shall* rubrics. These terms would be inappropriate for manual suggestions that are not directed toward a particular rite or tradition. Instead, we can think of these suggestions for the design and execution of worship as *metarubrics*. That is, they are principles that inform practice without being particularized for one rite or another. It is my hope that they will be found to be useful both in formal liturgical services and in free liturgies, as well as those in between.[1] In place of the prescriptive *may* and *shall* language, the tone here will be suggestive (e.g., "Let there be time for silence"). The implication in using this tone is that there is no absolute or liturgically correct way to do things, but there are best practices that can be employed by worship planners and leaders in communicating their intentions as worship unfolds in the presence of the assembly. In other words, these metarubrics are offered not in the optative (may) or imperative (shall) moods but in the indicative. These indications and descriptions of practice support the iconic, symbolic, and indexical qualities of worship signs so that there will be congruence between what we intend will happen in worship and what is experienced.

The suggestions offered in this manual are intended for use in a wide range of liturgical communities: traditional, free, and those in between. Still, it is understood that there are things appropriate in some communities that are not appropriate in others. The suggestions made here are not intended to be followed woodenly, nor are they all intended to apply to every worshiping community. If, however, faith communities can discover new expressions that are compatible with their own theology, they might rejoice in singing new songs or experimenting with new practices that come from other traditions. Given

---

1. For particular rites or orders of worship, see the worship books listed in the bibliography. Especially useful for churches that have no published denominational resources is the collection of worship texts contained in Brink and Witvliet, *The Worship Sourcebook*.

the gulfs that divide Christian worship practices today, wherever we might find commonality there is a point of celebration. As indicated in chapter 3, where worship streams run together, there is a river that makes glad the city of God.

At the conclusion of part 2, a sample of typical liturgies from various worship traditions is provided as a rough guideline for congregations seeking to rely on the historic wisdom of the church that is found in developed orders of worship. These ordinary services can be enriched as congregations make use of the local particularities that make each congregation distinct. It is a hallmark of missional theology that local opportunities and gifts of the Spirit guide the ministry of each place. When this happens in worship, it can be extraordinary.

The Sending

The sending forth of gathered worshipers is the pivotal moment when worship turns from adoration to action. Within the assembly, the congregation has attended to God's Word and responded to it in various ways. The people may have celebrated or remembered the sacraments of baptism and Holy Communion. The congregation has been prepared (or centered, to use the missional language) for the ardent work of Christian discipleship that takes place between one Sunday and another.[1] During this hour (*worship as adoration*), they have been encouraged, inspired, and met by the activity of the Triune God. In this final moment of worship, the gathered become the sent. They are not dismissed, as if worship were adjourned. They are sent forth in the enactment of God's mission in the local community and the world (*worship as action*). In this, they are participating in the work of the Trinity whereby the Father sends the Son to offer salvation and hope, and the Father and the Son send the Spirit to inspire and encourage the faithful. In the sending, worship redirects its focus from the liturgy of assembly to become the living liturgy of discipleship.

The sending portion of the liturgy is often overlooked as insignificant or inconsequential. The goal here is to restore the sending to its ritual potential. While it cannot and should not compete in duration with any other part of worship, it can be seen as a critical moment, the planning and execution of

1. As in part 1 of this book, the terms *Sunday worship* and *hour of adoration* are used here as shorthand references for a congregation's regular weekly services of worship, regardless of the day on which they are held or their length.

which requires care and foresight. Accordingly, the following principles indicate ways in which the elements of sending rites can be focused and compelling.

The Benediction

The service of adoration usually begins with a firm greeting or invitation spoken on God's behalf by the presider. The service concludes with another bold statement spoken on God's behalf that blesses the assembly as the people go forth into service. The benediction (from Latin to "speak a good word") is intended to bless the people on their way with the promise and assurance that the God who met them in the Word, the prayers, and the sacraments is also with them in the living liturgy of daily life. The blessing emphasizes the idea that the church moves forward into action with the Holy Spirit as the source of its inspiration and power. Two cautions about the pronouncement of the blessing: (1) The blessing is not a command given by the presider for people to go forth in service. This would suggest that Christian faith and service depend on the work of the faithful rather than the grace of God. The blessing does not command but impels people forth with the promise of God's grace in their practice of discipleship. If the Word and sacraments set the sails for God's people, the sending provides the promise of wind to fill them and move them inexorably. (2) Most inappropriate at this point in the service is a casual farewell. This has the iconic problem of suggesting that the gathering has been a social event rather than a spiritual assembly with the Creator at its center.

- Let the final blessing or benediction focus on sending God's people out into the world in Christian discipleship. The verbs in a benediction are active verbs with God as their subject. A benediction might take traditional form, as in the Aaronic blessing from Numbers 6:24–26 or the apostolic blessing of 2 Corinthians 13:13. Or it may be a word crafted by the presiding minister to offer hope to those who continue to worship through their Christian action in the world outside the church doors.
- Let the tone of the final blessing and the entire sending be one of encouragement and hope. May it be spoken with an urgency that indicates that action is the natural result of God's people gathering for adoration and centering. Let the blessing not be spoken tentatively but boldly, giving the promise that God goes with each individual as he or she moves outward into various ministries. It is always best when benedictions can be spoken from memory. Looking down at a book or a bulletin reduces the impact of the powerful words the leader intends to convey. The face and eyes communicate as well as the voice. (Leading in this way requires rehearsal.)

- The language of the sending can recapitulate the images and ideas that have been the focus of the service's Scripture, sermon, prayers, and songs.
- Let the speaker of the blessing face the congregation and use full, confident gestures to convey the power of the moment. Many gestures can be appropriate but the simplest is for the leader to stand erect with arms stretched outward in a natural, open reach. Allow the palms to face inward and slightly upward and the fingers to be gently curved. The larger the assembly, the wider the arms should be spread so that the gesture can be seen even at a distance.
- Note that in some traditions the benediction is intended to be spoken only by an ordained presider. This follows the theological idea that ordination bestows the church's authority for a person to speak on God's behalf. In settings where this is appropriate and when an ordained leader is not presiding, the practice is for the words of blessing to be adjusted so as to avoid pronouncement. For example, "The Lord bless you" becomes "The Lord bless us" when spoken by a lay leader.

Concluding Prayer

There are many kinds of prayer that might conclude worship. They are typically spoken by a leader to draw the worshipful dialogue to a close. The prayer is spoken on behalf of the people, usually giving thanks to God for the gifts bestowed during worship.

- If there is a concluding prayer in the worship service, let it not be a substitute for the blessing of the people. Let the leader be aware of the direction of address: the leader speaks to God in the prayer on behalf of the people and addresses the people on behalf of God in the benediction. If there is to be only one of these elements (prayer or benediction), let the benediction be spoken. In the dialogue that is worship, God has the final word. The "final word" image should not be taken literally, for there are fitting responses to a blessing, such as saying "Amen" or singing a sending song. But the image does underscore the relationship between the final prayer and the blessing.
- Whichever form of prayer is chosen, let the leader take care to craft the prayer wisely. This does not mean that the leader cannot improvise a prayer and respond to the spontaneity of the moment. It does suggest, however, that the prayer should be thoughtful, related to the images, themes, and texts of the worship service, and that the prayer leader should use language appropriate to the ritual moment. The sending calls for language that has intensity and focus. This is not the time for

rambling, stammering petitions; it is the time for words that accommodate the urgent business of invoking God's grace for the Christian action to follow. Like all elements of the sending, the concluding prayer leans forward toward the active worship that is to take place beyond the church doors.

Sending Song

Songs for the close of worship need to capture the tenor of the service, naturally. An Easter service will certainly resonate with joy whereas a funeral service may end more serenely. Generally, the sending song can be one that reflects on the images and messages conveyed during worship and that compels people forward into the week of Christian witness and service. The music is often upbeat and the mood is one of anticipation and hope. Most appropriate are the songs and hymns that speak to God's empowerment of ministry as believers go forth.

- Let the texts of sending songs and hymns focus on God's active leadership of the church in ministry rather than the activities of the faithful. All of worship should reflect the theological imperative that faith and Christian service are always gifts of grace and never the achievements of ardent persons.
- Generally, the tempo of sending music is lively. The quick step of a march or a dance is not inappropriate as a signal that the body of Christ is on the move. Music stirs a restful body to action.
- If worship planners find it difficult to locate appropriate sending songs, a congregation may wish to encourage its musicians young and old to create new song texts for existing hymn tunes or new songs altogether. Remember that newly created songs may prove effective for a moment of worship even if they are set aside thereafter. In such a case, they are simply one of the propers, as is the sermon.
- On festive occasions, the service may end (as it may have begun) with the parading of worship leaders. The gathering parade is called a *procession*; at the end of the service it is a *recession*. More is said below about the order and style of such a ritual (see chap. 8).

Commissioning

There may be occasions in the life of a missional congregation when church members undertake special mission activities. There is a growing trend in churches in North America to send house-building teams to Mexico and Caribbean countries, medical teams to Native American reservations and countries in the Two-Thirds World, evangelical missionaries to local and distant places, and so forth. The sending is the time to ritually celebrate the commencement of missions fostered by a congregation's ministry. At the appointed time:

- The presider calls forth the mission team to stand before the congregation for commissioning. If the list is not long, their names can be read aloud.

- The commissioning rite begins with a statement describing the missional activity to be undertaken. It is generally followed by a question put to the mission team regarding their commitment. For example, "Will you serve faithfully in this ministry, seeking God's guidance as you strive to do God's will? If so, answer, 'We will.'" The team responds.

- The act of commissioning is a strong statement of support given by a worship or congregational leader, sending the mission team forth with the congregation's encouragement and blessing. It usually contains words such as: "This congregation commissions you to . . ." It not only signals the commencement of the team's work, but it assures them that they are undertaking a congregational initiative that is consistent with its overall mission.

- Let the rite conclude with a prayer that God equip, inspire, and protect those being sent.

Announcements

The placement of announcements in worship is the bane of worship planners and leaders. Wherever they are placed, they often seem to be out of place. Many options are available as to where the announcements may appear, and there seems to be no universal agreement as to what is most appropriate. The announcements are discussed here because, though they may not necessarily be placed within the sending rite, the announcements are one of the key elements of worship that point the time of adoration toward the action that follows. They will also be discussed briefly in the following sections relating to gathering, Word, and sacraments. For those who are tempted to avoid announcements altogether, let it be remembered that there is no better time for the congregation to learn of opportunities for prayer and service than when the church has assembled. Announcements may not fit the flow of worship—seeming to many as if they are mere advertisements—but they connect the gathering to all that is about to take place in the faith community in the days ahead. There are opportunities for service to be announced, information about persons in the community that must be shared, reminders of meetings and classes that are scheduled, and so forth. The mention of these things has the effect of keeping the hour of adoration in tune with the hours of action that follow and the broader mission of the church. Therefore, the announcements should be given their due.

Still, they should not be overdrawn lest they eclipse the other activities of worship. Persons making announcements should speak with clarity and economy. Whether delivered in a serious tone, as when announcing a tragic event, or with joy and humor, they should be deliberate and well spoken.

The actual placement of announcements will be up to each local congregation. The following suggestions may be useful as a way to keep announcements in check and in proper relationship to the service of worship:

- Let the announcements be presented in various places, depending on their nature. General announcements might be offered as a service begins, along with any information that will guide people in following the service for the day.

- Some announcements are best given at the main time of prayer (sometimes known as the pastoral prayer or the prayer of the church). Announcements about persons for whom or events for which the assembly prays can be made immediately before the prayers are voiced. A few examples will be given below in the Word section as prayer is discussed as part of the people's response to hearing the Word.

- If announcements have to do with things occurring immediately following the service, they might be offered prior to the benediction. Here, they should be especially brief in order to maintain the urgency that the pivot from adoration to action calls for.

- Let new songs and musical refrains be taught and rehearsed prior to worship's opening song or invocation. The time to learn something new is not in the middle of a service but in preparation for it. Assuming people will simply catch on to a new song as it is employed in worship guarantees that most worshipers will be unable to participate in singing it.

8

The Gathering

When God's people return to services of worship from busy lives of activity and discipleship, they do so both to adore the God who created them and called them into service and to be re-centered in faith. They gather around the central signs of faith that can point them toward the activities of adoration as well as take them to the iconic border beyond which they can only imagine the presence and activity of God. While the gathering is the beginning of the hour of adoration, it is also the conclusion of the period of action. The mood is typically celebratory, as God's people reassemble for fellowship and centering.

The suggestions that follow have to do with both the design of the places where God's people gather and the ritual activities that occur during the commencement of the worship service.

Architecture and Furnishings

The site of Sunday worship can be outdoors, a home, a gymnasium, a theater, or a church building. It is a commonplace of missional ministry that the church is comprised not of a building but of the local body of Christ. When God's people assemble, regardless of where they gather, there are symbolic, architectural, and furnishing elements that the church, in its historic wisdom, has agreed on as useful for the purpose of adoration. The chief symbol of the Christian faith is the cross, but there are several other symbols and signs that represent and accompany the activities of worship. Key among them are a pulpit (sometimes called an ambo) or lectern for placement of Scripture, the Bible itself, a table (often called an altar), and a font or pool for baptisms. In addition, there are visual representations of many kinds that provide the indexical function of pointing to aspects of things ordinary and proper.

Symbols and Visual Imagery

Remember that symbols are signs with meanings assigned by tradition or communal experience. In using symbols and visual imagery in worship, the following suggestions may prove useful:

- Let the cross be large enough to be visible by all worshipers. When processions are appropriate, the cross should be one that can be carried on a pole at the head of the processional column. It can be lifted high for visibility and to signal the lifting of heads, voices, and spirits as worship begins.
- Let symbols be used economically. A single cross well placed will direct a worshiper's attention more eloquently than a chancel filled with crosses of various sizes and descriptions. If candles are used for illumination or decoration, they are typically found in pairs of single candles or candelabras placed on either side of the worship space. If the candle is used as a sign pointing to the presence of Christ, the Light of the World, a single candle well placed for visibility is all that is necessary. In liturgically formal settings, a Paschal candle serves this purpose. For visibility's sake, let the size of this candle be fitting for the size of the worship space.
- Symbols function best when they are clearly seen. Worship planners should be aware of sight lines in the worship space. Primary symbols require prime locations. Hiding them with furnishings, instruments, or music and microphone stands masks their visibility and undermines their impact. It is a theological principle that the most visible things in worship are those that bear the greatest significance for the community. If a communion table is eclipsed by a drum set and other instruments, it is clear that the worshiping community places greater significance on the activities of the worship band than on the activity of God in the sacrament.
- When used in service of adoration, electronic projection equipment can be effective. (Beware that it not be used in a gratuitous or controlling manner.) It can add to the visual imagery of worship and make for clear communication and presentation of worship texts. It can also free hands from holding hymnals or worship materials, allowing for free bodily participation in worship. Let projection screens be placed discreetly so as not to diminish the effectiveness of the central symbols around which the assembly gathers.

- Banners and hanging art can provide imagery that supports a theme, text, or season in worship. This is the place to employ artists of every age from the community. Some of the work will be intentionally simple and for short-term use. This is especially a place to employ the work of children, nearly all of whom are artistic. For temporary art, simple materials can be used, but they should not be so flimsy as to undermine the grace articulated by the artist within the medium. For more permanent installations, better materials can be used to honor the work of the creators and to inspire the perception of the worshipers. There is no reason for artists to be confined to the medium of synthetic felt for church banners. This cheap material cannot do justice to the conceptual inspiration of creative people. Many churches have talented quilters within their communities. Their work can provide richly textured and long-wearing banners.
- Materials and images drawn from local folk art traditions are appropriate for making worship culturally distinctive.
- Banners need not always depict texts and representational figures. Colors themselves can function symbolically. A community's artists will know how to turn color, form, and shape into meaningful visual imagery supportive of a day's or a season's worship.

Worship Space

The traditional cruciform (cross-shaped) layout of a church is now largely considered disadvantageous for worship. It places people on two sides of a central aisle, facing the chancel and the priests who preside there. The term *priests* is applicable here even in Protestant settings, since the architecture makes it seem unavoidable. One of the key elements of the Reformation was the notion of the priesthood of all believers. When architecture elevates and brings excessive focus to the leaders of worship, it suggests that they are functioning in an elite way. They are, in such settings, the only persons that a pew-bound worshiper faces. This problem is repeated in worship settings that are designed to imitate theaters and auditoriums. An egalitarian ecclesiology is signaled by seating that allows worshipers to (more or less) face one another with leaders situated in their place in the circle. An additional indexical problem with strict forward-facing seating is that it suggests that the geographic presence of God in the gathering is at the front, in an elevated and elite space, rather than in the midst of the people.

Today, there is a growing interest in making worship spaces flexible so that chairs can be moved to accommodate various configurations for worship. Where flexible space allows:

- Let the chairs be placed such that worshipers can face and see the body of Christ. This may mean a configuration of chairs placed in a semi- or full circle. Or it may allow for banks of chairs facing one another.

- Leaders need to be visible in order to perform their roles. Visibility can be achieved subtly, avoiding the sense that leaders are specially positioned to exercise power or demand attention. Slightly elevated, movable platforms can provide visibility for leaders as well as for a cross, a table, and a lectern.

- Let the leaders of worship sit in chairs comfortably situated facing the people. This emphasizes the sense that God's people have gathered, with their various roles of participation or leadership, around the central things of faith. When clergy and other leaders are seated facing the same direction as the congregation or facing each other from sides of the chancel, it serves to foster the indexical problem of separating the leaders from other worshipers (suggesting an elite status).

- When worship occurs in a setting outside of a church, certain things can be introduced to facilitate a worshipful assembly. First, the primary things need to be provided for: table, lectern, font, and cross. Additionally, banners and other simple and portable visual art can transform an ordinary space into a space set apart for adoration.

Acoustic Space

Attention to the way sound occupies a space is another consideration for worship spaces. In designing acoustics for worship, the first question to be asked is "which voices are the most important voices in the assembly?" The obvious answer is God's voice, which is typically heard through the human speech of the Scripture reader and the preacher. Accordingly, worship spaces need proper acoustics and/or amplification for orators to communicate clearly. A less obvious answer to the question is the voice of the body of Christ. If worship is a dialogue between God and God's people, then the people's response needs to be heard. Where possible, carpeting and seat cushions should be used sparingly so as to keep acoustic space lively. A worshiper should be able to hear herself when singing and speaking, as well as the voices of fellow worshipers. When the acoustics of the space are highly absorbent, a worshiper may have the impression that he is singing or speaking alone. This leads an ardent worshiper to speak or sing all the louder and the voice to become tired. Ideally, a worshiper should not only see one's brothers and sisters at worship, but should be able to hear them sing, speak, and breathe. Even if a person closes her eyes in silence during prayer, the sound of people breathing and sighing together is a sign that the people of God are gathered in adoration.

When tuning acoustics in worship spaces, let the balance between a clear solo communicator (such as the preacher) and the congregation's corporate voice (as in singing) lean in the congregation's favor. The speaker's voice can always be modified with electronic amplification. It would be impractical to amplify an entire congregation so that the voice of the assembly can be heard.

- Remember that improving electronic amplification in a space is not the same as improving its acoustic qualities. For listeners to hear an amplified speaker or singer clearly is desirable. But that is no substitute for an acoustic space that brings the voice of the assembly to life. A space that is sufficiently lively (or *wet*, to use acoustic jargon) will be equally effective for choral singing and for congregational participation.
- Effective use of electronic amplification requires rehearsal and regular testing. It is the responsibility of worship leaders and speakers to plan on a time for sound checks. Prudent speakers will practice in the worship space and give thought as to how they might proceed if the amplification system malfunctions.
- Let those who have the privilege in worship of having their voices amplified remember that their role is to serve the assembly, not to dominate or cover the assembly's voice. If the principle sound a worshiper hears during corporate responses is that of the amplified voice, then the speaker's volume probably needs to be turned down.[1] Proper volume is achieved when members of the congregation can hear prayer or song leaders distinctly *with* the voices of the people (rather than *instead of* the people).
- For preachers and other speakers, lavaliere and head microphones are preferable to handheld microphones. Speakers will want their hands free for gesture, page turning, holding the Bible, and so forth.

Clothing

Vestments, when worn in humility by servant-oriented worship leaders, can be useful for worship. They are signs pointing to various worship leadership roles.

- Albs are white robes worn by baptized persons, lay or clergy, who lead in worship. They are a point of baptismal remembrance, whether worn by acolytes, choir members, readers, or assisting and presiding ministers. Albs are typically used in churches with formal liturgical traditions.
- Stoles are narrow shawls draped over the shoulders of clergy. They are frequently designed with colors referencing liturgical seasons. Similarly

1. Today, as most Protestant traditions seek to downplay priestly roles and share worship leadership between clergy and laity, it should be noted that the abuse of the privilege of having one's voice amplified suggests, effectively, that the priest is the one with the microphone, even if that person is a song leader.

designed banners and cloths (called paraments) are often used to dress pulpits and communion tables.

- Preaching robes (also called Geneva gowns) are worn by preachers and other leaders. They are similar to and reflective of academic gowns. They point to the study that takes place in preparation for preaching. Geneva gowns are most often found in churches of the Reformed tradition.

- Choir robes can be of various designs and colors. They are used to indicate those called and prepared to perform musical leadership in worship and to provide a uniform appearance for the group.

- In churches with free liturgical traditions, vestments are typically not worn. The use of street or dress clothes points toward a theological conviction regarding egalitarianism between clergy and laity. When ordinary clothing is worn by worship leaders, let there be care as to its selection. What we wear is a clear signal pointing to how we value the hour of adoration and the leadership roles in which we are called to serve. Indexical problems occur when leaders dress in ways that undermine the important words they have to say.

Lectern and Bible

While it is necessary to provide a place to hold a central Bible for worship, it is not necessary to provide both a lectern and a pulpit (or ambo). Many churches are designed with both. In such settings, Scripture readings are typically presented from the lectern and the sermon is reserved for the pulpit. In the most traditionally designed churches, the pulpit is elevated so as to gain visibility and hearing for the preacher. This configuration, however, can suggest that the preacher has a heightened role and standing in the congregation.[2] Where possible:

- Let there be a single Bible and a single place in the chancel from which Scripture is read and proclaimed. That it may be used equally by lay readers and preachers points to the equality of the faithful and the priesthood of all believers.

- Let the Bible used in worship be one that is large enough to be a visible sign that God's Word is being read and proclaimed in the midst of the people. Larger Bibles also have the benefit of large print, making them easier to use for readers of all ages.

- Projecting the words of Scripture on a screen can be a useful means of involving the congregation in following or speaking aloud with Scripture readers. Even when texts are projected, leaders themselves should read directly from a Bible, held or visible on the lectern, signaling and supporting the scriptural source of the readings.

2. Indeed, the old joke is that the pulpit is elevated so as to be six feet above contradiction.

- In settings where readings from Scripture are printed in worship bulletins or on folders, it is all the more important for leaders to use a visible Bible. With the disposable nature of the printed material in the worshiper's hands, the permanence of God's Word needs to be underscored.
- Let the lectern and/or pulpit be used sparingly. They point to God's Word. When they are used as the convenient place from which to read announcements or offer prayers, their clear and singular index as a sign of God's Word becomes clouded. Let prayers and announcements be presented from another location where worship leaders sit facing the congregation. The use of cordless microphones makes this a convenient possibility.

Table

First, let us recall that the term *altar* is an Old Testament image for the place of sacrifice. One of the first theological moves of the Reformation was to unshackle the celebration of Holy Communion from the medieval sense of sacrificing Christ on local altars. The sacrificial death of Christ was understood by the Reformers as a once-and-for-all action of God that had nothing to do with the power of the priest to confect the body and blood of Christ from common elements. Accordingly, the furnishing on which the food for communion is placed should be called by its appropriate name: the table.

- Let the table be placed in a prominent position that points to the significance of the sacrament within the community. In most traditions, this would suggest central placement within the chancel.
- Let the table be large enough to fit the size of the worship space and signal the important ritual that is enacted there. In churches where the liturgical theology construes the real presence of Christ in the bread and wine, the table is usually large and permanently placed.
- Regardless of frequency of use, the presence of the table is a reminder of God's grace and is rightly displayed in the worship space at all services of adoration.
- To retain the clear and singular index of the table as a sign of Christ's love, the table should not serve as a catch-all for miscellaneous books, Bibles, hymnals, bulletins, collection plates, etc. Let bread and grape juice or wine be placed on the table, surrounded perhaps by a pair of candles for illumination and to signal honor.
- Sight lines for the table should be maintained, regardless of whether Holy Communion is celebrated at a given service, since the table not only serves to point to the love of Christ but also functions iconically as the border between the food we physically eat and the spiritual realm where God

meets God's people with love and forgiveness. Music and microphone stands, chairs, and other objects should not eclipse the table. This does not mean that leaders should avoid stepping or standing occasionally in front of the table.

Font/Pool

Likewise, the font or pool can be a constant reminder of God's grace through baptism when visibly placed. All suggestions regarding size, sight lines, and visual obstruction apply.

- Two sites are typically employed to provide visibility for the font or pool. One is at the entrance to the worship space. This points to the theological notion that God's people enter the faith through baptism. The other is at the front or center of the worship space, near the table, signaling the connection between the sacraments as means of God's grace.
- Because water is one of the great symbols of God's grace, the use of an abundance of water points both visibly and audibly to what God is doing in baptism. In traditions where a pool for full immersion is used, there is the strongest possible signal of baptism's significance in the life of faith.

Technology and Media

In addition to the statements made above regarding use of amplification and projection equipment, an important caveat needs to be made. Because the use of media (sound and lighting systems, cameras, projection systems, etc.) can be costly, time consuming, and culturally appealing, we must remember that technology and media *serve* worship and do not drive its content or form. Avoid allowing these tools to take center stage, impair liturgical movement, and obscure primary symbols and actions.

Elements of the Opening Rite

Greetings and Announcements

Leaders begin the service of worship in various ways, sometimes with casual greetings and folksy chatter, sometimes with a biblical greeting, and other times with a set of announcements. Regardless of how a congregation elects to begin its time of adoration, leaders can invite people into the gathering with a knowledge that they have come from days of active service and worship in the world. As previously they have been sent, here they attend to the need for God's people to come together again for fellowship and the spiritual refreshment of Word and sacrament. It is the responsibility of a worship leader to acknowledge these things in a greeting and to set a tone for the service and indicate its spirit and purpose. Accordingly:

- It is to be expected that worship leaders will rehearse their parts. They will do so in the worship space itself, practicing with microphones, doing a sound check, and going over their texts and readings as often as necessary to achieve meaningful communication. Prudent leaders will seek out the advice and direction of actors and drama coaches in the community to help them learn to perform their roles with grace and clarity.
- Here is the place for certain announcements: a declaration of the theme of the day; directions as to how worshipers can follow the service from a book, bulletin, or projection screen; alerts as to things that might be unusual or unexpected; and rehearsal of new songs.
- Let the mood of leaders generally be one of joy and hospitality, the volume of their voices raised in anticipation of the extraordinary things that will happen in the coming hour, displaying an attitude of genuine delight that God has called God's people together again. A contradiction in communication occurs when a rousing opening song is followed by a leader's statement that is flat, quiet, or lacking vitality. Let the moment resound with true joy.
- A scriptural greeting is appropriate following opening announcements. Though worship has already begun with people gathering in fellowship, prayer, and meditation, a greeting signals a more formal beginning of the dialogue between God and God's people. There are many places in the Bible to find such greetings, such as those used by Paul in 2 Corinthians 13:13 and Galatians 1:3–5. Scriptural greetings should be spoken with confidence and authority; they are God's own greeting and require a declarative tone. They are also best delivered from memory, with direct eye contact.
- Mutual greetings may also come at this time in the gathering, where people greet one another with peace.

Invocations and Calls to Worship

Invocations are prayers usually spoken by a leader on behalf of the congregation. The purpose of the invocation is to pray for the Spirit of God to be at work in the hour of gathering. Invocations acknowledge that God is the chief agent in worship—gathering, enlightening, listening, and forgiving. Leaders may craft their own prayers of invocation or use those printed in worship resources. As a general rule, if printed prayers are consulted, let them serve chiefly as models to be modified to fit the particular and proper occasions for local worship.

The call to worship is a statement by the presider inviting people to attend to the activities of worship. It may contain scriptural language or be wholly composed by the leader. The direction of communication is from the leader to the assembly.

- Miscommunication occurs when leaders forget the direction of address in these statements: to repeat, invocations are spoken as a prayer to God on behalf of God's people; calls to worship are spoken directly to God's people, inviting them to participation.
- A service of worship might contain one or two of these elements: greeting, invocation, and call to worship. Incorporating all three is unnecessary and ritually unwieldy.

Confession and Absolution or Assurance

The honest confession of sins either privately or corporately is an essential spiritual practice for faithful disciples. If done corporately in worship, it signals a strong Protestant impulse that private confession before a priest is not a requirement for faith. This is not to devalue the pastoral office of hearing and absolving sin privately, a spiritual practice sought out by many faithful Protestant and Catholic believers. Confession, when included in corporate worship, can appropriately come as part of the gathering rite. (It might also fittingly occur during a communion liturgy.) Prayers of confession can either be voiced by a leader on behalf of a congregation or spoken aloud by the assembly. When done in this manner, the words of confession are made available to the people on paper or on screen. Those crafting such prayers for the people should be mindful of the local and global issues that will particularize the prayers and make them fit for a given time, place, and people. When scriptural confessions are voiced (e.g., Psalms 51 and 130), additional particularized petitions may be added.

The pronouncement of absolution or pardon *always* follows corporate confession.[3] If there is any inviolable liturgical rule, this is it. (The only exception would be confessions offered on Good Friday. There is a strong penitential effect achieved when, on that day above all others, the confession lingers until the resounding absolution that finally comes two days later in the celebration of the resurrection on Easter.) Words of absolution are among the most powerful and meaningful spoken in worship. They indicate the good news of the gospel in concrete and immediate terms. In traditions with a high view of ordination, the presider typically offers a declarative statement of forgiveness

---

3. It must be noted that some traditions do not use absolutions or assurances of pardon following confessional prayers. If there is a practice I would like to encourage for use in all Christian assemblies, it is this. I have an equal commitment, as will be seen in the section on preaching, to the good news always being proclaimed in the sermon as well.

with words such as, "as a called and ordained minister of the church of Christ and by his authority, I declare the entire forgiveness of your sins." In traditions with a more guarded view of ordination, presiders—lay or clergy—will speak a word of assurance. These words are often directly from Scripture such as Jeremiah 33:8 or Romans 5:8–9.

- The tone of the absolution or assurance is one of confidence and joy.
- Confession and forgiveness are used weekly in some churches and occasionally in others. It is especially appropriate when Holy Communion is celebrated.
- There is one occasion, even if a Eucharistic service, where confession and absolution are unnecessary: In congregations where a strong tradition of reflection on repentance occurs during the season of Lent, confession can be omitted on Easter Sunday. When the people of Christ gather to approach the magnificent mysteries of resurrection and forgiveness that are viewed from the joyous vantage of Easter worship, the postponement of celebration for additional confession is untimely and out of place.

Entrance Songs

Like opening statements, entrance songs set the tone for services of adoration. They can serve as musical invocations or calls to worship as well as statements of solidarity as God's people gather with a common purpose. Generally, the tone of these opening songs reflects a sense of joy at the regrouping of God's people for the fellowship and centering of corporate worship. Also appropriate is music that reflects the theme of the day, the season, or the day's scriptural texts. Churches with traditional liturgies typically begin with a series of songs including an opening hymn, a song of praise (often featuring the text of the *Gloria in excelsis* from Luke's Christmas story), sung prayers (such as the *Kyrie eleison*, "Lord have mercy"), and a psalm. Lately, many congregations are following the move toward use of a set of songs that are assembled by worship leaders to draw worshipers into a deepening spiritual encounter as worship begins. Regardless of worship tradition or format, some basic guidelines apply to selection of music for the gathering:

- Let it be remembered that the human voice is the primary instrument of worship and that full participation of all worshipers is desired.
- Worship songs and hymns should reflect the corporate nature of worship. Indexical problems occur when first-person-singular texts are sung as gathering songs.
- Worship planners should select gathering songs that are highly participatory. Engaging worshipers at the outset sets a trajectory for full participation as worship unfolds.

- To ensure participation, let new songs be taught during the announcements or at other times.
- It is fitting to provide for graduated participation in songs with difficult or unknown melodies. For example, stanzas may be sung by a band or choir with refrains sung by the people.
- Variation in musical expression and idiom encourages participation.
- Gathering songs provide opportunity for bodily engagement, as people physically process into worship spaces or join in stationary dance as spirited music stirs them to life.
- Choirs and song leaders have the responsibility to draw people into participation in the gathering songs. They are to lead as servants of the assembly and avoid the temptation of performing for the assembly.
- Music is crafted, accompanied, and performed according to the best account standard described in chapter 4.

Miscellaneous Speech

Worship leaders uncomfortable with their roles of hospitality sometimes resort to chatter, filling the gathering rites with wordy explanations and nervous talk. Because rituals are symbols with shared meaning that is rich and multivalent, the more leaders fill them with chatter, the more they are reduced in their impact. Thoughtful worship leaders will recognize that some things need to be announced or clarified as worship unfolds, while other things are obvious. When something goes without saying, to mention it is redundant and an intrusion on the ritual moment. As a general rule, give spoken guidance through the service only when necessary. Otherwise, let the material on the screen, in the worship bulletin, or in the service book guide people. When it is obvious that many visitors are in attendance (as in weddings, funerals, or baptisms), the necessity for spoken guidance increases.

- Let worship leaders speak economically, intentionally, and at all times with a tone and style that befits the moment. A conversational tone is usually the right tone to strive for, while remembering that participating in the dialogue between God and God's people is a conversation with enlarged purpose.
- When possible, let gestures accompany spoken directions or substitute for them.
- It should also be noted that there is nothing wrong with quiet words spoken between worship leaders in order to facilitate the gathering. Better a few clarifications made discreetly in the chancel than large mistakes made because of misunderstandings.

- Nonetheless, mistakes in the execution of worship will occur, regardless of how carefully worship leaders plan and rehearse. Worship is a live event and its participants are entirely human. In such instances, the best thing to do is acknowledge the mistake with good humor and move on. Laughing at one's mistakes shows humility and grace. Laughter among the people breaks tension and releases them for continued participation.

- Let worship leaders use language that invites rather than commands or allows. "Please rise" or "please be seated" are more hospitable statements than "be seated" or "you may be seated." The latter statements imply that the leader is a supervisor rather than a host.

- It is common nowadays to qualify worship directions in deference to the differently abled: "Please rise if you are able." While an obvious courtesy, leaders may wish to think twice about following this pattern of invitation. First, it is redundant: obviously, only those who are able will stand. Those who are unable are not likely to feel obligated to do what is difficult for them, and we expect that fellow worshipers would understand if anyone were not to rise. Second, making mention of anyone's disability simply draws undue attention to the difference between persons. Polite society has always understood such things. It is hard to imagine that, in a zeal for correctness, we would begin to qualify all invitations: "those who can see, please read along" or "those who can hear, listen to the choir."

Movement

Worship is incarnational: it involves constant movement. Leaders gesture and move from one place to another. The assembly stands, sits, and kneels. People might also raise hands in prayer, process to communion, or dance to stirring music. Movement is a natural aspect of worship that is to be encouraged and planned for. The desire for full participation in worship is achieved when it involves not only the mind in prayerful assent but the entire person in response to music and prayer.

- Let worship leaders rehearse their movements in the worship space and choreograph their steps for economy. Let the leaders' movements be spare, avoiding attention except as intended.

- Wise leaders will consult with dancers and movement artists in their communities in order to help them comport themselves with dignity and grace.

- Leaders' gestures should be simple, unselfconscious, graceful, and hospitable. They should be generous enough to be seen and understood by all in the assembly. The prudent worship leader will practice gestures, perhaps before a mirror or a trusted colleague, so as to become familiar

and comfortable with them. Practice will save leaders from using meaningless, contradictory, or comical gestures. Among the comical are those
with inelegant hand postures (such as a claw shape) and the agitated,
palm-down, squashing gesture often used to get people to sit.

- Generally, the following simple gesture can be used to communicate a
  number of things: The presider stands erect with good posture and raises
  arms from his or her side in an open, inviting reach with palms upward
  and hands slightly curved. (This is the same gesture as described in the
  sending section above.) When people are seated, this gesture performed
  with a slight lift will indicate the presider's desire to have people stand.
  When they are standing, the gesture performed with a slight bow indicates his or her desire to have people sit. It is a fitting accompaniment
  to pronouncing a benediction, voicing a prayer on behalf of the people,
  welcoming people during a greeting, and pronouncing absolution.

- When performed meaningfully, a gesture can take the place of spoken
  directions such as "please rise" or "please be seated."

- Processions at the beginning of worship allow for the entrance rite to
  be fully embodied. Participants in the procession can be few, involving
  worship leaders only. They can also be grand and involve a cross bearer
  (crucifer), acolytes bearing tapers for lighting candles, banner bearers,
  a person bearing the Bible, choir members, readers and prayer leaders,
  and assisting and presiding ministers. In the most formal liturgies, the
  processional lineup follows this order. If bishops or other dignitaries are
  in attendance, they usually walk at the end of the procession. Even in
  less formal liturgies, the usual protocol calls for the cross to lead the way
  both into and out of church during the recessional. On special occasions
  (such as the Easter vigil) processions can involve the entire worshiping
  assembly, as they meet informally outside the church doors and proceed
  into the worship space during the gathering songs.

- Processions are occasions to call on the dance talent in a community.
  Dancers can add choreography and special skill to what might otherwise
  be an ordinary trouping of persons from one place to another.

- Children—dancers and artists all—are especially eager to join in processions and delight in waving banners and palms (as on Palm Sunday).
  Their joyful participation can lift the hearts and bodies of those who,
  by virtue of disinterest or disability, elect not to participate in a congregational procession.

- Services of worship that begin with a procession usually end with a
  recession, with people retreating in the same order as they originally
  advanced.

9

The Word

One of the ways that God's people are centered in worship is to hear and respond to God's Word. Scripture is read and proclaimed; silence may be provided for meditation and reflection. A creed may be spoken, prayers are usually offered in intercession for God's people, and songs are sung. The Word portion of worship allows for the active engagement of all people in the dialogue of worship. People attend as God speaks; then, the people respond as God listens. The Word typically comes in two forms: reading Scripture and preaching.

Reading Scripture

Churches in every tradition understand the value of hearing Scripture read during worship. This ancient practice, begun in the Old Testament period (2 Kings 23:1–2), speaks to the enduring nature of God's Word as the guide and good news for the life of the faithful. The mission of God in today's churches and local ministries is informed, inspired, and corrected by the mission established in Scripture. This means that missional congregations will seek ample opportunity to hear God's Word. The power of scriptural words to transform lives today comes not from the charisma or eloquence of a reader but from the Holy Spirit as God touches us through this timeless gift. Some churches, especially those with free liturgies, read a single Bible passage in worship and provide preaching on that lesson. Others use as many as four Scripture readings in a typical service of worship: an Old Testament reading, a psalm, an

Epistle reading, and a Gospel reading. These lessons are usually coordinated as propers for given days and seasons. The standard source for this fourfold system is the Revised Common Lectionary.[1] Given the significance of the Bible in the life of God's people, it seems advisable that congregations draw deeply from the well of Scripture during worship by hearing from several portions of the Bible. Regarding the selection of scriptural texts for worship:

- Let the psalms be spoken and sung as hymns of praise and prayers of lament. Though frequently omitted, use of the psalms provides a historic connection to the worship of ancient Israel, the worship of Jesus's time, and the church of all times and places. As prayers, they speak timelessly to every attitude of the heart. The psalms are also rich resources for imagery for prayers and preaching.
- Selection of psalms and lessons for a given service of worship needs to be made well in advance in order for missional congregations to draw on the resources of their faith communities in providing art and music in worship. Such coordination is made easy when the lectionary is used. In lieu of the lectionary, preachers and worship planners need to work together. Worship planning teams can include preachers, various worship leaders, choir and band directors, and artists. Their timely coordination can produce extraordinary moments of praise and adoration.
- Preachers usually take the lead in choosing lessons for worship or selecting readings to preach on from the four lectionary texts provided for each Sunday. Because the sermon holds central place in worship, preachers rightly lead in establishing the tone and theme for worship. Wise preachers know that leading this discussion is not the same as dominating it.

Prayers for Illumination

Preparation for hearing the readings in worship is formalized in some congregations and among certain traditions. Prayers for illumination are prayers offered by the reader invoking the Holy Spirit to act through the reading and hearing of the Word, even as the Spirit inspired its creation. The prayer emphasizes that hearing Scripture itself, not just preaching on the Word, is transformative.

1. This resource is an ecumenical listing of readings assembled in coordination with the liturgical year. It is *revised* in that it is a revision (in 1983 and again in 1994) of a three-year lectionary system established in 1963 (though based on ancient lectionary use) by the Roman Catholic Church. It is *common* in that it is used, with some variation, by most mainline Protestant denominations (especially English-speaking congregations) as well as Roman Catholic churches around the world. The lectionary represents a three-year cycle of readings coordinated with Gospel readings from Matthew (Year A), Mark (Year B), and Luke (Year C). There are numerous print and online resources for the Revised Common Lectionary.

- Prayers for illumination can be drawn from the language and imagery of Scripture, especially the texts selected for the day.
- Prayers for illumination are brief. They prepare listeners for hearing and do not eclipse the Word.

Introductions and Conclusions to Scripture Readings

In introducing textual readings, the leader need not cite chapter and verse. A simple statement will suffice, such as "a reading from the prophet Isaiah" or "a reading from Luke's Christmas story." In some instances, the reading is made more intelligible by a thoughtful word of explanation or introduction. If a Gospel reading depicts Jesus involved in a dispute, it will be useful to provide a brief word of explanation as to the topic, issue, or concern being addressed. If a Pauline text is an excerpt from one of the author's lengthy admonishments, it is fitting to put the reading in context. Some readings, on the other hand, do not require explanation. For example, a Gospel parable usually stands on its own. Psalms, also, are usually understood as prayers of praise or lament and do not require commentary. Let readers study their texts well and determine whether or not a word of explanation is necessary to help people understand the reading.

- Where a statement of explanation before a reading is desirable, let readers limit themselves to one or, at most, two sentences. More than that is an intrusion on the Word.
- At the conclusion of a reading, it is customary for readers to lead the people in a response, saying, for example, "The Word of the Lord" or "The Word of God for the people of God." The congregation responds with "Thanks be to God" or another brief reply. Leaders can be creative here and craft various statements fitting for the occasion.
- There is a strong custom among certain traditions for the assembly to stand when the Gospel reading is announced. This points to the understanding that Christ is present in the reading of the Word. The people stand, as if directly in his presence.
- In churches with traditional liturgies, a Gospel acclamation is typically offered. This may be said or sung and usually incorporates one or more "alleluias," except when they are omitted during the season of Lent. The acclamation is a brief statement, often from Scripture, acknowledging Christ as the living Word of God (see Luke 9:35 or John 6:68).
- Gospel lessons are often introduced (following the acclamation) with these or similar words: "The gospel of our Lord according to . . ." The traditional congregational response is "Glory to you, O Lord." Following the reading, the people respond with "Praise to you, O Christ."

- On special occasions, traditionally liturgical churches sometimes enact a Gospel procession, where the Bible is removed from its stand and carried into the midst of the gathering, accompanied by candles (held by acolytes) and the preacher. From the midst of the people, the preacher reads the Gospel lesson. The Bible is then processionally returned to its stand before the preacher begins the sermon.

Oral Interpretation of the Readings

Bringing a written text to life in the hearing of an audience is an art that is related to oratory and drama. Oral interpretation calls on the reader to study a text, discern an adequate interpretation of it, and practice its oral presentation with an eye toward phrasing, use of pause, inflection, emphasis, tempo, tone, volume, eye contact, gesture, and diction. This vast and important topic requires its own textbook.[2] This manual offers a number of basic suggestions for readers seeking to bring their interpretations to life in worship.

REGARDING WHO SHOULD READ THE LESSONS IN WORSHIP

- Let persons with suitable spiritual gifts for vocal clarity, personal energy, and willingness both to interpret texts and to involve their bodies in bringing the interpretation to life be selected as readers in worship. While most people learn to read aloud in grade school, there are always people within each community of faith that have special gifts for creating interest in a reading and communicating its meaning. Those with experience in debate, theater, teaching, and other modes of oral communication typically have the skills needed to render lessons in meaningful and lively ways.
- Those with special skills for bringing the Word to life prove useful as teachers where teams of readers are developed within congregations. They can be especially helpful in selecting and training children and youth to serve in this ministry. It is both inspiring and humbling to adults when they hear young people read Scripture with clarity and meaning. Children (as well as adults) should always be well prepared when reading for worship. Careful training teaches them proper skills along with an awareness of the magnitude of the privilege of speaking God's Word to God's people.
- Let readers remember that they are speaking the living Word of God. It is a mistake, if not a sin, to make it appear uninteresting or boring. Examples of slipshod preparation and poor reading in worship abound. Such laziness and inattention to this critical aspect of Christian worship is inexcusable.

2. See Schmit, *Public Reading of Scripture.*

REGARDING PREPARATION OF THE READINGS

- Let readers prepare well in advance and begin by studying the readings. The following steps can be used to study the text: (1) Read the lesson and its surrounding contextual material; (2) seek interpretive suggestions from Bible commentaries (often found in church libraries or pastors' studies); (3) establish an understanding of the reading and move toward crafting an interpretation that brings that meaning forward.

- Readers will then rehearse the reading to establish proper pacing, placement of pauses, development of mood, volume, and emphasis. Wise readers know that as they change the placement of word emphasis within a phrase, they also change meaning (e.g., "*I* don't know the man" and "I *don't* know the man" have slightly different meanings). They also understand that commas are not sure indicators of the need for a pause. Trial and error will bring the reader to a decision as to which techniques will yield the fairest interpretation.

- Let readers note that to read a lesson in a plain manner, without interpretation, is to *misinterpret* the text. Every text is more interesting than a flat reading discloses.

- Prudent readers will not only arrive at an adequate plan for interpretation of a text but will also mark their copy of the text with cues to guide the moment of presentation. Like musicians who mark the performance copies of their music, readers can be guided in delivery by insights captured on paper during rehearsal.

- To provide themselves with a readable and mark-able copy of the text, readers can type and print the Scripture lesson in large font. Let the reader remember to place the marked copy of the text within the pages of an actual Bible during the presentation. This reinforces the indexical sign that points to the reading as God's Word.

CONCERNING USE OF THE BODY IN READING

- Generally, the reader should stand erect, with good posture. Because breath control is critical to vocal production, the chest cavity should be raised and ready to receive deep breaths to fuel sound production.

- Eye contact with the audience is important but should not become compulsive. A few glances at the listeners, especially at the voicing of key phrases, will suffice for a reading.

- As much as possible, the head should be held high, so as to avoid constricting the throat and the larynx.

- Facial gesture is a natural and important accompaniment to vocal interpretation of a text.

- Hand gestures during readings are unnecessary. The hands can rest gently at one's side, rest on the sides of the lectern, hold the Bible as the lesson is read, or be used to keep one's place in the reading.
- The rest of the body needs to remain calm during readings. An exception occurs when the presenter of a text recites from memory. In these cases, the reader is free to move about, enacting the reading in a dramatic and physical way.

Creative Readings

Scripture can be brought to life in many ways. The following are suggestions for creative ways to present texts in worship:

- The most basic creative method of presenting Scripture is to read it dramatically. Doing this well requires time and skill. While it is a fine practice for a congregation to follow along with a reading in a Bible or on screen, how powerful it can be when the reading is so imaginative that listeners are compelled to watch the reader lest they miss something.
- Readings can be divided and spoken by two or more persons. This is especially effective when the text contains dialogue. Each person can assume the voice of a character in the narrative. One voice will be assigned the role of narrator.
- Choral readings are presented by a group of persons. They do not move about to enact the readings but stand or sit in a visible place. The choral reading text is divided into solo and ensemble portions. A theatrical director, like a choir director, is needed to coordinate the activities of the group.
- Scriptural texts are often set to music. Choirs, bands, and soloists can fittingly learn musical settings of biblical texts and present them for the hearing of God's people. In such cases, the singers understand that they are not leading the performance of the congregation. In the role of proclamation, they perform the piece as a musical interpretation of the text presented to the people. If a reading is offered by a reader, it is not inappropriate for the same lesson to be offered by musicians directly following or at a later point in the service. The musical rendition bears the same interpretive and proclamatory value as the textually based words spoken by a preacher.[3]

Preaching

The topic of preaching is vaster than even that of oral interpretation of Scripture, and the literature is historical, immeasurable, and varied. Five key prin-

3. Thus, Bach has been called the Fifth Evangelist.

ciples will be provided here that relate the task of preaching to the mission of the church and the missional character of worship.

Preaching Is Textual

There are many things that pass for preaching today, and not all of them can be considered proclamation of God's Word. Preaching is biblical. It is derived from careful and prayerful consideration of the scriptural text(s). Any substitutions for an inspired Word prepared by a textual preacher are inappropriate for the portion of the worship service called the sermon. There are many appropriate times in the life of a congregation for general teaching or to offer pastoral opinion. The sermon is reserved for God's Word, thus, God's opinion. The preacher's job is to set aside presumptions about what God has to say and to seek that Word through study and prayer.

- Missional preaching understands that biblical texts are interpreted in light of local considerations. Preachers are informed about the meaning of texts when they engage in conversation about them with people in the community and read them in light of their local pastoral ministry. A good practice is to begin study on preaching text(s) early in the week and to take the text(s) out for a walk with them as preachers go about their public ministry.
- Preachers interested in discovering and proclaiming God's mission for their congregations will submit to biblical texts and use the skills of language and exegesis to look carefully at what God is saying in them and doing through them today.

Preaching Is Contextual

The sermon is one of the principal propers of worship. It is designed for a particular time, place, and people. This means that it is one of the chief ways that worship maintains a connection to missional interests. It is entirely about what God has to say and what God wants to do in a given moment within a community of faith. Thus, the preacher plays a particularly important role in missional communities, interpreting God's vision and broadcasting it for the congregation to understand and embrace. Accordingly, missional preaching will contend with

- congregational, as well as local community issues and opportunities
- regional, national, and global issues, whether religious, social, political, or related to weather and disasters
- cultural issues, especially those that compete with the faithful life of discipleship

- the honest situations—the joys, concerns, desires, values, habits, sins, and laments—of listeners

Missional preaching will also take into account

- the ethnic, economic, and educational makeup of the congregation, striving to speak in a style that meets the expectations for local public communication
- the temporary nature of a timely sermon; the most pertinent sermon in a given time and place will not likely serve another setting or moment as fittingly as it does its *proper* time and place

Preaching Is Theological

It goes without saying, perhaps, that missional preaching will accurately express and teach orthodox Christian theology. Let two things be emphasized here. First, while most Christians hold to a central orthodoxy, within which we can claim to be universally catholic (united) in our understanding of the faith, the distinctive aspects of theology that distinguish the denominations and traditions of the faith are to be honored and upheld by preachers. The historic wisdom of the church is that many voices are needed around the theological table. Preachers cannot presume that what God desires to do in a local community is to make Roman Catholics become Lutherans and to make Presbyterians become Pentecostals. The care given by denominations and church bodies regarding ordination and polity is to be safeguarded by preachers. This means, for example, that a sermon dealing with baptism in a Baptist church (where infant baptism is denied) should be different from one presented in an Anglican church.

Second, among the first precepts of Christian faith is universal agreement regarding the good news of God's grace. Preachers, therefore, will take care that every sermon proclaim, in some manner, this basic message. There is no clearer message within the history of the church, the history of missions, and the ministry of missional congregations than this: God desires to reconcile people through forgiveness of sins. This is the good news that the church has offered every people in every age. It is an imperative that missional preaching proclaim some aspect of this good news in every sermon. Not every aspect of the good news need be proclaimed in each sermon; the text will always be the guide as to which word of promise or comfort the sermon will announce. But every sermon—as does the full arc of the biblical narrative—will contain a proclamation of good news. If it does not, it is neither missional nor any other kind of effective preaching.

Preaching Speaks to the Mind of the Listener

For preaching to be effective, it must be clear. Let preachers write and rewrite their material, sifting it for logic, cohesion, and unity.

- While some traditions hold the expectation that the sermon will unfold in three or more points, congregations will always be blessed when a preacher acquires the skill to present a *single*, clear idea from Scripture.
- If there are to be more points of development, let them each be lucid and unambiguous. If the preacher follows an inductive method, let the final goal toward which the sermon is striving always be in mind.[4]
- For preachers who speak without notes or pulpit materials, let them rehearse aloud so as to make the sermon's delivery fluid and accurate to their intended goals, free from digression and redundancy. Prudent preachers understand that preaching without notes is not the same thing as memorizing their sermon. Better than rote memorization is *internalization* of material so that it will be at the preacher's command as it is spoken.
- The wise preacher will understand that while there is a teaching dimension to all preaching, and while some sermons are intentionally designed as teaching sermons, there is a general distinction to be made between teaching and preaching. There are many appropriate times within the life of a congregation for teaching (e.g., Bible study, denominational doctrine and polity classes, confirmation and new member classes, and parenting classes). Let missionally minded preachers understand that their pulpit time is reserved for proclamation of God's Word, mission, and promise.

Preaching Speaks to the Heart of the Listener

At a time when sermons are often considered boring and irrelevant, let preachers understand that the creation of interest in a sermon is within both their responsibility and their grasp. While speaking to the mind requires clear and unambiguous language, speaking to the heart involves lively delivery of carefully wrought, inherently interesting material. Learning to be an effective communicator of the gospel involves

- writing and rewriting, so as to strive for language that captures the imagination, fires the senses, and holds people's interest
- use of repetition, metaphor, simile, and all other common figures of speech that are taught as effectual means of written communication
- rehearsal of the sermon with an eye toward the use of gesture, pause, pacing, volume, tone, and the effect of one's voice within the space
- the use of humor and irony, as long as they serve and do not dominate a message

4. Inductive preaching unfolds as a journey and does not announce its purpose or point up front. Deductive preaching, the most common type of sermon prior to the late twentieth century, presents propositions that are announced and developed.

Responding to the Word

Within the dialogue of worship, there are many ways that people respond to hearing God's Word. Vocally, they might sing, recite creeds, and pray. Silently, they might meditate and offer their treasure to God. Physically, they might bow, kneel, fold hands, make the sign of the cross, and dance.

Song

Sung responses can accompany the reading of psalms and lessons, such as in the Gospel acclamation. They also frequently follow the sermon. This song or hymn of the day, as it is sometimes called, typically reinforces or reflects on the message of the sermon or its related scriptural text. As preachers and worship leaders select songs and hymns for sermon response, let them remember these points:

- The song of the day is intended to involve people directly in vocal response. Songs and hymns that are well known and easy to participate in are best. Songs performed by soloists, bands, or choirs at this point cannot achieve the level of involvement that this moment calls for.
- The first response to a thoughtful sermon is silence. If there is a song of the day, let it not begin too soon, thereby interrupting people's natural inclination to think about the message just spoken. It is the calling of preachers to speak with the confidence that through them, God is speaking; let the listeners linger in awe and gratitude for the promises heard.
- Let preachers (and other leaders) avoid the temptation to announce the song or hymn of the day following the sermon. It is usually obvious when a song follows and that people are expected to sing it. Rather, after a suitable moment of silence, let the song's introductory music give people time to find it (on a screen or in a worship folder or hymnal) and prepare to sing. Only when it is not obvious should a leader briefly and clearly announce where the song is to be found (e.g., "The hymn is number 381"). The goal here is to let sermon, silence, and song be an uninterrupted sequence of hearing and response. The more a leader fills it with chatter, the less impact the sequence will have.

Creeds

The ecumenical creeds (the Apostles' Creed and the Nicene Creed are the two most commonly used) have historically been used as a response to hearing God's Word. To recite the creed together allows a congregation to join with one voice in speaking the belief they hold in common with Christians of all times and places. The creeds typically follow the sermon or the song of the day. (Some orders of worship place them between the reading of the lessons and the sermon.) Leaders can invite participation in the creeds simply. If a sermon theme (such as baptism) provides opportunity, the leader might design an invitation drawing on the theme: "Let us speak together of the faith in which we are baptized." Otherwise, it is sufficient to say, "The Apostles' Creed" and proceed in leading the recitation.

- Let the leader speak first, with confidence. The congregation will follow.
- Unless there is an intentionally designed teaching moment, the creeds do not require explanation. Worshipers young and old learn the historic wisdom of the church at worship more through experience and repetition than through worship burdened with teaching moments. (In other words, worship is the school of the church and it is *always* teaching, even when it is not designed to be didactic.)

Prayer

God speaks to the body of Christ in worship during the reading and proclaiming of Scripture. God listens to the people during their prayers. They may occur in many places in worship, such as an invocation or a prayer of the day at the beginning, prayers of illumination before the readings, prayers beginning or concluding sermons, intercessory prayers following the sermon, prayers during the sacraments, and concluding prayers during the sending. Wherever they occur, certain principles apply as to the content, language, and leadership of prayer used in corporate worship.

REGARDING THE LANGUAGE OF PRAYERS

- When leaders speak prayers on behalf of the people, they are voicing petitions that they expect people will respond to with strong assent—such as "Amen." Let them prepare prayers that speak in a corporate voice and are in a style of speech familiar to the people. The aim, again, is to be conversational yet purposeful and dignified.
- Those with gifts for creative writing can be recruited as prayer leaders. Their poetic talents can produce prayers that are evocative and engaging. Let the poetry of prayer serve the assembly and not seek to impress the people.
- While it is perfectly admissible to use printed prayers found in worship resource books, online, and in hymnals, leaders of prayer in local congregations can consult these materials also as models for composing their own prayers. Like preaching, prayers are most effective when they are written with the local context in mind and honestly address the circumstances of the people.

- Prayers spoken on behalf of the people do not need to be printed for people to follow. They give aural assent to them as the prayers are spoken by a leader. Those spoken by all worshipers will need to be printed in worship bulletins or projected on screens. Let them be well crafted and practiced by worship planners in advance. Written language may seem appropriate until speaking it aloud reveals that certain combinations of words and phrases are difficult to articulate vocally. Even prayers taken from trusted print resources should be tested for use; published materials are often not as carefully edited as necessary.

- Let prayer writers and leaders use varied and creative images for God. "Father" and "Father God" are appropriate addresses for God but frequently used to the exclusion of all other terms. Psalms and hymns are rich resources for finding new ways to address God. Also, the lessons appointed for worship may provide imagery that can be used in prayer to harmonize the conversation between what God is saying and the way that people respond. As a general rule, where congregations use the traditional trinitarian address ("Father, Son, and Holy Spirit") in creeds and formulaic texts, let leaders seek additional, imaginative ways to address God in sermon and prayer. Each form of address (even calling God "Father") is a metaphor. Let the ways we think about the persons and nature of God expand by seeking apt metaphors to increase our awareness.

- Another overused practice is the attempt to achieve humility by qualifying the prayer: "Lord, we just pray that . . ." While the humble stance of the prayer leader is admirable, the congregation hears a tentativeness that is inappropriate for the moment. Scripture tells us to pray with confidence. Let prayer leaders do so with the expectation that nothing is too great to ask from the God of the universe and that God will hear and respond.

Concerning the Content of Intercessory Prayers

- Every level of context is under consideration for the people's prayer: personal, congregational, community, regional, national, and global. The mission of God is both particularized in each location and related to the work and concerns of the church around the world.

- Let prayers reflect the special concern God has locally and globally for the poor, the oppressed, the hungry, the sick, and for justice and peace.

- When local issues are raised in prayer, it is appropriate for the prayer to begin with a brief announcement of the names and situations for which the community prays. Let the announcement not be artificially imbedded in the prayer (as in, "O God, we pray today for Helen, who is recovering from surgery in room 232 in the hospital . . ."). In this way, the announcements are addressed directly to the people and the prayer is reserved for the people's direct address to God. A few examples:

"As we join our hearts in prayer today, let us remember Helen, who is recovering from surgery in room 232 of the hospital. She is happy to receive visitors during the coming week. Let us pray."

"We pray today for the soldiers, marines, and airmen of our community who are serving overseas: [name each person]."

"In the coming week, our congregation will undertake a partnership with local government as part of a faith-based initiative. We pray today that it will touch the lives of our community to bring wholeness and healing. Let us join in prayer."

- Prayers for leaders and politicians are appropriate in public worship. Inappropriate are prayers that call for political assent. For example, praying for godly leadership and fair elections is appropriate; praying that one candidate win over another will certainly be disputed by people in the assembly. Prayer leaders can voice their petitions in such a way that wins assent ("Amen") from the people while honestly contending with difficult issues. For example, "As our nation wages war in a foreign land, we ask for your protection for our troops and your forgiveness that in our human weakness our nations have not been able to arrive at peaceful resolution to our conflicts."

- When prayers of adoration, confession, lament, and thanksgiving are not included elsewhere in a service, they can be made part of the intercessory prayers.

Regarding the Use of Silence during Prayer

Part of the dialogue of worship takes place as people hear God speaking as that still, small voice. They require silence to hear that level of conversation with God. Silence also affords them the opportunity to meditate on Scripture that has been read and proclaimed and to quietly lift their own hearts in prayer. Let there be opportunities for silence in worship. It is especially appropriate following strong moments of proclamation (such as the sermon or a performed choral anthem), between petitions during intercessory prayers, and during celebration of Holy Communion. Congregations unaccustomed to the use of silence may need to be trained in its value for worship. In such cases, silence can be introduced gradually. Let worship planners and leaders understand that silence means that voices as well as musical instruments are tacet.

Concerning the Leadership of Corporate Prayer

- Let leaders speak clearly, with confidence, knowing that they voice the longings and pleadings of the people of God.

- The direction of address in prayer is from people to God. Let leaders not confuse the direction of address, nor offer misdirected admonishment to the people in the midst of the prayers. (As a bad example, "O God, help us to become more involved in Bible study in this congregation because the people of this church are slow to open your Word.")
- Prayers can be spoken from a neutral place. As noted above, offering prayers from the pulpit or communion table reduces the indexical value of having these signs point toward singular things.

THE FORM OF CORPORATE PRAYER

There are numerous forms for corporate prayer. A number of sample forms are listed below:

- Responsive prayer: a leader speaks petitions, finishing each with a prompt for a congregational reply, such as:

    Leader: Lord, hear our prayer.

    People: Your mercy is great.

    Leaders can be creative in generating new ways to shape this conversation.
- Pastoral prayer (usually spoken only by a presider): The congregation listens in silent assent until the final "Amen."
- Litany: A series of petitions are begun by a leader and concluded by the assembly. Often, the concluding line is a repeated one:

    Leader: For peace among nations,

    People: we seek your grace, O God.

    Leader: For favorable weather and a good harvest,

    People: we seek your grace, O God.

    [*Etc.*]
- Bidding prayer: The leader calls or bids people to pray for specific things and then provides time during which people offer silent, prayerful response:

    Leader: I ask your prayers for our pastors and their families.

    Silence for individual prayer.

    Leader: I ask your prayers for the mission of our church.

    Silence.

    [*Etc.*]
- Free prayer: A leader invites worshipers to speak their petitions aloud in the assembly. Sometimes these are assented to with a formalized congregational response, such as "hear our prayer."

- Written prayers: The leader will invite people to pray a prepared text that has been printed or projected for the congregation's use. The invitation is simple and direct. "Let us pray" or other hospitable words are appropriate. When using this form, the leader begins reading the prayer confidently; the congregation follows. In some cases, worship planners may wish to formalize the opening of the prayer by placing the address to God in the voice of the leader. The congregation responds by speaking the prayer with the leader.

> Leader: Let us pray. Merciful God,
>
> People: We give you thanks for the beauty of the earth and the recent rains that have nourished it . . .

As the assembly voices a corporate prayer, the leader who initiated it will continue speaking audibly, leading the pace and tone of the prayer. In some cases, the written prayer will take the form of a collect.[5]

THE LORD'S PRAYER (SOMETIMES CALLED THE PATER NOSTER, FROM THE LATIN "OUR FATHER")

Certainly, this has been one of the chief ordinaries in worship through the Christian ages. Little needs to be said about it, except to encourage its regular use and to remind leaders that from the moment it was given (see Matt. 6:9–13 and Luke 11:1–4), it was the church's corporate prayer and should be voiced together by the people. It usually follows the intercessory prayers or is incorporated as part of the communion liturgy. Its use at other times could hardly be considered inappropriate.

---

5. See sidebar 3.5 on use of the collect.

10

The Sacraments

The celebration of baptism and Holy Communion is as old as the Christian church and still takes central place in nearly all forms of Christian worship. Some congregations, especially those in Orthodox, Catholic, Anglican, and Episcopal traditions, celebrate the Eucharist weekly, even daily. Due to influences of the liturgical renewal movement, many Protestant congregations are now celebrating communion more frequently, even weekly. Baptisms in all traditions are scheduled as needed or in coordination with a liturgical calendar. When baptism and Holy Communion are not celebrated at services of corporate worship, they can still be remembered in various ways. Doing so is theologically appropriate: the people of God gather as baptized people around the gifts of God's grace. Remembering the sacraments in worship is also a missional impulse: it helps congregations anticipate, in their adoration, the Christian action that follows. The sacraments are means of grace that God uses to call, inspire, and feed disciples for the service and proclamation they take into the world. Sacramental remembrance can be explicit:

- Sacramental images and metaphors are mentioned in prayers and other worship texts.
- The common elements of water, bread, and wine are referenced in prayer, song, and sermon.
- Baptismal and Eucharistic symbols are visible in the worship space. Chief among them are the font/pool and table.
- Rites of baptismal recommitment (sometimes called *confirmation* or *affirmation of baptism*) or thanksgiving for baptism are included as

part of the gathering or in response to the Word. Water is sometimes sprinkled (by dipping a pine bough into a bowl and lightly spraying it over the people, for example) in baptismal remembrance. For some, this may smack too much of Roman Catholic practice (sprinkling the congregation with holy water). For many Protestants, it is a refreshing and tangible sign of their own baptism.

The practice of baptism and Holy Communion varies greatly from one denomination or tradition to another. Often, the very things that distinguish one church body from another have particularly to do with the practice and theology concerning the sacraments. Therefore, it will not be possible to provide rubrics for the execution of sacramental rites for every tradition. Still, there are a number of general things that can be suggested for use in most churches. Here we may see that the common practice of certain traditions can inform and enrich that of all.

Concerning Baptism

- Let baptisms be done during the time of corporate worship. Private baptisms are reserved (in most traditions) for emergency situations. Otherwise, it is fitting for the entire gathering to participate in bringing new brothers and sisters into their midst and membership. Let pastors have the confidence, in baptismal planning, to hold a firm line with people who insist that they want their (or their child's) baptism done privately. Their shyness can be graciously met by a congregation that is accustomed to welcoming new people with warmth. People can also be reminded that the focus in baptism is on what God is doing, rather than on what they say or do or wear.
- The celebration of baptism in public gives the congregation a chance to meet new members or celebrate the commitment of those who take this step in faith. It also allows them an opportunity for renewing their own baptismal vows.
- White baptismal gowns or coverings are appropriately worn by the baptized. This is common in many traditions, regardless of the church's stance on infant or believer baptisms. Infants are often dressed in white dresses or bibs; adults are regularly immersed in modest white gowns. This is not only historic, going back to the early practice of the church, but it also points to the scriptural image (see Rom. 13:14) of putting on Christ. Two extensions of the white gown image are provided when worship leaders (from among the baptized) wear a white alb and when the coffin of a believer is draped with a white pall.
- As much as possible, let the sign of water be used abundantly. Full immersion, though not practiced by all churches, is still appropriate in

most. Where this is impractical, let the use of water be richly seen and
heard. Ordinary moments become extraordinary when leaders engage
the imaginations and the senses of the congregation. If, in the process,
leaders become wet, so be it. Full immersion baptisms actually require
ministers to stand in the water with the baptized. Churches with drier
traditions can learn from their free-spirited cousins.

Concerning the Celebration of Holy Communion

The practices here are so denominationally varied, only a few general suggestions seem appropriate.

- Like baptism, communion is a corporate action. When private communion is practiced—as in taking the sacrament to the homebound—let it
  be connected in various ways to the corporate worship of the congregation. Members of the church may form a group to take the sacrament
  to the infirm. Readings from the Sunday service can be read, followed
  by a brief summary of the sermon's message. Where possible, it is appropriate to ritually send persons from the Sunday assembly along with
  portions of the bread and wine (or grape juice) directly to the home
  bound. This practice connects the overall mission of the church with
  the life and service of these travelling communion ministers as well as
  those who are being fed.
- Let leaders speak the words of the communion liturgy with confidence.
  Whether the Eucharist is seen theologically as a sign of Christ's presence
  or a symbol of his grace, the witness to it is bold and our invitation to
  it is wholehearted.
- Let presiding ministers be cautious in handling the communion elements
  during the rite. They should especially try to avoid any action that suggests to the people that they are manufacturing the body of Christ out of
  bread and wine. While this is nearer the theology of the Roman Catholic
  Church, the liturgical renewal movement has made this a questionable
  practice even there. Among Protestants of every kind, such confection-
  ary actions (such as breaking the bread precisely as the words "he took
  bread and broke it" are spoken) are untenable. (See chap. 5 for further
  explanation of this indexical problem.)
- Regarding distribution of the bread and wine (or grape juice), it is common in the rubrics of some worship manuals to indicate that the presiding
  and assisting ministers serve themselves first and then take the elements
  to the people. Let presiders and assisting ministers, rather, follow the
  scriptural injunction that leaders serve others (see Luke 22:25–27) before
  themselves.

Conclusion

The hope that initiated and guided this book is that there is much to be celebrated in Christian worship today and that there is much we can share with and learn from each other, regardless of denomination or tradition. More unites us than divides us. This attempt to renew worship practice springs from the growing missional focus of congregational ministry across North America and the globe. It is fed by the present-day openness toward the rich use of art and imagery in worship and the growing embrace among twenty-first-century people of mystery and historic wisdom. Above all, it seeks to challenge Christians to see their hour of worship as integrally related and connected to their work of service and discipleship in the world. I conclude with a prayer that the church of our age find reconciliation in the face of ongoing battles over worship as we learn to listen to one another and learn to use best practices and forms, whether they come from history, ecumenical opponents, or the insights of artists and children.

God of All Ages, God of All Peoples: You call us, gather us in your presence, feed us, and send us out as your disciples. Without your gifts of grace, we cannot come to you or serve you. Let your Spirit flow within our congregations and communities of faith around the world, bringing fresh insight, inspiring imaginations, opening hearts, compelling us to faithfulness. Assure us of your promises in Word and sacrament that we might worthily adore you and serve you with joy. Let this be our worship, we pray through Christ our Lord. Amen.

Appendix

Orthodox (Eastern Orthodox) Worship

There are many expressions of Orthodox Christianity (e.g., Greek, Russian, Polish, Albanian, Cypriot, etc.). Their liturgies are highly developed and each has its distinctive qualities. Generally, the Orthodox Church follows what is called the Divine Liturgy of St. John Chrysostom. The following order of worship is a summary of the vast ritual movement and prayer that make up an Orthodox service of worship.

The Gathering

Proskomedia (the priest prepares the bread and wine for communion in advance)

Greeting

Litany of Peace (or *Kyrie eleison*, "Lord have mercy")

Hymn of Incarnation

Antiphon (sung or said by the people)

The Little Entrance (a procession involving the priest and the ritual carrying of a Gospel Book)

Prayers proper for the day are said

A traditional hymn (the Thrice Holy Hymn) is sung

The Word

The lessons are read, along with prayers appointed for the day

The Gospel, with appointed prayers and acclamation, is presented

Sermon

Intercessions are offered

The Sacraments (The Mass)

Prayers and hymns are sung

The Great Entrance (the bread and wine are brought forward)

The Litany of Peace and the sharing of the peace between worshipers

The Nicene Creed

Prayers of Consecration, Invocation, and Thanksgiving

The Lord's Prayer

Hymns and prayers in preparation for receiving the bread and wine

Distribution of bread and wine, with accompanying prayers

Post-communion Prayer of Thanksgiving

The Sending

Benediction

Closing prayers

Dismissal (note that *dismissal* is the term typically associated with this portion of the sending rite in Orthodox usage, as well as in Roman usage, as indicated below)

The Roman Catholic Mass

The Catholic Mass is little changed in form from its medieval order. Since the reforms of Vatican II, it is usually presented in the local vernacular, although Latin versions can be found. The ordinaries of the Mass (marked with an asterisk) are always included and are still known by their Latin names (indicated below in italics).

The Gathering

Entrance Song or Psalm

Greeting

Sprinkling with holy water or penitential rite (optional)

*Kyrie eleison**

*Gloria in excelsis**

Prayer of the Day

The Word

Old Testament Lesson

Responsorial Psalm

Epistle Lesson

Gospel Acclamation

Gospel Lesson

Sermon (often called the Homily)

*Credo** or Creed (usually the Nicene Creed)

Intercessions (or Prayers of the Faithful)

The Sacrament (The Mass)

Offering (or Presentation of Gifts, along with Preparation of the Altar)

The Eucharistic Prayer, including the Great Thanksgiving, a Preface appointed for the day

Institution Narrative and the Lord's Prayer; it also includes the *Sanctus** and *Benedictus**

Sharing the Peace

The Fraction (breaking the bread) and *Agnus Dei**

Distribution of bread and wine

Prayer after Communion

The Sending

Blessing or Benediction

Sending Song

Dismissal

Liturgically Traditional Order of Worship

This traditional liturgy (largely following the Catholic order of worship) is typically used, with variation, by Anglicans, Episcopalians, and Lutherans, as well as others. Indicated here is a typical service of Holy Communion.

The Gathering

Confession and Absolution (optional)

Entrance Song or Hymn

Greeting

Kyrie eleison

Song of Praise (often the *Gloria in excelsis*)

Collect or Prayer of the Day

The Word

Old Testament Lesson
Psalm
Epistle Lesson
Gospel Acclamation
Gospel Lesson
Sermon
Hymn or Song of the Day
Creed
Intercessory Prayers (or Prayer of the Church)
Sharing the Peace

The Sacrament (The Communion Rite)

Offering
The Eucharistic Prayer, including the Great Thanksgiving, a Preface appointed for the day, the Institution Narrative, and the Lord's Prayer; it can also include the *Sanctus* and *Benedictus*
Agnus Dei
Distribution of bread and wine
Prayer after Communion

The Sending

Blessing or Benediction
Concluding Prayer
Sending Song
Sending Charge (e.g., "Go in peace to serve the Lord")

Moderate Liturgical Order of Worship

This is a large category with a great deal of variation. Thus, only a generalization can be presented. These kinds of liturgies are used principally by Methodist congregations and churches in the Reformed traditions (Presbyterian, Dutch Reformed, etc.) as well as some others. Lutherans drawn to freedom of liturgical expression as well as free churches with a relatively formal approach to liturgy may order their worship similar to this pattern. Listed here are the primary elements of these orders placed in their typical sequence. In services where Communion is not celebrated, the service may include all of these elements except the Sacrament portion.

The Gathering

Informal prayer, singing, and testimonies may occur as people gather

Greeting (sometimes a choral Introit serves as the Greeting)

Invocation or Call to Worship

Hymn or Song

Opening Prayers and Praise (sometimes a set of contemporary songs is sung)

Prayer of Confession and a Declaration of Pardon may occur here (or later, as a response to the Word)

The Word

Prayer for Illumination

From one to three lessons are read, usually an Old Testament, Epistle, and Gospel Reading; a psalm can also be said or sung

Hymn or Song of the Day (sung here or following the sermon)

Sermon

Apostles' Creed (optional)

Concerns and Prayers (Intercessions or Pastoral Prayer)

The Sacrament

Offering (followed by the singing of a Doxology or other song)

Prayer of Thanksgiving, Institution Narrative, followed by the Lord's Prayer

Giving the bread and cup

Prayer of Thanksgiving for Communion

The Sending

Blessing or Benediction

Hymn or Song (which may be preceded or followed by a Dismissal)

Free Church Liturgies

These orders of worship are used by churches and congregations that exercise freedom in the way services are structured. Again, the order here can only be generalized. (Among some churches, a simple form colloquially known as the "hymn sandwich" provides the order: hymn, prayer, Scripture, sermon, hymn.) Nonetheless, the orders of worship in free churches tend to fall into certain patterns that become more or less fixed in use. Baptist, Adventist, nondenomi-national churches, and Pentecostal churches are among those who follow such free liturgies. In Holiness and Pentecostal churches, spontaneity and free prayer (sometimes in glossolalia) are customary. The variation in practice is wide. Accordingly, the most basic order of worship is indicated here.

The Gathering

Invocation or Call to Worship

Opening Hymn or set of Praise Songs (the time of praise is especially im-portant among Holiness and Pentecostal churches)

Welcome and Prayer

The Word

Scripture reading (one or more lessons)

Offering followed by Doxology or a Song

Sermon

Call for Repentance or Conversion

Prayer

Hymn or Song

The Sacrament

If baptism or Communion are to be celebrated, they may occur here (or before the sermon); the most common practice calls for monthly Communion

The Sending

Prayer

Blessing

Hymn or Song

Bibliography

Anderson, Herbert, and Edward Foley. *Mighty Stories, Dangerous Rituals: Weaving Together the Human and the Divine.* San Francisco: Jossey-Bass, 1998.

Aune, Michael B. "Ritual Practice: Into the World, Into Each Human Heart." In *Inside Out: Worship in an Age of Mission,* edited by Thomas H. Schattauer, 151–80. Minneapolis: Fortress, 1999.

Austin, J. L. *How to Do Things with Words.* Cambridge, MA: Harvard University Press, 1975.

Bangert, Mark P. "Holy Communion: Taste and See." In *Inside Out: Worship in an Age of Mission,* edited by Thomas H. Schattauer, 59–86. Minneapolis: Fortress, 1999.

Baptism, Eucharist, and Ministry. Faith and Order Paper No. 111. Geneva: World Council of Churches, 1982.

Barrett, Lois Y., ed. *Treasure in Clay Jars: Patterns in Missional Faithfulness.* Grand Rapids: Eerdmans, 2004.

Bartow, Charles L. *God's Human Speech: A Practical Theology of Proclamation.* Grand Rapids: Eerdmans, 1997.

Bateman, Herbert W., IV, ed. *Authentic Worship: Hearing Scripture's Voice, Applying Its Truths.* Grand Rapids: Kregel, 2002.

Beach, Nancy. *An Hour on Sunday: Creating Moments of Transformation and Wonder.* Grand Rapids: Zondervan, 2004.

Begbie, Jeremy. *Theology, Music, and Time.* Cambridge: Cambridge University Press, 2000.

Bevans, Stephen B. *Models of Contextual Theology.* Maryknoll, NY: Orbis, 2004.

Blackwell, Albert L. *The Sacred in Music.* Louisville: Westminster John Knox, 1999.

Blauw, Johannes. *The Missionary Nature of the Church: A Survey of the Biblical Theology of Mission*. Grand Rapids: Eerdmans, 1962.

Bliese, Richard. "The Mission Matrix: Mapping Out the Complexities of a Missional Ecclesiology." *Word and World: Theology for Christian Ministry* 26, no. 3 (Summer 2006): 237–48.

Bliese, Richard H., and Craig Van Gelder, eds. *The Evangelizing Church: A Lutheran Contribution*. Minneapolis: Fortress, 2005.

The Book of Common Prayer and Administration of the Sacraments and Other Rites and Ceremonies of the Church: Together with the Psalter or Psalms of David. New York: Seabury, 1979.

Book of Common Worship. Louisville: Westminster John Knox, 1993.

Bosch, David Jacobus. *Transforming Mission: Paradigm Shifts in Theology of Mission*. American Society of Missiology 16. Maryknoll, NY: Orbis, 1991.

Bradshaw, Paul, ed. *The New Westminster Dictionary of Liturgy and Worship*. Louisville: Westminster John Knox, 2002.

Branson, Mark Lau. "Ecclesiology and Leadership for the Missional Church." In *The Missional Church in Context*, edited by Craig Van Gelder, 94–126. Grand Rapids: Eerdmans, 2007.

Brink, Emily R., and John D. Witvliet, eds. *The Worship Sourcebook*. Grand Rapids: Calvin Institute of Christian Worship, Faith Alive Christian Resources, and Baker Books, 2004.

Brownson, James V., Inagrace T. Dietterich, Barry A. Harvey, and Charles C. West, eds. *StormFront: The Good News of God*. The Gospel and Our Culture Series. Grand Rapids: Eerdmans, 2003.

Calvin, John. *Institutes of the Christian Religion*. Translated by John Allen. Vol. 1. Philadelphia: Presbyterian Board, 1844.

Carson, D. A., ed. *Worship: Adoration and Action*. Grand Rapids: Baker Academic, 1993.

Carson, D. A., ed., with Mark Ashton, R. Kent Hughes, and Timothy J. Keller. *Worship by the Book*. Grand Rapids: Zondervan, 2002.

Chan, Simon. *Liturgical Theology: The Church as Worshiping Community*. Downers Grove, IL: InterVarsity, 2006.

Clapp, Rodney. *A Peculiar People: The Church as Culture in a Post-Christian Society*. Downers Grove, IL: InterVarsity, 1996.

Constitution on the Sacred Liturgy: Sacrosanctum Concilium. 1963. http://www.vatican.va/archive/hist_councils/ii_vatican_council/documents/vat-ii_const_19631204_sacrosanctum-concilium_en.html

Costen, Melva Wilson. *African American Christian Worship*. Nashville: Abingdon, 1993.

Crouch, Andy. "A Humbling Experience: Contemporary Worship's Simple Aesthetic." In *Worship at the Next Level*, edited by Tim A. Dearborn and Scott Coil, 131–35. Grand Rapids: Baker Books, 2004.

Dally, John Addison. *Choosing the Kingdom: Missional Preaching for the Household of God*. Herndon, VA: Alban Institute, 2008.

Danesi, Marcel. *Of Cigarettes, High Heels, and Other Interesting Things*. New York: St. Martin's, 1999.

Daniels, Harold M. *To God Alone Be Glory: The Story and Sources of the Book of Common Worship*. Louisville: Geneva, 2003.

David, Hans T., and Arthur Mendel. *The Bach Reader: A Life of Johann Sebastian Bach in Letters and Documents*. Rev. ed. New York: Norton, 1955.

Dawn, Marva J. *Reaching Out without Dumbing Down: A Theology of Worship for the Turn-of-the-Century Culture*. Grand Rapids: Eerdmans, 1995.

———. *A Royal "Waste" of Time: The Splendor of Worshiping God and Being Church for the World*. Grand Rapids: Eerdmans, 1999.

Dearborn Tim A., and Scott Coil. *Worship at the Next Level*. Grand Rapids: Baker Books, 2004.

A Directory for the Public Worship of God. Church of Scotland, 1645.

Driver, Tom F. *Liberating Rites: Understanding the Transformative Power of Ritual*. Boulder, CO: Westview, 1998.

Duck, Ruth C. *Finding Words for Worship: A Guide for Leaders*. Louisville: Westminster John Knox, 1995.

Dyrness, William A. *Reformed Theology and Visual Culture: The Protestant Imagination from Calvin to Edwards*. Cambridge: Cambridge University Press, 2004.

———. *Visual Faith: Art, Theology, and Worship in Dialogue*. Grand Rapids: Baker Academic, 2001.

Edwards, Jonathan. *Religious Affections*. Carlisle, UK: Banner of Truth Trust, 1961.

Edwards, O. C., Jr. *A History of Preaching*. 2 vols. Nashville: Abingdon, 2004.

Elkins, Heather Murray. *Worshiping Women: Re-Forming God's People for Praise*. Nashville: Abingdon, 1994.

Eliot, T. S. *The Complete Poems and Plays, 1909–1950*. New York: Harcourt, Brace, 1952.

Ellingson, Stephen. *The Megachurch and the Mainline: Remaking Religious Tradition in the Twenty-first Century*. Chicago: University of Chicago Press, 2007.

Ellis, Christopher. "Baptists in Britain." In *The Oxford History of Christian Worship*, edited by Karen Westerfield Tucker and Geoffrey Wainwright, 560–73. Oxford: Oxford University Press, 2006.

Evangelical Lutheran Worship. Minneapolis: Fortress, 2006.

Fagerberg, David W. *What Is Liturgical Theology? A Study in Methodology*. Collegeville, MN: Liturgical Press, 1992.

Farhadian, Charles E., ed. *Christian Worship Worldwide: Expanding Horizons, Deepening Practices*. Grand Rapids: Eerdmans, 2007.

Frankforter, A. Daniel. *Stones for Bread: A Critique of Contemporary Worship*. Louisville: Westminster John Knox, 2001.

Gaither, Gloria. "Worship Wars." Unpublished address at North Anderson Church of God. Anderson, Indiana. August 13, 2006.

Gibbs, Eddie. *Church Next: Quantum Changes in How We Do Ministry*. Downers Grove, IL: InterVarsity, 2000.

———. *Leadership Next: Changing Leaders in a Changing Culture*. Downers Grove, IL: InterVarsity, 2005.

González, Justo L., ed. *¡Alabadle! Hispanic Christian Worship*. Nashville: Abingdon, 1996.

Guder, Darrell L. *The Continuing Conversion of the Church*. The Gospel and Our Culture Series. Grand Rapids: Eerdmans, 2000.

———, ed. *Missional Church: A Vision for the Sending of the Church in North America*. The Gospel and Our Culture Series. Grand Rapids: Eerdmans, 1998.

Hawn, C. Michael. *Gather into One: Praying and Singing Globally*. Grand Rapids: Eerdmans, 2003.

———. *One Bread, One Body: Exploring Cultural Diversity in Worship*. Herndon, VA: Alban Institute, 2003.

Headley, Carolyn, and Mark Earey. *Mission and Liturgical Worship*. Cambridge, UK: Grove Books, 2002.

Hiebert, Paul G., R. Daniel Shaw, and Tite Tiénou. *Understanding Folk Religion: A Christian Response to Popular Beliefs and Practices*. Grand Rapids: Baker Academic, 1999.

Hoffman, Lawrence A. *The Art of Public Prayer: Not for Clergy Only*. Washington, DC: Pastoral, 1988.

———. *Beyond the Text: A Holistic Approach to Liturgy*. Bloomington/Indianapolis: Indiana University Press, 1989.

Huck, Gabe, ed. *A Sourcebook about Liturgy*. Chicago: Liturgy Training Publications, 1994.

Hughes, Graham. *Worship as Meaning: A Liturgical Theology for Late Modernity*. Cambridge: Cambridge University Press, 2003.

Hunsberger, George R. *Bearing the Witness of the Spirit: Lesslie Newbigin's Theology of Cultural Plurality.* Grand Rapids: Eerdmans, 1998.

Hunsberger, George R., and Craig Van Gelder, eds. *The Church between Gospel and Culture: The Emerging Mission in North America.* The Gospel and Our Culture Series. Grand Rapids: Eerdmans, 1996.

Hurtado, Larry W. *At the Origins of Christian Worship.* Grand Rapids: Eerdmans, 1999.

Hustad, Donald P. *True Worship: Reclaiming the Wonder and Majesty.* Carol Stream, IL: Hope, 1998.

Jenkins, Philip. *The Next Christendom: The Coming of Global Christianity.* New York: Oxford University Press, 2002.

Jenson, Robert W. *Visible Words.* Philadelphia: Fortress, 1978.

Johnson, Todd E., ed. *The Conviction of Things Not Seen: Worship and Ministry in the Twenty-first Century.* Grand Rapids: Brazos, 2002.

———. "Disconnected Rituals: The Origins of the Seeker Service Movement." In *The Conviction of Things Not Seen: Worship and Ministry in the Twenty-first Century,* edited by Todd E. Johnson, 53–66. Grand Rapids: Brazos, 2002.

———. "Liturgical Links: Toward a Theology of Free Church Worship." Unpublished address at the installation of Todd E. Johnson in the Brehm Chair for Worship, Theology, and the Arts at Fuller Theological Seminary, Pasadena, CA. May 22, 2007.

Justin Martyr. *First Apology.* In *Early Christian Fathers,* translated and edited by Cyril C. Richardson, 225–89. New York: Macmillan, 1976.

Kapikian, Catherine. *Art in Service of the Sacred.* Edited by Kathy Black. Nashville: Abingdon, 2006.

Kavanagh, Aidan. *Elements of Rite: A Handbook of Liturgical Style.* New York: Pueblo, 1994.

Keifert, Patrick. *We Are Here Now: A Missional Journey of Spiritual Discovery; A New Missional Era.* Eagle, ID: Allelon, 2006.

———. *Welcoming the Stranger: A Public Theology of Worship and Evangelism.* Minneapolis: Fortress, 1992.

Keillor, Garrison. "In Search of Lake Wobegon: It's in Central Minnesota, According to Its Creator." *National Geographic Magazine,* December 2000, 86–109.

Kimball, Dan. *Emerging Worship: Creating Worship Gatherings for New Generations.* Grand Rapids: Zondervan, 2004.

Koester, Anne Y., ed. *Liturgy and Justice: To Worship God in Spirit and Truth.* Collegeville, MN: Liturgical Press, 2002.

Kraft, Charles. *Christianity and Culture: A Study in Dynamic Biblical Theologizing in Cross-Cultural Perspective.* Maryknoll, NY: Orbis, 1995.

Lange, Dirk G., and Dwight W. Vogel, eds. *Ordo: Bath, Word, Prayer, Table.* Akron, OH: OSL, 2005.

Langer, Susanne K. *Feeling and Form.* New York: Scribner's Sons, 1953.

Langford, Andy. *Transitions in Worship: Moving from Traditional to Contemporary.* Nashville: Abingdon, 1999.

———, ed. *United Methodist Book of Worship.* Nashville: United Methodist, 1992.

Lathrop, Gordon W. "Bath, Word, Prayer, Table: Reflections on Doing the Liturgical *Ordo* in a Postmodern Time." In *Ordo: Bath, Word, Prayer, Table,* edited by Dirk G. Lange and Dwight W. Vogel, 216–28. Akron, OH: OSL, 2005.

———. *Holy Ground: A Liturgical Cosmology.* Minneapolis: Fortress, 2003.

———. *Holy People: A Liturgical Ecclesiology.* Minneapolis: Fortress, 1999.

———. *Holy Things: A Liturgical Theology.* Minneapolis: Fortress, 1993.

———. *The Pastor: A Spirituality.* Minneapolis: Fortress, 2006.

———. *What Are the Essentials of Christian Worship?* Minneapolis: Fortress, 1994.

Lathrop, Gordon W., and Timothy J. Wengert. *Christian Assembly: Marks of the Church in a Pluralistic Age.* Minneapolis: Fortress, 2004.

Lischer, Richard. *The End of Words: The Language of Reconciliation in a Culture of Violence.* Grand Rapids: Eerdmans, 2005.

Long, Thomas G. *Beyond the Worship Wars: Building Vital and Faithful Worship.* Herndon, VA: Alban Institute, 2001.

Luther, Martin. *Luther's Large Catechism.* Translated by J. N. Lenker. Minneapolis: Fortress, 1967.

———. *Luther's Works.* Edited and translated by Charles M. Jacobs and E. Theodore Bachmann. Vol. 35. Philadelphia: Fortress, 1960.

———. *Luther's Works: Liturgy and Hymns.* Edited and translated by Ulrich S. Leupold, Helmut T. Lehmann, and Paul Zeller Strodach. Vol. 53. Philadelphia: Fortress, 1965.

———. *The Lutheran Handbook.* Minneapolis: Fortress, 2005.

———. "Small Catechism." In *The Book of Concord,* translated and edited by Theodore G. Tappert, 337–56. Philadelphia: Fortress, 1959.

Manual for Worship and Service. Mississauga, ON: Canadian Baptist Ministries, 1998.

Maynard-Reid, Pedrito. *Diverse Worship: African-American, Caribbean and Hispanic Perspectives.* Downers Grove, IL: InterVarsity, 2000.

McKinney, Lora-Ellen. *Total Praise! An Orientation to Black Baptist Belief and Worship.* Valley Forge, PA: Judson, 2003.

Meeks, Blair Gilmer, ed. *The Landscape of Praise: Readings in Liturgical Renewal.* Valley Forge, PA: Trinity International, 1996.

Montefiore, Hugh, ed. *The Gospel and Contemporary Culture.* London: Cassell Academic, 1992.

Myklebust, Olav Guttorm. *The Study of Missions in Theology Education: An Historical Inquiry into the Place of World Evangelisation in Western Protestant Ministerial Training, with Particular Reference to Alexander Duff's Chair of Evangelistic Theology, Egede-Instituttet, Oslo.* Oslo: Egede instituttet; hovedkommisjon Land og kirke, 1955.

Navarro, Kevin J. *The Complete Worship Leader.* Grand Rapids: Baker Books, 2001.

Neill, Stephen. *A History of Christian Mission.* Rev. ed. New York: Penguin, 1986.

Nes, Solrun. *The Mystical Language of Icons.* Grand Rapids: Eerdmans, 2004.

Nessan, Craig L. *Beyond Maintenance to Mission: A Theology of Congregation.* Minneapolis: Fortress, 1999.

Newbigin, Lesslie. *Foolishness to the Greeks.* Grand Rapids: Eerdmans, 1986.

———. *The Gospel in a Pluralist Society.* Grand Rapids: Eerdmans, 1989.

———. *The Open Secret.* Grand Rapids: Eerdmans, 1978.

———. *The Other Side of 1984.* Geneva: World Council of Churches, 1983.

Old, Hughes Oliphant. *Guides to the Reformed Tradition: Worship.* Atlanta: John Knox, 1984.

Ott, Craig, and Harold A. Netland, eds. *Globalizing Theology: Belief and Practice in an Era of World Christianity.* Grand Rapids: Baker Academic, 2006.

Parry, Robin. *Worshiping Trinity: Coming Back to the Heart of Worship.* Milton Keynes, UK: Paternoster, 2005.

Pfatteicher, Philip H. *Liturgical Spirituality.* Harrisburg, PA: Trinity International, 1997.

———. *The School of the Church: Worship and Christian Formation.* Valley Forge, PA: Trinity International, 1995.

Pfatteicher, Philip H., Carlos R. Messerli, and Inter-Lutheran Commission on Worship. *Manual on the Liturgy: The Lutheran Book of Worship.* Minneapolis: Fortress, 1978.

Philip, T. V. *Edinburgh to Salvador: Twentieth Century Ecumenical Missiology; A Historical Study of the Ecumenical Discussions on Mission.* Delhi: CSS & ISPCK, 1999.

Pickthorn, William E. *Minister's Manual*. 3 vols. Springfield, MO: Gospel, 1965.

Piper, John. *Let the Nations Be Glad!: The Supremacy of God in Missions*. 2nd ed. Grand Rapids: Baker Academic, 2003.

Plantinga, Cornelius, Jr., and Sue A. Rozeboom. *Discerning the Spirits: A Guide to Thinking about Christian Worship Today*. Grand Rapids: Eerdmans, 2003.

Pocock, Michael, Gailyn van Rheenen, and Douglas McConnell. *The Changing Face of World Missions: Engaging Contemporary Issues and Trends*. Encountering Mission Series. Grand Rapids: Baker Academic, 2005.

Pohl, Christine D. *Making Room: Recovering Hospitality as a Christian Tradition*. Grand Rapids: Eerdmans, 1999.

Renewing Worship. *Principles for Worship*. Minneapolis: Fortress, 2002.

Rice, Howard L., and James C. Huffstutler. *Reformed Worship*. Louisville: Geneva, 2001.

Richardson, Cyril C., trans. and ed. *Early Christian Fathers*. New York: Macmillan, 1976.

Riddell, Mike, Mark Pierson, and Cathy Kirkpatrick. "New Approaches to Worship." In *Worship at the Next Level*, edited by Tim A. Dearborn and Scott Coil, 136–46. Grand Rapids: Baker Books, 2004.

Robeck, Cecil M. *Azusa Street Mission and Revival: The Birth of the Global Pentecostal Movement*. Nashville: Nelson, 2006.

Rognlien, Bob. *Experiential Worship: Encountering God with Heart, Soul, Mind, and Strength*. Colorado Springs: NavPress, 2005.

Rosin, H. H. *'Missio Dei': An Examination of the Origin, Contents and Function of the Term in Protestant Missiological Discussion*. Leiden: Interuniversity Institute for Missiological and Ecumenical Research, Department of Missiology, 1972.

Routley, Erik. *Church Music and the Christian Faith*. Carol Stream, IL: Agape, 1978.

Roxburgh, Alan J., and Fred Romanuk. *The Missional Leader: Equipping Your Church to Reach a Changing World*. San Francisco: Jossey-Bass, 2006.

Saliers, Don E. *Worship and Spirituality*. 2nd ed. Akron, OH: OSL, 1996.

———. *Worship as Theology: Foretaste of Glory Divine*. Nashville: Abingdon, 1989.

Scalise, Charles J. *Bridging the Gap: Connecting What You Learned in Seminary with What You Find in the Congregation*. Nashville: Abingdon, 2003.

Schattauer, Thomas H., ed. *Inside Out: Worship in an Age of Mission*. Minneapolis: Fortress, 1999.

———. "Liturgical Assembly as Locus of Mission." In *Inside Out*, edited by Thomas H. Schattauer, 1–22. Minneapolis: Fortress, 1999.

Scheer, Greg. *The Art of Worship: A Musician's Guide to Leading Modern Worship.* Grand Rapids: Baker Books, 2006.

Scherer, James A. *Gospel, Church, and Kingdom: Comparative Studies in World Mission Theology.* Minneapolis: Augsburg, 1987.

Schillebeeckx, Edward. "Towards a Rediscovery of the Christian Sacrament: Ritualizing Religious Elements in Daily Life." In *Ordo: Bath, Word, Prayer, Table*, edited by Dirk G. Lange and Dwight W. Vogel, 6–34. Akron, OH: OSL, 2005.

Schmemann, Alexander. *Introduction to Liturgical Theology.* Translated by Asheleigh E. Moorehouse. New York: St. Vladimir's Seminary Press, 1986.

Schmit, Clayton J. "Art for Faith's Sake." In *Worship at the Next Level*, edited by Tim A. Dearborn and Scott Coil, 156–62. Grand Rapids: Baker Books, 2004.

———. *Public Reading of Scripture: A Handbook.* Nashville: Abingdon, 2002.

———. *Too Deep for Words: A Theology of Liturgical Expression.* Louisville: Westminster John Knox, 2002.

———. "The Word, Beauty, and a Place Set Apart: An Interview with Bill and Dee Brehm." *Theology, News and Notes* 48, no. 2 (Fall 2001): 18.

Schmit, Clayton J., and Jana Childers, eds. *Performing the Word: Bringing the Sermon to Life.* Grand Rapids: Baker Academic, 2008.

Schreiter, Robert J. *The New Catholicity: Theology between the Global and the Local.* Maryknoll, NY: Orbis, 1999.

Sedmak, Clemens. *Doing Local Theology: A Guide for Artisans of a New Humanity.* Maryknoll, NY: Orbis, 2002.

Senn, Frank C. *Christian Liturgy: Catholic and Evangelical.* Minneapolis: Fortress, 1997.

———. *The People's Work: A Social History of the Liturgy.* Minneapolis: Fortress, 2006.

Shenk, Wilbert R. *Exploring Church Growth.* Grand Rapids: Eerdmans, 1983.

Smith, Kathleen S. *Stilling the Storm: Worship and Congregational Leadership in Difficult Times.* Herndon, VA: Alban Institute, 2006.

Stapert, Calvin R. *A New Song for an Old World: Musical Thought in the Early Church.* Grand Rapids: Eerdmans, 2007.

Steiner, George. *Real Presences.* Chicago: University of Chicago Press, 1989.

Stutzman, Linford L., and George R. Hunsberger. "The Public Witness of Worship." In *Treasure in Clay Jars: Patterns in Missional Faithfulness*, edited by Lois Y. Barrett, 100–16. Grand Rapids: Eerdmans, 2004.

Tappert, Theodore G., trans. and ed. *The Book of Concord: The Confessions of the Evangelical Lutheran Church*. Philadelphia: Fortress, 1959.

This Far by Faith: An African American Resource for Worship. Minneapolis: Fortress, 1999.

Tisdale, Leonora Tubbs. *Preaching as Local Theology and Folk Art*. Minneapolis: Fortress, 1997.

Tucker, Karen Westerfield, and Geoffrey Wainwright, eds. *The Oxford History of Christian Worship*. Oxford: Oxford University Press, 2006.

The United Methodist Book of Worship. Nashville: United Methodist, 1992.

Van Gelder, Craig, ed. *Confident Witness–Changing World: Rediscovering the Gospel in North America*. Grand Rapids: Eerdmans, 1999.

————. *The Essence of the Church: A Community Created by the Spirit*. Grand Rapids: Baker Books, 2000.

————, ed. *The Missional Church in Context*. Grand Rapids: Eerdmans, 2007.

Verduin, Leonard, trans. *The Complete Writings of Menno Simons*. Scottdale, PA: Herald, 1956.

Volf, Miroslav. "Worship as Adoration and Action: Reflections of a Christian Way of Being-in-the-World." In *Worship*, edited by D. A. Carson, 203–11. Grand Rapids: Baker Academic, 1993.

Walls, Andrew F. *The Missionary Movement in Christian History: Studies in the Transmission of Faith*. Maryknoll, NY: Orbis, 1996.

Webber, Robert E., ed. *The Biblical Foundations of Christian Worship*. The Complete Library of Christian Worship 1. Peabody, MA: Hendrickson, 1993.

————, ed. *The Ministries of Christian Worship*. The Complete Library of Christian Worship 7. Peabody, MA: Hendrickson, 1993.

————, ed. *Music and the Arts in Christian Worship: Book One and Book Two*. The Complete Library of Christian Worship 4. Peabody, MA: Hendrickson, 1994.

————. *Planning Blended Worship*. Nashville: Abingdon, 1998.

————, ed. *The Renewal of Sunday Worship*. The Complete Library of Christian Worship 3. Peabody, MA: Hendrickson, 1993.

————, ed. *The Sacred Action of Christian Worship*. The Complete Library of Christian Worship 6. Peabody, MA: Hendrickson, 1993.

———, ed. *The Services of the Christian Year*. The Complete Library of Christian Worship 5. Peabody, MA: Hendrickson, 1993.

———, ed. *Twenty Centuries of Christian Worship*. The Complete Library of Christian Worship 2. Peabody, MA: Hendrickson, 1994.

———. *Worship Is a Verb: Eight Principles for Transforming Worship*. Peabody, MA: Hendrickson, 1992.

———, ed. *Worship Old and New*. Rev. ed. Grand Rapids: Zondervan, 1994.

White, James F. *A Brief History of Christian Worship*. Nashville: Abingdon, 1993.

———. *Documents of Christian Worship: Descriptive and Interpretive Sources*. Louisville: Westminster John Knox, 1992.

———. *Introduction to Christian Worship*. Rev. ed. Nashville: Abingdon, 1980.

———. *The Sacraments in Protestant Practice and Faith*. Nashville: Abingdon, 1999.

———. "The Spatial Setting." In *The Oxford History of Christian Worship*, edited by Karen Westerfield Tucker and Geoffrey Wainwright, 793–816. Oxford: Oxford University Press, 2006.

Wiersbe, Warren W. *Real Worship: Playground, Battleground, or Holy Ground?* 2nd ed. Grand Rapids: Baker Books, 2000.

Witvliet, John D. "Beyond Style: Rethinking the Role of Music in Worship." In *The Conviction of Things Not Seen: Worship and Ministry in the Twenty-first Century*, edited by Todd Johnson, 67–81. Grand Rapids: Brazos, 2002.

———. *The Biblical Psalms in Worship: A Brief Introduction and Guide to Resources*. Grand Rapids: Eerdmans, 2007.

———. *Worship Seeking Understanding: Windows into Christian Practice*. Grand Rapids: Baker Academic, 2003.

Work, Telford. "Pentecostal and Charismatic Worship." In *The Oxford History of Christian Worship*, edited by Karen Tucker and Geoffrey Wainwright, 574–85. Oxford: Oxford University Press, 2006.

Wright, N. T. *For All God's Worth: True Worship and the Calling of the Church*. Grand Rapids: Eerdmans, 1997.

———. *Surprised by Hope: Rethinking Heaven, the Resurrection, and the Mission of the Church*. New York: Harper, 2008.

Wuthnow, Robert. *All in Sync: How Music and Art Are Revitalizing American Religion*. Berkeley: University of California Press, 2003.

Zwingli, Ulrich. "On the Lord's Supper" (1526). In *Zwingli and Bullinger*. Library of Christian Classics. Louisville: Westminster John Knox, 1979.

Index

engaging
worship